AN INTRODUCTION TO
Landscape Architecture

AN INTRODUCTION TO
Landscape Architecture

Michael Laurie

Department of Landscape Architecture
University of California, Berkeley

AMERICAN ELSEVIER
PUBLISHING COMPANY, INC.
NEW YORK • LONDON • AMSTERDAM

AMERICAN ELSEVIER PUBLISHING COMPANY, INC.
52 Vanderbilt Avenue, New York, N.Y. 10017

ELSEVIER SCIENTIFIC PUBLISHING COMPANY
335 Jan Van Galenstraat. P.O. Box 211
Amsterdam, The Netherlands

Library of Congress Cataloging in Publication Data   Laurie, Michael.   An introduction to landscape architecture.   Bibliography: p.   Includes index.   1. Landscape architecture. I. Title   SB472.L38 712   74-3728   ISBN 0-444-00146-8   ISBN 0-444-00171-9 pbk.

Designed by Ellen Blissman

Manufactured in the United States of America.

CONTENTS

PREFACE

This book consists of a series of essays on various aspects of landscape architecture as it has developed in recent years. We are now faced with new and challenging environmental problems of land use, conservation, landscape design, and planning. A rational approach to the solution of such problems draws upon the earth and biological sciences and the principles of conservation as well as the behavioral and social sciences. The health of the ecosystem and of the people is the basis on which concepts are developed.

The theoretical base I seek to establish is broad and applies at the scale of the region as well as that of the garden or courtyard and everything between. The central idea is a process which synthesizes ecological and social data relevant to the particular situation or task, resulting in either land use policy or detailed design form as the case may be. The interrelationship of the products is fundamental. Policies regarding the use of land at a regional level depend on a detailed understanding of criteria for various land uses and their impact on the land. Conversely, regional characteristics become determinants of form in house and garden design.

The "what" and the "why" as well as the "how" are integral parts of the theory. That is to say, program formulation is as important as the technology of construction and implementation. We cannot stand aside from value judgments nor can we ignore certain aspects of the problem because they are not specified in the client's brief or program. Our role in society must be positive, constructive, and informative, an advocacy for quality and long term values. This book addresses itself to the fulfillment of that role.

The essays are short statements on different subjects and are introductions rather than comprehensive reviews. They draw on my personal knowledge and experience so that the examples or case studies are random but, I hope, meaningful. They also draw extensively on the varied but limited literature in landscape architecture and related fields. I have included an historical review because I believe it is helpful to see what we are doing today in the context of the past. It also helps us to appreciate the origins of forms and concepts and the development of ideas and attitudes which are part of our present consciousness. Many of the historical sketches are based on several sources in an attempt to portray the concepts. They are thus often combinations of the way the place looks today, the way it appeared in early prints and illustrations, and the way I think the designer intended it to look. I have not included a discussion of basic design principles, aesthetics or graphic communication. That is not to suggest that they are unimportant but rather that they are to some extent separate from a deterministic theory of form.

Inasmuch as the book is a general overview of the field of landscape architecture and its component disciplines, it is suitable as a text for an introductory course for students of landscape architecture and others in related fields with an interest in environmental design and planning.

ACKNOWLEDGMENTS

It is clearly impossible to acknowledge all the people who have contributed to the content and ideas set out in this book. The Bibliography represents most of them. I have been fortunate in the last twenty years in meeting or having the opportunity to listen to most of the distinguished landscape architects and many architects, planners, and environmentalists primarily in the United Kingdom and in America, but including visitors from elsewhere. It is inevitable that they will find thoughts here which originated with them.

I wish to recognize specifically six people who have been very influential in the development of my concept of landscape architecture: my father, Ian M. Laurie, who introduced me at an early age to plants and planting, the nub of landscape architecture; Frank Clark, who taught me the importance of the interrelationship between disciplines and how the study of history made the present meaningful; Dame Sylvia Crowe, in whose office I had my first job and from whom I learned, among other values, what dedication was; Professors Ian McHarg and Karl Lin, great teachers when I was a student at the University of Pennsylvania in 1960 and who directed me toward the theory of this text; and Professor H. L. Vaughan at Berkeley, from whom I learned much, including how to decide what was important and what was not, and then how to say it clearly.

In addition to these must be added my students at Berkeley, who in the last ten years in more ways than they will ever know have challenged and inspired me. This is appropriate company with which to express my indebtedness to Lawrence J. Fricker, long-standing friend and critic, who read the manuscript at an early stage and advised me on improvements. I take this opportunity also to acknowledge the encouragement of my colleagues in the Department of Landscape Architecture and the College of Environmental Design at Berkeley who have helped me to come to grips with many of the issues in the book. My special thanks to Russell Beatty, who read the entire draft and helped me considerably with the chapter on planting design, and to Clare Cooper-Marcus, to whom I am indebted for several ideas included in the chapter on social and psychological factors, and to Tom Brown, who provided film and literature references for Chapter Two. I also wish to thank Roger Osbaldeston for the additional musical notes he prepared for the same chapter.

I have received considerable assistance with photographs to illustrate the text. Specific acknowledgments are given for pictures that are not my own, but I wish to thank particularly William Garnett for kindly allowing me to use several of his fine aerial photographs, R. Burton Litton for several magnificent landscapes, Peter Kostrikin for taking, developing, and printing photographs specially for the book, Robert Sabbattini for permission to use his photographs published earlier in Landmark '72, Trinidad Juarez for specially taken photos, photographic work, and graphics, and Willfred Hoover for printing many of my photographs.

Further thanks are due to Ava Lydecker, who typed early drafts of the manuscript, to Yee Sen Lee, who prepared the Bibliography, to Professor Jot Carpenter, who read the manuscript and gave me helpful criticism and guidance, and to the book production staff of American Elsevier for their patience and assistance, especially Robert Goodman for his encouragement during the book's early stages. Many others, individuals in agencies, libraries, universities, and private offices, are unfortunately too numerous to mention, but their assistance is not forgotten. My thanks to all who have helped in the production of this book.

Michael Laurie—
Berkeley, California

ix

1. NATURE AND MAN: LANDSCAPE ARCHITECTURE

Since land is one of the basic commodities of the world, its planning for use and conservation is a central political and social issue. Land becomes landscape when it is described or seen in terms of its physiographic and environmental characteristics. Landscape varies according to these characteristics and according to the historical impact of man on it. Thus landscape is a reflection of dynamic, natural, and social systems. Landscape architecture is concerned with the planning and design of land and water for use by society on the basis of an understanding of these systems. "Planning" implies a futuristic approach to land: land is regarded as a resource to be considered in relation to the demands and predicted needs of society and its values. "Design" refers to the qualitative and functional arrangement of parcels of land set aside in the planning process for some specific social purpose such as housing, education, or recreation.

ENVIRONMENTAL FRAMEWORK

Clearly, these considerations are no recent preoccupation of man and society; indeed the conscious planning and arrangement of land for agricultural and social purposes has been going on since the earliest civilizations of China, Egypt, and the Middle East. The rice terraces of the Orient (Fig. 1.1) and the earliest recorded domestic garden at Thebes (Fig. 2.2) are both very clear examples of conscious land-

Fig. 1.1 Pattern of rice fields in China illustrates the I-thou relationship between man and nature.

scape manipulation. Our approach to land use and design today is inevitably conditioned by this backlog of experience, tradition, and practice, and our perception of landscape and attitude toward nature are influenced by the cultural context from which each one of us has grown and the society in which we presently exist.

The words planning, design, and use suggest man-made or man-regulated landscape. By definition, there is of course no such thing as an entirely man-made landscape. There are rather degrees of

Fig. 1.2 The criteria for modern highway construction frequently results in drastic changes to the landscape. As technology has increased so has the degree to which we can change the face of the earth and the speed at which it can be accomplished.

adaptation of natural systems by man. For example, the California Indians changed or modified very little the landscape in which they lived, whereas the physical impact of the state Highways Department is clearly great (Fig. 1.2). Yet in both cases the landscapes can be said to have been modified and used. Moreover, there are two types of adaptation. Adaptation may be related to man's use of the land for growing crops, raising stock, or supplying resources, or it can take the form of "impressions" made on the land as an expression of philosophical and artis-

1

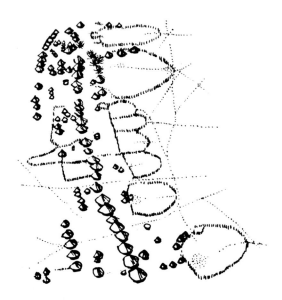

Fig. 1.3 The I-thou relationship between man and nature is manifest in the layout of an African tribal village.

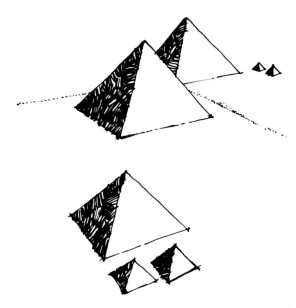

Fig. 1.4 The pyramids of Egypt, a reflection of increasing self confidence of man in nature.

tic urges, the needs of the soul. The second type is represented by the great gardens of the world such as the Villa Lante, a product of the fifteenth-century Renaissance in Italy (Fig 2.20). Throughout the history of civilization there is ample evidence of both.

As technology has increased, so has the degree to which we can change the face of the earth and the speed at which this change can be accomplished. The primitive digging stick and the modern excavator are used for basically the same purpose but have clearly different potential. These two tools may be associated with two basic relationships between man and nature, the I-thou and the I-it, which are defined by E. A. Gutkind.[1] The I-thou represents

1. E. A. Gutkind, *Our World from the Air* (New York: Doubleday, 1952).

a mutual adaptation between man and nature, whereas the I-it reflects an estrangement.

Gutkind identifies four stages in man's changing attitude to his environment over the known period of civilization. The first stage in the I-thou tradition is characterized by fear—fear of the unpredictable forces of nature with an accompanying desire for security. This is the general pattern of primitive societies who form hunting and self-sustaining agricultural groups in which the individual recognizes the need for the cooperation of other individuals to survive. These primitive societies have a very direct relationship with the landscape which they work and in which they live, and the relationship of the people to the external world is imbued with symbolism. In terms of physical form, Gutkind regards the

organic interdependency of primitive villages and fields and the layout of tribal settlements as reflections of this stage (Fig. 1.3).

The second stage is one of growing self-confidence leading to a more rational adaptation of the environment for different needs. Nonetheless, man accepts the challenge of nature as a discipline and the I-thou relationship persists. In this stage people work with nature on the basis of understanding its processes and knowing man's limitations in terms of manipulating them. Landscape is regarded as a resource and it is recognized that the continuation of crop yield year by year depends on refertilization of fields and careful management and husbandry. The rice terraces and fields of China and the Orient, the regulation of rivers for the irrigation of crops as in the ancient civilizations of the Middle East, and the pyramids and temples of Egypt are physical manifestations of this stage (Figs. 1.1 and 1.4). So too is the Medieval town with its church and castle and organic winding street pattern closely related to physiographic features (Fig. 2.13).

The third stage has led to our present situation and is the one advanced technological societies are still in; this is the stage of aggression and conquest. The adjustments to the environment of the second stage are replaced by exploitation and waste of natural resources. This I-it relationship may be symbolized by the contemporary automobile-oriented, spreading urban region with its hinterland of felled forests, worked-out mineral deposits, and polluted rivers (Figs. 1.5, 1.6, 1.7, 1.8, 1.9, and 1.10). Gutkind argues that it is the result of the depersonalization of nature through scientific specialization in the nineteenth century which weakened the awareness of the total relationship between man and nature.

The fourth stage lies, according to Gutkind, in the

Fig. 1.5 Los Angeles, an auto oriented spreading urban region symbolic of an I-it relationship between man and nature (early 1950's).
Photograph by William A. Garnett.

Fig. 1.6 As early as 1949, smog in Los Angeles (Hollywood) reached intolerable levels, result of a neglected relationship between the physiographic form of the landscape, the climatic pattern and dependence on the individual automobile for transportation.
Photograph by William A. Garnett.

future. He describes it as an age of responsibility and unification. The I-it attitude is seen transformed into renewed understanding and insight into the workings of nature resulting in social awareness and more sensitive adjustments to environmental conditions. This new attitude depends on the science of ecology. There is already some evidence of this fourth phase. The Tennessee Valley Authority project of the 1930s (Fig. 3.6) and more recent river basin planning studies for the Delaware and Potomac recognize the implications of ecological relationships and the hydrologic cycle in land use planning and management. The work of the Association of Bay Area Governments and the Bay Conservation and Development Commission in California also is symptomatic of the new attitude that is slowly gaining acceptance world wide (Fig. 1.11).

In many ways Gutkind's statement or belief is similar to the hope expressed by Kenneth Boulding.[2] Boulding suggests that we are in the process of a great transition as a result of changes in science and technology, in the physical machinery of society and in the utilization of physical energy. His theme is simply that if we can avoid the entropy trap: the wasteful consumption of energy, and the war trap, which we seem to have difficulty in doing, and *if* we can learn to use the enormous potential of the great transition for good rather than for evil, then we may indeed be able to achieve Gutkind's fourth phase. Although this seems difficult, the option is open and one of the responsibilities of the environmental professions including landscape architecture must be to demonstrate and advocate this alternative to their clients and to the public in every possible

2. Kenneth Boulding, *The Meaning of the 20th Century: The Great Transition* (New York: Harper and Row, 1964).

Fig. 1.7 Chicago (1967).
Photograph by William A. Garnett.

Fig. 1.8 Transportation between cities and the need for building materials have their impact on the hinterland. Highway 1, Northern California (1967).
Photograph by William A. Garnett.

way and at every possible moment since it is the only reasonable alternative for survival.

According to the optimists then there is evidence that we are emerging (or at least can emerge) from a brutal, insensitive, and ignorant sense of priorities and are approaching a new age of enlightenment in which the reshaping of the environment is seen in terms of land and landscape as a resource, to be planned and designed first according to the principles of the natural sciences and ecology and second to meet people's basic needs for physical and mental health and happiness according to the principles of the social and behavioral sciences.

Thus in a theory of landscape architecture responsive to this new approach we must understand the natural processes that constitute and have formed the landscape and the social processes that result in, or represent, the use of the landscape or environment and the way in which it is perceived. Next we need a methodology for analysis, evaluation, synthesis, and problem solving. And finally we need a technology to match the solution so that it may be implemented. The planning technology involves political and economic procedures; the design involves building and planting.

In addition, landscape architecture must be based on a set of values. This is perhaps the most difficult part of this approach to acquire. Natural and social science, methodology, and technology can be learned; values have to be lived and felt. We need to develop a set of priorities and subscribe to a land ethic related to our belief in the "alternative for survival," in which short term profit at the expense of long term regeneration and conservation of resources would be unthinkable. Environmental impact must be seen in a regional context. Quantity must be equated with quality. We must learn to make judg-

ments in terms of what is considered best for the common good and the future of mankind. The professional must present such considered judgments to the investment banker, government agency chiefs, and others in whose hands lie the ultimate decisions—even though his recommendations may be at variance with their programs.

THE PROFESSION OF LANDSCAPE ARCHITECTURE

Before proceeding further with this theoretical framework it is perhaps useful to discuss earlier and other interpretations of the term landscape architecture. It is a difficult title, for the words seem to contradict one another: landscape and architecture, the one dynamic and ever changing, the other static and finite. Professionals frequently find it frustrating that their role in society has been consistently misunderstood. Landscape gardening is the usual interpretation, but the terms site planning, urban design, and environmental planning are frequently added to the names of landscape architecture firms as a means of expressing their broader concerns and capabilities.

Frederick Law Olmsted, designer of New York's Central Park, coined the term *landscape architect* in 1858. And in case any of us think it is a difficult name to live with we should know that he apparently chose it in preference to his second alternative, "rural embellisher." Olmsted was a prolific man and in addition to city parks he also planned complete urban open space systems, city and traffic patterns, subdivisions, university campuses, and private estates. In addition, he was active in the conservation movement and in 1865 was largely responsible for the first area of scenic landscape, Yosemite Valley in

Fig. 1.9 Derelict land resulting from the gold mining dredging operations in California (see also fig. 3.5). Such disregard for the landscape is characteristic of the intense l-it attitude of man toward nature in the 19th Century.
Photograph by William A. Garnett (1953).

California, being set aside for public use and enjoyment. All this he called "landscape architecture," so it is not surprising that there has been some confusion about what landscape architects do. Olmsted had no training in the profession which he established at the age of 40. His previous experience in farming and engineering, his ability in writing and management, and his romantic disposition fitted him for the role he adopted. Others, such as Horace Cleveland and Charles Eliot, followed in his footsteps and in 1901 the first complete program in landscape architecture was established at Harvard University.

Since these auspicious beginnings, the prestige of the profession waxed and waned. Landscape architects found themselves in competition with other environmentalists of the nineteenth century: architects, engineers, surveyors, foresters, park superintendents, and city planners. The city planning profession emerged out of landscape architecture in 1907.

Thus from being responsible for some very large and important work in the nineteenth century, the landscape profession entered a somewhat less ambitious but nonetheless quite flamboyant phase in the early 1900s with greater emphasis on large estates, gardens, and small scale site planning. During the depression years of the 1930s, landscape architects became involved in larger scale work again, playing a significant role in the various public works programs, particularly those of the U.S. National Parks Service. Since World War II, however, the work of landscape architects, often operating as members of a team, has changed to include the restoration of derelict land, regional and urban landscape analysis and planning, and site planning for housing, schools, and large scale industrial plants. These now form a major portion of the landscape architecture carried on in public agencies and private practice. In spite of this, the contribution of the landscape architect to the overall development and maintenance of a stimulating, agreeable, and viable environment may not appear to be very great. People of landscape sensitivity and expertise do not occupy all the positions from which decisions affecting landscape are made. However, it is also true that landscape work does not always have an immediately perceptible impact and the effectiveness of planting and land use decisions or policies may not be appreciable for twenty to thirty years. The landscape of the first new towns in England, for example, is just beginning to achieve the effect and visual qualities that were in the minds of the designers twenty-five years ago, and war housing built in the United States has

Fig. 1.10 Strip mine near Farmington, Illinois (1965). The scale of operation is characteristic of the I-it phase of the man-nature relationship. The mechanical shovel is higher than a five-storey building. The intended restoration of the land to agriculture reflects the 4th stage of understanding and responsibility.
Photograph by William A. Garnett.

DEVELOPED SPACE

Predominantly Residential

Predominantly Basic Employment

Airports, Military and Institutions · 3

Community Centers · ●

Regional Highways · —

OPEN SPACE

Controlled development

Permanent open space

Fig. 1.11 Regional plan, 1970-1990. This plan prepared by the Association of Bay Area Governments in 1970 includes nine counties and attempts an overview of major land uses and transportation. Metropolitan rapid transit (not shown) presently connects eleven of the community centers and is projected to connect all of the centers shown on the plan.

Fig. 1.12 (a) and (b) The impact of time is clearly seen in photographs of the same place taken 10 years apart. The ability to project such change and development is the key to Landscape Architecture. See also Figs 7.9, 7.10 and 7.11.

often been demolished, leaving mature trees for a replacement project.

This fourth dimension, time, is an important aspect of landscape architecture (Fig. 1.12). Olmsted talked of the far-reaching conception that the designer must have in developing "a picture so great that nature shall be employed upon it for generations, before the work he has arranged for her shall realize his intentions."

CONCEPTUAL DEFINITION OF LANDSCAPE ARCHITECTURE

To bring us closer to a meaningful definition of landscape architecture for today let us look briefly at some earlier concepts. Hubbard and Kimball refer to landscape architecture as primarily a fine art whose "most important function is to create and preserve beauty in the surroundings of human habitations and in the broader natural scenery of the country; but it is also concerned with promoting the comfort, convenience and health of urban populations, which have scanty access to rural scenery, and urgently need to have their hurrying workaday lives refreshed and calmed by the beautiful and reposeful sights and sounds which nature, aided by the landscape art, can abundantly provide."[3] This definition reflects Olmsted's belief that contact with natural landscape was essential to human morality, health, and happiness.

Garrett Eckbo defines landscape architecture as covering

"that portion of the landscape which is developed or shaped by man, beyond buildings, roads, or utilities and up to wild nature, designed primarily as space for human living (not including agriculture, forestry). It is the establishment of relations between building, surfacing, and other outdoor construction, earth, rock forms, bodies of water, plants and open space, and the general form and character of the landscape; but with primary emphasis on the human content, the relationship between people and landscape, between human beings and three-dimensional outdoor space quantitatively and qualitatively."[4]

This definition is essentially concerned with site planning and the relations between people and design in that context. Thus it is more limited in scope than that of Hubbard and Kimball.

Eckbo's definition is related to the concept expressed by others that landscape architecture is an extension of architecture by other means. They are regarded as the same job. It is argued that until about the end of the eighteenth century no architect would have considered himself incapable of designing the space between buildings or the space around buildings, that is, gardens and landscape. The people we think of as the great landscapists of the eighteenth century thought of themselves as architects as much as gardeners; for example, in England Lancelot Brown, called Capability Brown, built as many houses as he did gardens, although the quality of the houses is not thought to be too high. Conversely, some of the people we think of as great architects of eighteenth-century England, like William Kent, were also great landscape architects, and Kent saw no incompatibility between the two pursuits. Chiswick House and Garden, which Kent designed, illustrate his skill at both. Joseph Paxton is another famous gardener who practiced architecture. His design for Crystal Palace, a landmark in the evolution of modern architecture, was the result of his work in

3. H. V. Hubbard and Theodora Kimball, *An Introduction to the Study of Landscape Design* (New York: Macmillan, 1917).

4. Garrett Eckbo, *Landscape for Living* (New York: Architectural Record, 1950).

greenhouse construction at Chatsworth where he made a great garden for the Duke of Devonshire. Paxton was also to become a leader in the design of public urban parks in nineteenth-century England. According to this theory the differences between architecture and landscape architecture occur in the means, techniques, and materials.

However true this may be, Brian Hackett points to another essential difference between landscape architecture and other design professions. This is the medium in which we work, the landscape, capable of change and growth, which has existed for millions of years and will doubtless continue to exist. "All that we can and should do is to modify or adapt the landscape to fit the new program." Thus the constraints inherent in the ecological cycles and environmental processes of a landscape limit the opportunities for an individualistic approach to design which is more possible in engineering, architecture, or industry.[5]

More recently Elizabeth Kassler points out that "the oldest gardens of China and Japan were the works of poets, painters and philosophers but in our part of the world (the West) Landscape Art has generally been considered a form of Architecture." She continues,

"As it becomes obvious that we have applied ourselves with more whim than wisdom to the critical problem of how best to live on this earth, or rather with this earth, we begin to realize that the work of fitting people to the land and fitting the land to people must be undertaken with much the same care for action and interaction that a forester might apply to his far simpler problem of ecology. And since a measure of beauty seems to be the happy byproduct of any ecological approach to land use, it is unlikely that our physical environment will be ugly if it is planned to respect both the nature of man and the nature of nature."[6]

Kassler challenges the concept that landscape is a form of architecture and suggests that landscape architecture would do better to draw its determinants of form from scientific knowledge and research in ecology and behavioral studies as well as from painting, sculpture, and architecture. She thus identifies broader responsibilities for the landscape architect to see beyond the boundaries of his design project and to become involved with and understand the larger region in which his project lies, where the impact of numerous projects and developments represents another level of concern for him.

It can be seen that the definition of the profession has varied over the years in an attempt to match its goals with the problems and needs of society. Recently the American Society of Landscape Architects amended its official definition to include "stewardship of the land" as one of its commitments. By its very nature, then, landscape architecture is a profession of the future; landscape planning and landscape design are acts of faith. Those who talk of landscape architecture being "architecture by other means" are usually architects. But landscape is architecture only in a spatial manner and its principles are hardly related to a profession whose products are very soon obsolete, with life spans often much shorter than the time it takes for a tree to reach maturity.

COMPONENTS OF PRACTICE IN LANDSCAPE ARCHITECTURE

Over the years, and especially since World War II, the realm of landscape architecture has diversified and classified its activities in response to the needs of a changing world. There now appear to be three clearly definable, related types of activity. First there is landscape planning and assessment. This has a strong ecological and natural science base and is concerned with the systematic evaluation of large areas of land in terms of the land's suitability or capability for any likely future use. The process usually involves a team of specialists. It may result in a land use plan or policy, affecting, for example, the distribution and type of development or land use, the alignment of highways, the location of industrial plants, the conservation of water, soil, and amenity values, and the use of the countryside for recreation. The study area usually coincides with a natural physiographic region such as the watershed of a major river or some other logical unit of land; unfortunately these seldom coincide with legal jurisdictions, county and state boundaries. The planning function may at times be less comprehensive and concentrate on the impact of major proposals on the environment or the identification of land suitable for one major use such as recreation.

The second activity of landscape architects is site planning. This represents the more conventional kind of landscape architecture and within this realm lies landscape design. Site planning is the process in which the analysis of the site and the requirements of the program for the use of the site are brought together in creative synthesis. Elements and facilities are located on the land in functional relationships and in a manner fully responsive to the characteristics of the site and its region.

Finally, there is detailed landscape design. This is the selection of components, materials, and plants and their combination as solutions to limited and

5. Brian Hackett, "Landscape Student and Teacher," *Institute of Landscape Architects Journal*, 81 (February 1968).
6. Elizabeth Kassler, *Modern Gardens and the Landscape* (New York: Doubleday, 1964).

well-defined problems; paving, steps, fountains, and so forth. This is the process through which specific quality is given to the diagrammatic spaces and areas of the site plan.

There is clearly an interrelationship among these three aspects of landscape architecture: landscape planning, site planning, and detailed landscape design. The wider landscape is the context for the site, which in turn is the framework within which lie the details. But just as it is reasonable to expect that small scale projects such as a garden or park should be influenced by and respond to the larger environment, so it is true that criteria for certain large scale land planning decisions depend on an understanding of the details of design and technology in siting houses, roads, and facilities. Practitioners have to understand both scales to do either of them with responsibility and sensitivity.

A THEORY OF LANDSCAPE ARCHITECTURE

I have now mentioned the five major components of a theory: natural process, social processes, methodology, technology, and values. Whatever the scale or emphasis of operation, these five components are consistently relevant. Social and natural factors must permeate every facet of a profession that is concerned with people and land. Problem solving, planning, and design methods apply at all scales. Good judgment is consistently required.

Consider how natural factors data are relevant to both planning and design. At the regional scale, the impact of development or change in use on a landscape must clearly be known and evaluated before a policy to allow such action is set. An inventory of the natural factors, including geology, soils, hydrology, topography, climate, vegetation, and wildlife and the ecological relationships between them is fundamental to an understanding of the ecosystem to which change is contemplated. Equally important is an analysis of visual quality. Land use policy can thus be made on the basis of the known vulnerability or resistance of the landscape. In other circumstances the natural processes which add up to a given landscape at a given moment in its evolution may, as at Grand Canyon and elsewhere, constitute a resource to be preserved and managed as a public trust (Fig. 1.13). On a smaller scale, soil and geological conditions may be critical in the determination of the cost and form of building foundations: where it is most suitable to build and where it is not. The sun, wind, and rain are important factors of design where the development of comfort zones for human activity or the growth of plants is a primary objective. Thus in many ways the natural factors of site or region interact in the process of landscape planning and design.

The social factors apply equally at various scales. In site planning and landscape design, cultural variation in the use and appreciation of open space and parks and the physical and social needs of the young and old are some of the many variables to be considered in a design process that aims to be responsive to social values and human needs. In decisions related to appropriation of landscape for recreation and aesthetic value people's perception of the environment and the behavioral patterns and tendencies of people in the out-of-doors are clearly relevant. It is important that designers understand the impact of environment on behavior and also appreciate the basic human need to manipulate and control the environment.

Technology is the means by which a design is implemented or on which a policy depends. Some of it changes year by year as new materials and machinery and techniques are developed. Its role in the three types of landscape architecture is clear. Specific areas of technology include plants, planting and ecological succession, soil science, hydrology and sewage treatment, microclimate control, surface drainage, erosion control, hard surfaces, and maintenance.

Design methodology involves systems whereby conflicts can be identified and landscape problems defined. It is a process in which all relevant factors and variables can be given values and brought to bear on the development of a solution to the problem. Computer graphics, analytical techniques, and notation systems aid in this process. In addition, there is much to commend an investigation of the creative process as proposed by Halprin.[7] He suggests scoring techniques, as in music or choreography, as a device to open up and make visible the design process. This, according to Halprin, allows more people to participate in design and decision making and facilitates the generation of new ways to plan and design large scale complex environments and regions leading to more humanistic solutions.

The objective of combining these components is the development of a basis from which landscape planning and detailed design can be made responsive to human behavioral patterns (people) and specific situation characteristics (the setting). Since both will vary in terms of culture, region, and neighborhood there can be no panaceas and no preconceived solutions. Thus analysis of social and natural factors is critical in comprehensive problem definition leading to unique and appropriate design form and plan relationships.

7. Lawrence Halprin, *R.S.V.P. Cycles* (New York: Braziller, 1970).

ations in vegetative cover from north to south slopes, from meadow to subarctic plateau, from river valley to rocky talus constitute exact responses to the range of environmental conditions created by the physiographic differentiation of the landscape. In turn, the wildlife distribution is dictated by the type and extent of the vegetation. No one aspect of the pattern is without cause or consequence. All merge irrevocably into a self-sustaining and evolving ecological system, representing the resolution of the natural forces and processes up to a specific moment in time. The parallel is perhaps limited, but it is this sense of ultimate resolution of form-giving forces with a built-in potential for change that should be the goal of the landscape planner and designer.

Suggested Readings

Landscape Architecture

Colvin, Brenda, *Land and Landscape.*
Eckbo, Garrett, *Landscape for Living*, Ch. 2.
Eckbo, Garrett, *Urban Landscape Design.*
Newton, Norman T., *Design on the Land*, Ch. XXVI, "Founding of the American Society of Landscape Architects."
Simonds, John O., *Landscape Architecture.*

Environmental Problems

Blake, Peter, *God's Own Junkyard.*
Darling, F. Fraser, *Wilderness and Plenty.*
Dasmann, Raymond F., *The Destruction of California.*
Gutkind, Erwin A., *Our World From the Air.*
Kahn, Herman, *The Year 2000.*
McHarg, Ian, *Design with Nature,* "The Plight," p. 19–29.
Scientific American, Cities.
Tunnard, Christopher and Boris Pushkarev, *Man-Made America–Chaos or Control.*
The film "Multiply and Subdue the Earth" (McHarg).

Fig. 1.13 The form of natural landscapes is a direct reflection of the processes of nature. Man made form should ideally be equally responsive to social processes and equally dynamic.

The process of design, the aim of which is the evolution of forms and relationships suited to the needs of people, may be compared to the fundamental form-giving processes which have created the geomorphology of the great natural landscapes of the world. Here the visual form of the land's surface—valleys and ridges, water-filled basins, and jagged peaks—represents an evolutionary stage in the interaction between the geological structure and the agents of erosion. The forms we see result from the response of inorganic material to a set of imposed conditions of weathering (Fig. 1.13). The vari-

2. THE GARDEN IN HISTORY

The meaning of the word garden can be traced to the Hebrew *gan,* to protect or defend, implying a fence or enclosure, and *oden* or *eden,* meaning pleasure or delight. Thus in the contemporary English word garden we have a combination of the two, meaning the enclosure of land for pleasure and delight.

The history of the pleasure garden is reviewed here for several reasons. Each type of garden is a reflection of the concurrent man/nature relationship and may be seen as an ordering of the environment according to an image of an ideal world. In addition, the great gardens of history constitute a vocabulary of landscape design on which recent practice has been built.

ORIGINS OF THE GARDEN CONCEPT

The concept of the pleasure garden perhaps originates in mythology, whereas its layout and organization seem to derive from ancient cultivation and irrigation practices. Most of the major religious faiths describe gardens or paradise at the beginning of time or the end of life on earth. The promised garden of Mohammed was said to be filled with groves of trees and fountains. Here enjoyments which lasted for mere moments on earth were prolonged for a thousand years. There are also legends of the Garden of Eden in which God placed Adam and Eve. This is described in Genesis I and II as a park planted by God in which there were all kinds of trees, delightful to see and good to eat and, of course, the tree in the center that yielded knowledge of good and evil. There was also a river which branched into four streams on leaving the park. The image is vivid and persistent even in modern times. Everyone knows what is meant by Eden. This universal knowledge gives meaning to book titles such as *East of Eden* or *Eden in Jeopardy.* Similarly, a nightclub called The Garden of Eden needs no further explanation.

In addition to the symbolism attached to the garden, early civilizations attributed special meaning and significance to certain trees and plants such as the olive, the thorn, the fig, and the vine. In times when starvation was a recurring phenomenon, it is not unnatural that trees, the longest living things known to man, should be revered for the fertility, life, and nourishment they represented.

Thus in our deepest ancestry there are strong myths and legends whose meaning may now be obscure but which, nonetheless, were influential in early thought and civilization. They are still part of our cultural heritage and partly responsible for the attitudes and emotions we hold today and, no doubt, for our unquenchable interest in plants, gardens, and gardening.

BABYLON, EGYPT, AND PERSIA

If the origins of garden layout and form also lie in agricultural practices, we may regard the fenced vegetable patch as the prototype. As leisured segments of society could be supported by the productivity of settled civilizations, such as those of the Euphrates Valley around 3500 BC, so gardens were made for pleasure. True to their origins, the dimensions and shape of planting beds were those of the fields. Irrigation channels and ponds were incorporated for functional reasons, as well as for the sensuous enjoyment of water in a hot climate. Shade was provided by forest trees planted in regular groves, and the garden was protected with a wall to keep out animals and intruders. The heads of state and the ruling classes lived in palace complexes of sun-baked brick with gardens of this type. The Hanging Gardens of Babylon were unique. This great monument is said to have occupied four acres and to have risen in a series of planted and irrigated roof terraces to a height of 300 feet from which views of the valley and the surrounding desert were obtained (Fig. 2.1).

The Nile Valley was another center of early civilization. Egypt's long period of pre-eminence lasted from 3500 to 500 BC. The religious and symbolic significance of certain trees and flowers such as the lotus, the papyrus, and the date palm gave rise to the

Fig. 2.1 Hanging Gardens of Babylon, 3,500 B.C.

Note on the figures in Chapters 2, 3, 4 and 5:

Many of the historical sketches are based on several sources in an attempt to portray the concepts. They are thus often combinations of the way the place looks today, the way it appeared in early prints and illustrations, and the way I think the designer intended it to look.

Fig. 2.2 The house and garden of an Egyptian government official at Thebes, 2,000 B.C.

use of plants for ornamental purposes. The rich built residences and walled gardens in the agricultural countryside. The officials' garden at Thebes, of which there are good records, is probably typical. It consists of a rectangular and axial arrangement of flower beds, ponds, enclosures, and a vine trellis under which one walked from the gate to the house. Fruit trees were planted for shade. There were irrigation channels and garden pavilions and the garden was surrounded by a high wall (Fig. 2.2).

Much later, about 500 BC, the kings of Persia created lavish formal gardens for delight, consecrated to joy, love, health, and luxury. A Persian palace garden of this era would have irrigation channels running through it as though it were a field of some economic crop. Here, guarded by high lookout towers and walls, fruit trees and scented flowers, including roses and violets, were cultivated between rills of water emanating from a central fountain as four basic channels, symbolic of the cosmic cross or

the four branches of the river rising in Eden mentioned in the Book of Genesis. The Persian garden has been described by Sorensen[1] as a stylization of the agricultural landscape employing water for irrigation and air cooling and imbued with religious and symbolic significance (Fig. 2.3). This strong tradition persisted into the Persian Empire of the sixth century. Garden carpets of this and later eras illus-

1. Carl T. Sorensen, *The Origin of Garden Art* (Kobenhavn: Danish Architectural Press, 1963).

Fig. 2.3 The concept of the Persian palace included an open relationship between garden and architecture with ever-present basins of water (500 B.C.-600A.D.).

Fig. 2.4 The Court of the Lyons, Alhambra, Spain.

trate similar arrangements: irrigation systems supporting cool, shady environments, symbols of paradise, filled with exotic fruits and flowers.

SPAIN

The Islamic garden concept of Middle Eastern origin was then taken from one empire or civilization to another and finally brought to North Africa by the Moors and eventually introduced into Spain in

the thirteenth century, where the theme of the paradise garden was combined with the atrium of Roman origin: Thus what we have come to call the Spanish garden is given earliest form at the Alhambra at Granada, Spain. A comparison of Persian palaces and the Court of the Lyons at Granada illustrates the similarities in architecture, courtyard design, and the use of water (Fig. 2.4). Similar open pavilions permit the free flow of air. Water is used symbolically and as a cooling agent.

The Alhambra was a fortified palace built on high ground. It developed in stages between 1350 and 1500, and, as a result, its series of chambers and enclosed courtyards is without any connecting organization (Fig. 2.5). The form of the complex is a response to the climate. The outside is hostile, hot, and dusty. The inside is shaded, cool, and protected by thick walls. Since the entire structure is perched on high ground, the windows which provide views out over the landscape also permit breezes to blow in. Rooms associated with pools of water thus provide a primitive but successful air conditioning system (Fig. 2.6). Channels of water ran not only in the courtyards but sometimes also actually into and through the buildings, lowering temperatures and providing the cooling sound of running water.

Fig. 2.5 Probable plan of the Alhambra at some point between 1238 and 1358 (more recent additions are omitted). The Generaliffe is at the upper right.

Fig. 2.6 The Court of the Myrtles, Alhambra, Spain. Breezes blowing from outside across the water basin act as an air conditioning system for the palace.

MEXICO AND CALIFORNIA

The courtyard or patio closely linked to the living rooms and corridors of the house is the distinguishing characteristic of the Spanish garden. If we pursue this cultural tradition and climatic type, we find them not surprisingly in the Spanish Empire of the New World. From Mexico, expeditions explored Alta California in the late eighteenth century and the series of missions built by Junipero Serra and his monks between 1769 and 1821 incorporated courtyards with central fountain or well, diagonal paths, and plantings of imported fruit trees, herbs, and flowers, surrounded by arcades (Fig. 2.7). Domestic homesteads, too, adopted similar arrangements, well-suited to the California climate and style of life at that time and clearly derived from the Spanish pattern. (Fig. 2.8). This phenomenon and its subsequent revival in the 1920s will be discussed later. But consider at the moment the compelling qualities of this garden concept which evolved from the experience and form of the Persian and early Middle Eastern cultures 5,000 years earlier and 10,000 miles away. In suitable climates, a house type with a private family patio and direct indoor/outdoor connections remains a valid form in the second half of the twentieth century regardless of all social and material advances.

Fig. 2.7 Plan of Mission San Juan Capistrano (1776). The missions of California introduced the architectural forms of Spain—arcades and enclosed courtyards.

Fig. 2.8 Plan of an early California homestead (1858). The central source of water and the architectural enclosure are Spanish in origin.

ANCIENT GREECE AND ROME

There is little concern with gardens in early Greek history. The private home seems to have been a very modest affair in comparison with the important social places such as the agora and gymnasium, theater and sacred groves. The living rooms of the house faced onto an inner court which was often paved and decorated with statues and plants in pots (Fig. 2.9). Distant palaces of the Greek empire, particularly in the time of Alexander the Great, are said to have had elaborate gardens inspired by those of Persia and Egypt.

The Roman house basically followed the Greek pattern. Houses were built flush to the street with inward-facing rooms connected by colonnades and opening onto an open square or atrium. The gardens were essentially social sanctuaries, enclosed shelters from the fierce sun, wind, dust, and noise of the streets. Since shade was provided by the surrounding portico, there was little need for trees. Planting, if any, was chiefly in pots or raised beds, and stone water basins, marble tables, and small statues were frequently used to embellish the courts (Fig. 2.10).

Since much of the original wealth of Rome came from the surrounding agricultural landscape, many aristocrats built villas outside Rome. Cicero is said

Fig. 2.9 Greek house, at Prienne (300 B.C.).

Fig. 2.10 Roman house at Pompeii (50 B.C.).

Fig. 2.11 Pliny's villa at Laurentinum (100 A.D.).

to have owned about eighteen such country homes. In AD 100 Pliny the Younger built a villa seventeen miles from Rome at Laurentinum, where the garden was chiefly planted with fig and mulberry trees. The formal layout included a well-stocked kitchen garden, cloisters, a summer house, and a terrace with fragrant flowers. The villa, situated on water for a cooler climate, is basically a farm house set in fields (Fig. 2.11). Hadrian's villa at Tivoli, built between AD 117 and 138, was much more elaborate and extensive, since it was used for many years as a government center. It was in fact a large estate containing many buildings, pools and water basins, terraces and statues. Although the garden units which make up the complex are architectural, there was no overall design concept within which to fit later additions (Fig. 2.12). The layout included a wooded park area, called the Valley of the Tempe, representative of a legendary forest said to have stood at the foot of Mount Olympus. Such a feature was no doubt regarded by the eighteenth-century Romantic movement as evidence that the ancient Romans practiced irregularity in gardening.

MEDIEVAL EUROPE

The Medieval period of European history occupied the time between the disintegration of the Roman Empire and the emergence of Modern Europe in the fifteenth century. The sense of community isolation within a hostile landscape is perfectly evoked in Hesse's novel *Narcissus and Goldmund*. The dark ages were characterized by war, turmoil, and plague. Pleasure gardens were unusual within the dense fortified cities and towns (Fig. 2.13). Space which

was available was used functionally for growing food or medicinal herbs. Gardens also were devoted to this purpose within the walls of castles and baronial strongholds (Fig. 2.14). In the monasteries more extensive areas were planted with fruit trees, vines, vegetables, and altar flowers (Fig. 2.15), but the most important element was the physic garden planted with sixteen different herbs which were the basis of drugs and medical science (Fig. 2.16). These herbs were concocted into lotions and preparations to treat various illnesses. For example, lemon balm was used for dog and scorpion bites, camomile for disease of the liver and also for migraine. Myrtle was recommended for many ailments including ulcers, spitting of blood, and fractured joints. Toward the end of the period, with the easing of political conflict, the development of trade and accumulation of wealth, Medieval gardens attached to castles and country houses became larger, more elaborate, and designed for pleasure as well as utility. Herb gardens and orchards were important basic elements of the walled gardens, which were embellished with grass-covered seats, fountains, flower beds, arbors, clipped shrubs, and fish ponds. Within the enclosure, pleasure pursuits took place; jesters entertained their lords and ladies who danced, ate meals, and made love in the gardens (Fig. 2.17).

The ballads of troubadors and early manuscripts describe Medieval gardens in terms of an emerging idyllic image of nature. The grass is always intensely green, lawns always sprinkled with fresh wildflowers. The water emanating from fountains and wells is crystal clear. There is no pollution. The air is fresh, the sky is cloudless and bright blue. Trees are in blossom. Birds sing sweetly and mate happily. The time is always spring. The garden provided sensuous pleasures: the scent of flowers and

Fig. 2.12 Hadrian's villa at Tivoli (117-138 A.D.). A series of buildings and courts built over a long period of time without any co-ordinating plan. The Valley of the Tempe is in the lower left (1).

blossom, the coolness of shade cast by the trees and arbors, rest and relaxation, and the acoustic delights of bird song and running water. This is the image of the Medieval garden and no doubt it matched the reality. Its intimacy, simplicity, beauty, and delight are appealing and appropriate to twentieth-century life styles.

Carl Theodore Sorensen, the Danish landscape historian, suggests that the great sense of craftsman-

Fig. 2.14 Medieval fortified castle with minimal space for a garden.

Fig. 2.13 Italian hill town of the Middle Ages, little space or need for gardens and parks.

Fig. 2.15 A Medieval monastery with a series of enclosed gardens for herbs, vines and vegetables.

Fig. 2.16 A monastery herb garden. Detail of a woodcut by an anonymous artist from Fior di Virtu Hystoriato, Florence, 1519. The Metropolitan Museum of Art, Harris Brisbane Dick Fund, 1925.

Fig. 2.17 A Medieval garden. Woodcut from Crescentius' De Agricultura Vulgare, Venice, 1519. The Metropolitan Museum of Art, Harris Brisbane Dick Fund, 1934.

ship associated with these gardens of the Middle Ages forms the basis for the gardener working as an artist in the subsequent history of garden design. Craftsmanship, an essential component of the Middle Ages, with its craft guilds and an inventiveness capable of solving all kinds of practical problems, ultimately became associated with aesthetics or ornament. This combination raises life to a higher level or to what British art historian Kenneth Clark defines as civilization.

Thus in gardening the craft produced edges and divisions, plots, dimensions, and shapes suited to cultivation practice, irrigation, tilling, and gathering. But as the idea of an ornamental pleasure garden developed, so the edges and divisions of functional origin became less practical and became ends in themselves. Thus their arrangement became an art as well as a craft.

ITALY

As the Middle Ages progressed from barbarism into an ordered political system based on commerce, so the wealthy aristocracy which it supported turned their attention to refinement. Circumstances made this possible first in Italy in the fifteenth century. Kings, princes, and merchants of the Italian city-states looked back to the Roman Empire for inspiration and guidance. Thus the Renaissance was initiated. Music, art, literature, science, and architecture became major preoccupations of the new enlightened age. In garden design, which held an equal place with the other arts, the most important influence was the writing of Pliny on gardens, paraphrased by Alberti in the second half of the fifteenth century. The theory proposed that the garden be strongly linked to the house by loggias and other architectural extensions into the landscape. Terraces and stairways were recommended to overcome the difficulties of uneven terrain, and an avenue or axis should link up all elements and spaces of the plan.

The gardens of the early Renaissance were designed as intellectual retreats where scholars and artists could work and debate in the coolness of the countryside away from the heat and frustrations of the cities in summer. The Villa Medici, designed by Michelozzo for Cosimo de' Medici around 1450, is an early expression of Alberti's principles (Fig. 2.18). The banker Medici selected the site on a hillside outside Florence overlooking the plain where it would catch the breeze. Thus it allowed the view which Alberti prescribed. Because of the hillside location, several terraces were required to fit the villa

Fig. 2.18   The Villa Medici (1450).

into the land. The entrance driveway followed the contours along the hillside arriving at the top terrace in front of the villa. The house was connected to the garden by a loggia or arcade. However, the relationship between the upper and lower terrace is indirect. The necessary connection was not celebrated with an elaborate staircase as it would have been in the sixteenth century. Behind the house and cut off from the rest of the garden is the giardino segreto, or secret garden. This was a place in which to be alone, secret, hidden and quiet, as opposed to the rest of the garden which would be more public, used by visitors and guests, and permeated with servants.

Bramante's plan for the Belvedere Garden of the Vatican (1503) introduced architectural steps as a major garden design feature to link terraces. The great hillside Italian gardens of subsequent dates developed this new element to its fullest potential. The use of water, which was readily available in the hills, favored for summer villas, was also exploited in elaborate gardens.

Perhaps the greatest example of expertise in stairways and waterworks is the Villa d'Este, designed by Pirro Ligorio in 1575 (Fig. 2.19). Here all the essential characteristics of the prototypical Italian garden are in evidence. Dense shade as a contrast to the bright Mediterranean sunlight was provided by the

Fig. 2.19 The Villa D'Este (1575).

arrangement of avenues of tall cypress, pleached alleys, and arbors. Sculpture and architectural features were placed throughout the garden to enliven it by contrast with natural forms and textures and also to provide an architectural relationship with the house or villa. On the steep slopes, terraces and flat areas were carved out, supported by retaining walls, and connected with a variety of stairs, flights of steps, and ramps. Water, diverted from a river at a higher point, was directed through the gardens in the form of cascades, fountains, jets, and reflecting pools. These provided visual and sensuous delight and also served as an irrigation system. The presence of water together with shade contributed to the much desired coolness which the garden was expected to provide. Boxwood and other shrubs were clipped and arranged in linear patterns to be seen from above, but the use of flowering plants was rare. The entire layout was organized axially. Avenues of trees were used to emphasize perspective and to frame views of the landscape beyond the garden. The house and garden were designed in one process, as a unity.

The entrance is at the lower level and the visitor progressed through the garden with its various sculpture and fountains and other features and points of interest to the palace above. This provided a kinetic and sensuous experience, an unfolding of events before entering the building. A spectacular composition, it was designed for effect and to impress those who visited it.

The Villa Lante, built earlier than d'Este, is less Baroque, on a smaller scale, and more intimate (Fig. 2.20). Its design was directly related to an existing village (Fig. 2.21). An avenue runs between its marketplace and the front gate. The villa itself is two houses, or one house split into two by the garden, whose axis divides it. In addition, since the garden runs from the front gate between the villas to the top of the hillside, there is front garden and a back garden. These two facts make it an unusual and interesting design. Sylvia Crowe speaks of the progression of water from a rustic quality at the top, gradually increasing in sophistication as it is chan-

Fig. 2.20 The Villa Lante (1560).

Fig. 2.21 Plan of the Villa Lante, showing the relationship of the garden to the adjoining village. Note also the large enclosed informal woodland.

nelized and formed into jets and waterfalls until it reaches the bottom in an elaborate architectural water parterre.[2] On the other hand, since (as in the Villa d'Este) the garden is approached from the bottom, the actual experience sequence would in all probability be the reverse. The garden is a progression of events with changing views, symbolic meaning, and increasing enclosure. At certain points jets of water were designed to spray unsuspecting guests, and a stone dining table in the upper garden utilized the water in its center for cooling wine and floating dishes back and forth. As one rises up the hill, the parterre on the lower level is revealed and the surrounding town and landscape beyond the

2. Sylvia Crowe, *Garden Design* (London: Country Life, 1958).

wall also become progressively more visible. The enclosed garden was an oasis or paradise in contrast to the misery and squalor in the adjacent village and surrounding agricultural landscape.

In both of these gardens there is an inspired combination of site and concept. The qualities of the site are respectfully molded into a strong architectural composition. This provides an intense contrast between natural and man-made forms, which is often the essence of visual satisfaction in landscape design. Moreover, the site is enriched with detail appropriate and related to the overall concept yet providing variety and surprise within an intelligible whole. This relationship between detail and site plan is handled in such a way that each would be incomplete without the other. These are enduring principles in design.

FRANCE

Conditions of peace and prosperity essential for a renaissance came to France later. The aristocracy's enthusiasm to assimilate the artistic developments of Italy was dampened by the Hundred Years' War with England until the end of the fifteenth century. In 1495 Charles VIII of France made an expedition to Naples and returned with twenty-one Italian artists, a considerably quantity of *objets d'art,* and ambitions to build in the Italian manner. Subsequently, the gardens of the ancient châteaux at Amboise and Blois were altered and additions were made to reflect the Italian aesthetic. But it was difficult to achieve the prescribed unity between the new gardens and the existing buildings surrounded by protective moats and fortifications. At Blois, due to the lay of the land, new formal gardens were laid out at an oblique angle to the château. At Chantilly, the original castle occupied an island, making a direct house and garden relationship impossible (Fig. 2.22). At Fontainebleau, where Francis I rebuilt and decorated the palace with the help of a second importation of Italian artists in 1525, gardens were laid out beyond the moat separate from the châteaux.

It became obvious that only by building completely new châteaux and gardens at the same time could the proper effect be realized. This was done at Ancy-le-Franc (1546) and Château d'Anet (1548) and at numerous places thereafter. However, even though the protective moat served no defensive function after the invention of gunpowder, the French insisted on including a symbolic moat around many of the new châteaux.

In the seventeenth century France reached her greatest period of wealth and power and, in addition, became the major arbiter of taste throughout Europe. The French garden is particularly noted for it use of parterres. The origin of the parterre lay in the use of low hedges to separate one kind of herb from another in the Medieval physic garden. The functional divisions became ornamental in themselves and frequently there was nothing contained within them. Sometimes colored gravel or clay and sometimes flower and foliage plants were used. Jacques Boyceau developed the art of the parterre and a theory of garden design which prepared the ground for the celebrated work of André Le Nôtre in the mid-seventeenth-century.

The climate and landscape of northern France played a role in determining the basic characteristics of the French garden and also accounted for some differences between the prototypical French and Italian gardens. Northern France is comparatively flat and wooded. The gardens thus tended to appear as clearings in a forest and the gentle topography had to be treated with subtlety to create distinct differentiation of levels or terraces from which to view the parterres. Views out were limited. Slowly moving rivers and low-lying marshland lent themselves to the development of canals, moats, and expanses of still water. The use of fountains and cascades is thus less typical in the French than in the Italian garden. The few fountains in northern France were achieved at great expense and with considerable ingenuity.

The strong axial layout, symmetry, mathematical proportions, and infinite perspective of the seventeenth-century French garden reflect the wealth and power and rigid social structure of France and the evolving concept of man's ascendancy over nature. Hunting practices in the forest land surrounding the gardens required the cutting of alleys radiating from a central point. These provided sight lines and facilitated maneuverability. This "star" pattern was incorporated in the design of the garden and also in urban form, as demonstrated in the radiating avenues of Versailles, Paris, and Washington, D.C.

Two masterpieces by André Le Nôtre, Vaux-le-Vicomte (1650–1661) (Figs. 2.23 and 2.24) and Versailles (1661) (Figs. 2.25 and 2.26), represent the ultimate expression of the concept of a geometrically ordered landscape. Vaux is a perfect example of house and garden unity. It was designed by a team

Fig. 2.22 Chantilly, France in the 16th Century. A direct relationship between the ancient castle and the new formal gardens is prevented by the defensive moat.

consisting of André Le Nôtre, the gardener, and Le Brun and Le Vau, architects. The scale of the enterprise was, for those days, enormous. The project provided employment for hundreds of workers, some of whose families were displaced by the removal of three villages which lay in the way of the design. The area of the estate measured approximately ¾ mile by 1½ miles. However, the formal garden itself was a smaller area around the palace. The plan looks simple, rigid and symmetrical, but it is actually rich and varied on either side of the main axis with a number of surprises. The land was carefully shaped as it sloped away from the palace in such a way that the river, which was canalized, could not be seen until the last minute. From the other side of the river, looking back, the entire facade of the palace is seen reflected in the square pond. The garden is a mathematical exercise with carefully worked out proportions and optical effects. The palace itself is surrounded by a moat, a symbolic feature carried over from earlier traditions.

The garden belonged to Fouquet, Finance Minister to Louis XIV, and was frequented by large crowds of courtiers and officials, nobles, and their servants. It was a stage set for display and ceremony where fetes and concerts were held, boating took place on the river and hunting in the surrounding park, and the whole environment and social routine had all the qualities of an exclusive country club.

The King, jealous of Fouquet's social and artistic triumph, imprisoned him and took his design team to a small hunting lodge at Versailles. Within seven years, the original garden of 250 acres was enlarged to an estate of 15,000 acres, and the facade of the palace was extended to 1,325 feet in length. Although the garden itself may seem small in relation to the entire planned area, its axial lines are extended out into the landscape in the form of hunting rides forming star intersections where they meet and reradiate. It was an even greater undertaking than Vaux-le-Vicomte.

In spite of the technical difficulties, there were 14,000 fountains at Versailles. The palace was the focus of a new city of Versailles built to house the 20,000 people connected with the French Court. The palace itself accommodated 1,000 noblemen with their 4,000 servants. The distance from the palace to the beginning of the canal is ¾ mile (a gentle slope). The canal is 4,000 feet or almost 1 mile long beyond that and 300 feet wide. The principles of the French garden are clearly illustrated; the strong central axis leading to the horizon runs straight through the Sun King's bedchamber. It is a clear expression of the power of man over nature and, of course, of one man over other men, of divine right. The surrounding forest forms a strong enclosure to the garden. Views out are restricted to those provided by the alleys. The garden space is tightly closed around the main axis at the tapis vert. Within the forest to the left and right of the central open space are all kinds of gardens, waterworks, small theaters, and other contrived fantasies for the amusement of King and courtiers. As at Vaux-le-Vicomte, the gardens were designed for use by many people at one time. Versailles was the center of government with all the diplomatic, political, and entertainment functions that implied. The gardens provided an outdoor setting in keeping with the grandeur of the palace.

Fig. 2.23   Plan of Vaux-le-Vicomte (1650-61).

Fig. 2.24 Vaux-le-Vicomte (1650-61).

Fig. 2.26   Versailles (1661-65).

Fig. 2.25   Plan of Versailles (1662-65).

Fig. 2.27 Longleat, England (1685-1711).

THE FORMAL GARDEN IN ENGLAND

The influence of the French garden was enormous, especially in Holland and England. Their scale and rich design were impressive to all who saw them. The French tradition in England became pre-eminent after the restoration of the Stuart kings at the beginning of the seventeenth century. Contemporary views show the unsuitability of the rigid forms when superimposed on the undulating English agricultural landscapes. The intimate outdoor room quality of the Tudor garden was destroyed; parterres replaced knot gardens, and wells and simple fountains were replaced with formal pools and elaborate waterworks. Le Nôtre is thought to have designed the gardens of Greenwich Palace for Charles II, but the professional gardeners London and Wise were the chief exponents of the French garden in England, and they completed work which attempted to recreate the essential symmetry and monumentality of the French style at Hampton Court (1699), Longleat (1685–1711) (Fig. 2.27), and Chatsworth (1680–1690)

At Longleat, the natural river was formed into square and rectangular basins and furnished with fountains. Parterres were laid out within an architectural framework, but the avenues of trees superimposed on an open, undulating agricultural landscape looked quite different from the hunting rides cut out of the forests of France. At Greenwich, the topography of the site did not match the formality of the plan, nor was anything done to make it do so. Even at Hampton Court, where the land was more level, the French garden style did not fit well on the open landscape. In other words, due perhaps to inept design and certainly to the different qualities of the English landscape, the French gardens in England were poor imitations of the great models on which they were based.

Fig. 2.28 A town residence, Salem, Massachusetts (18th Century). 1. stable 2. toolyard 3. arbor 4. flower garden 5. vegetables 6. bee hives.

COLONIAL GARDENS

It was inevitable that both French and British settlers should bring to the American colonies the seventeenth-century garden forms from their homelands. In the north settlers of predominantly yeoman stock perpetuated the cottage gardens they had been accustomed to in England. This was essentially a utilitarian garden with little sense of aesthetics in its plan. In Massachusetts settlers from a higher economic background took the English manor house and garden as a prototype. Typically, these early American gardens were not large, were enclosed with fences or hedges, and had a central axis path leading through beds of flowers and vegetables, edged with clipped plants, to an arbor, summer house, or dovecote at the end (Fig. 2.28). The formal arrangements hinted at a desire to be stylish in the French manner but gardens in the United States were created under very different social and economic conditions.

The south, with its tradition of landed gentry and a different type of society and government, was more conducive to the development of extensive gardens (Fig. 2.29). Their inspiration came from imported gardening literature and European travel. The fine palace gardens of Williamsburg (1699) show clearly the European formal garden influence. At Middleton Place (1741) (Fig. 2.30), the formal gardens and the large rectangular lake reminiscent of French moats or the water basins at Versailles illustrate the strength of the French influence. This influence in America stretched well into the nineteenth century despite the evolution of the landscape garden in England in the early eighteenth century.

Fig. 2.29 Typical town garden in Virginia (18th Century). 1. kitchen 2. dairy 3. smoke house 4. stables 5. vegetables 6. grapes.

Fig. 2.30 Middleton Place South Carolina (1741). 1. house 2. formal pool 3. terracing.

ENGLAND

The landscape garden was an entirely different concept and its origins were varied. The English countryside with its rolling hills, winding streams, and scattered trees, which was inherently unsuited to the French garden, was inevitably a strong influence. The formal gardens of France were associated with despotic government distasteful to the democratic and rights-conscious Englishmen of the eighteenth century. An antithesis to the formal garden would thus be more acceptable. The emerging Romantic movement produced poetry and paintings which extolled the beauties of nature and landscape. The grand tour which all cultured Englishmen made through the Alps to Italy brought them in contact with rugged, picturesque scenery. Scenes such as they would see on the tour were represented on the canvases of Nicolas Poussin, Salvador Rosa, and Claude Lorrain. The paintings were not actual views but compositions of typical elements selected and arranged for emphasis—craggy mountains, rivers, pastoral plains, ruined castles and monuments, lakes, and wind-blown trees. Many included classical temples and groups of allegorical figures. In addition to the landscape and its stylization in the paintings, the visitor to Italy saw the famous villas and their gardens in an appealing, romantic state of disrepair. The travelers began to see landscape through the eyes of the painter and consequently on their return to England found their stiff formal gardens uninteresting and unattractive. One other influence was the Orient, which was opened to trade in the seventeenth century. Scenes on imported porcelain and lacquer work depicted natural gardens, lakes, and waterfalls and the aesthetic and attitude which they represented were influential in the development of a

Fig. 2.31 Plan of Katsura Palace, Japan (early 17th Century). The informal landscape was symbolic.

Fig. 2.32 Blenheim Palace as laid out by Henry Wise in 1705. Note 1. the straight entrance from the village, 2. the parterre in front of the house, and the radiating avenues in the woodland.

new system of gardening in England (Fig. 2.31).

The landscape garden was a product of the Romantic movement. Its form was based on direct observation of nature and the principles of painting. Surprise, variety, concealment, and the development of idyllic prospects became the goals of the art of landscape. The manipulation of nature's undulating contours according to Hogarth's serpentine "line of beauty" and the articulation of light and shade much as a painter would do became the preoccupation of all men of taste and culture in eighteenth-century England and ultimately all over Europe and

in America in the nineteenth century. Where they existed, the parterre and terrace of the formal garden were replaced with rolling grassland, clumps of trees, lakes, meandering rivers, and serpentine drives (Figs. 2.32 and 2.33). In the early examples the scene was embellished at suitable points with temples, bridges, and sculptures.

Of fundamental importance was the elimination of the visual break between garden and landscape. One of the techniques for eliminating this break was the sunken fence. This allowed the eye to see straight out to the countryside while at the same time keep-

ing deer and stock out of the garden proper. It is a technique with potential for use today in contemporary landscape design (Fig. 2.34).

William Kent argued that the validity of the system was due to two important factors: first its moral integrity and second its Classical derivations. For example, he said that bronze fountains cast to look like trees, trees clipped to look like stone, and other such trappings found at Versailles were dishonest or at least foolish. A natural cascade or serpentine stream was purer in concept than a jet of muddy water drawn up at great expense from a marsh. The

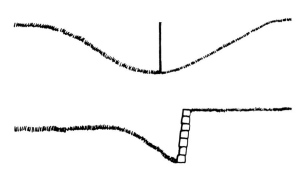

Fig. 2.33 Blenheim Palace as altered by Lancelot Brown in 1758. Note 1. the new winding approach from the village, 2. the irregular plantings and the sunk fence in front of the house replacing the parterre.

Fig. 2.34 Two versions of the sunk fence,—a technique of the 18th Century landscape garden used to eliminate visual boundaries between garden and landscape.

taste for the irregular and natural was thus considered highly moral. The Classical origins of irregularity were more difficult to identify. However, it was found that Classical authority practiced regularity in building and irregularity in gardens. The Valley of the Tempe at Hadrian's villa was evidence of this (Fig. 2.12). Thus, just as Palladian architecture was established as Classically correct, so too was the irregular garden.

By the third decade of the century, the revolution in garden design was well under way. It was led at first by so-called amateurs such as Henry Hoare,

who started work at Stourhead in 1725 (Fig. 2.35). The garden was set in a valley in which a stream was dammed to create an irregular lake. This cannot be seen from the house above, a Palladian villa, and, conversely, the house is not seen from the garden. The only connection between the two is an obelisk, which can be seen both from the house and from a specific point in the garden. A path was laid out around the shore of the lake connecting a series of "events," and the garden was properly experienced by following the route in the prescribed direction. The tour might take a day even though the dis-

tance was not great. The garden was arranged according to the rules of landscape painting, and in fact in this particular case the garden was based on a painting by Claude Lorrain. The bridge at the starting point, the Temple of Flora, and the Pantheon set out in the garden are similar in form and disposition to those in the painting.

A further level of appreciation was the mythological or literary allusions associated with each feature. As one walked, new vistas and views were revealed and the visitor was brought obliquely to buildings and places seen earlier. At one point the path leads

Fig. 2.35b   Stourhead, England (1725).

underground into a cool grotto with a moss-covered statue of Neptune; ferns, and the sound of running water. It is a conscious change in environment to evoke physiologically as well as intellectually images of a legendary underwater kingdom. A rocky opening at water level reveals the Temple of Flora across the lake already visited.

Stourhead is thus a sequence of experiences. Many have intellectual meaning and are conceived and appreciated on the basis of a knowledge of mythology and poetry. In addition, the environmental qualities of light, temperature, texture, and sound together with visual impressions add sensations which, combined with the first level of reaction, make a complete experience. A modern movie is perhaps the closest comparison in which an image,

Fig. 2.35a   Stourhead, England (1725). *Key to plan:* 1. house, 2. obelisk, 3. Paradise Temple, 4. grotto, 5. watch cottage, 6. Pantheon Temple, 7. Sun Temple, 8. St. Peter's Church.

Fig. 2.36 Rousham, England (1738-1740). View from the house into the landscape embellished with a mill and distant romantic ruin.

Fig. 2.37 Rousham, England (1738-1740). Plan shows the placing of elements in the landscape to improve the view. 1. mill and miller's house, 2. ruin, 3. house, 4. garden.

the meaning associated with it, and the response can be predetermined.

Bright flowering plants were not favored in the landscape garden. The rhododendrons that can be seen at Stourhead today were not part of the original planting. These were planted later and now stimulate a controversy between "purists" and the National Trust, who own and maintain the garden for the public. The National Trust say that the visiting public like azaleas. The purists would like the rhododendrons removed.

William Kent was the first professional to design gardens in the new manner. At Rousham, built between 1738 and 1740, Kent planned the entire view from the existing house and built a miller's cottage and a ruin on a distant hill to complete the romantic composition (Fig. 2.36). Thus the design consideration extended to the entire landscape visible from the house. The cumulative effect of this approach has resulted in the way the English landscape looks today. It has been designed and is a composite of views from many country houses. The garden at Rousham lies to one side of the house and includes a classical arcade, a serpentine rivulet, a grotto, cascades, and evocative statues placed within clearings in a woodland and connected with vistas and walks (Fig. 2.37).

By the mid-eighteenth century, the new style in gardening was widely accepted. Lancelot Brown, called Capability Brown, became the leading exponent and was in great demand. Unlike Kent, he did not approve of architectural features in the garden.

Fig. 2.38 Blenheim, England (18th Century).

Terraces and parterres were to be cleared away from the base of the house until nothing was left except grass, which came right up to the foundations. A sunken fence would eliminate the visual boundary, and the seemingly contiguous landscape would be planted irregularly with trees in clumps or groups on undulating ground. If possible, a stream would be dammed to form a lake as at Blenheim, and made to fit naturally without awkwardness into the landscape (Figs. 2.33 and 2.38). The appearance of these landscapes depended on good estate management and productive agriculture, for they encompassed working farms and fields. In addition, the making of picturesque landscapes which would blend visually into the existing natural system depended on an understanding of ecological principles.

In the late eighteenth and early nineteenth century Humphry Repton published a theory of landscape gardening and became the leading exponent of the style.[3] Repton modified Brown's ruthless formula and favored the restoration of the terrace to connect the house to the garden. In a satirical essay Repton was referred to as Mr. Milestone because of a trick whereby the milestones set on the driveway leading to the house were set at less than a mile apart. In this we see evidence of appreciation based on quantity and size reflecting on the prestige of the owners. A technique of more importance were his "redbooks," which illustrated his proposals with "before" and "after" drawings or watercolors (Figs. 2.39 and 2.40). Comparison of these showed how a quiet, uninteresting meadow and stream could be transformed into a beautiful landscape with serpentine lake and irregular plantations as an environment for a castlelike establishment set on a broad terrace (Fig. 2.41).

3. Humphry Repton, *Sketches and Hints on Landscape Gardening* (London: W. Bulmer, 1794).

Fig. 2.39 An impression of Redbook drawing by Repton showing a house in a bland landscape—a parody of Brown's "formula" (1803).

Fig. 2.40 The "after" illustration by Repton showed the introduction of a terrace and outbuildings, a romantic lake and picturesque planting (1803).

Fig. 2.41 Proposal for a country house by Repton (19th Century).

UNITED STATES

In due course the romantic landscape garden was adopted in America. Thomas Jefferson's remodeling of the Monticello gardens (Fig. 2.42) and the simple lawn and plantations introduced at Mount Vernon in 1737 (Fig. 2.43) are early indications of a change in American taste. Some of the first completely new landscape gardens were designed by Andre Parmentier, a Belgian who established a nursery in Brooklyn in 1824. In 1828 he wrote an essay praising the picturesque style and opposing the formalism then prevalent in America. He subsequently laid out the grounds of several large estates along the Hudson River before his death in 1830.

Fig. 2.42   Monticello, Virginia (1796).

Fig. 2.43   Mount Vernon (1737).

Parmentier was succeeded by Andrew Jackson Downing as champion of the landscape garden. Downing's theory,[4] published in 1841, was based on the work of Repton and embodied the same theory of the picturesque. His arguments in favor of the beauties of natural landscape, woods, and plantations and the aesthetic and moral values to be obtained from them were so convincing that all new gardens in association with the increasing number of suburban villas were laid out in the Romantic idiom (Fig. 2.44). His book was moralistic in tone, stressing the refinement and sophistication needed to appreciate the subtleties of natural forms. By the middle of the nineteenth century Downing had established himself as a tastemaker in gardening matters on the East Coast in America. He was adopted by the wealthy owners of estates on the Hudson River. Here he created very creditable landscapes in the English manner but with care to emphasize the particular qualities of each site. Illustrations in his book show prototypical villas for people of middle income (Fig. 2.45). Families are seen posed somewhat awkwardly or having tea on a lawn enclosed with conifers and shrubberies or commanding a view of a distant mountain landscape. Such villa gardens of the Victorian era were too small to

4. Andrew Jackson Downing, *A Treatise on the Theory and Practice of Landscape Gardening: Adapted to North America* (Boston: C. C. Little and Co., 1841).

Fig. 2.45 Villa and landscape garden as advocated by A. J. Downing (19th Century).

Fig. 2.44 Plan of suburban Villa Garden by Andrew Jackson Downing (1841). 1. lawn, 2. kitchen garden, 3. picturesque garden, 4. flower garden.

achieve the landscape effect, and this conflict between concept and the lack of space in which to carry it out contributed to the disintegration of the garden into the hodgepodge of flower beds and shrubberies which it became in the later nineteenth century.

Downing established and popularized the Romantic landscape garden as a tradition in America. It was part of a larger interest in nature and the American landscape, which will be discussed in Chapter Three. In the adoption of an informal and natural style of landscape design which recognized the constraints and potentials of each site we can detect the roots of a landscape philosophy held and advocated strongly by Frederick Law Olmsted as he entered practice in 1856. Since that time Olmsted, Eliot, Cleveland, and others in the field subscribed to a new way of doing things, which emphasized nature, and natural looks, with soft edges and curving lines as a contrast to urbanism in the form of one building or a whole city. An East Coast tradition was developed in practice and taught at Harvard University and other schools which gave courses in landscape architecture.

CALIFORNIA

It was noted previously that the early homesteads of California derived from an entirely different tradition whose roots lay in Islam and Spain. Retired Mexican soldiers and pioneer ranchers in the California of the early nineteenth century built adobe houses with covered porches around a central space or courtyard which was used as a social area for conducting ranch business and family affairs. The courtyards were also frequently used for growing vegetables, fruit, and some flowers. The plan of one such ranch establishment in the Santa Clara Valley about 1858 shows two gardens (Fig. 2.46). One was enclosed on three sides by the whitewashed adobe walls of the rooms, which were connected by a covered veranda or arcade. The arrangement was formal with flower beds, rose hedges, and clipped cypress. Gravel walks led to a fountain or well in the center. An orchard or orange grove enclosed the fourth side. The second garden contained a grape arbor and a chapel. The configuration of this homestead conceded a close affinity with outdoor life. It was simple in design, and its form was related to the practical aspects of irrigation and the cultivation of produce and flowering plants.

With the cession of California to the United States in 1848, the region became susceptible to the life style, fashions, and attitudes of the East Coast, which included, as we have seen, a taste for landscape gardens. Thus in California the adobe architecture and patio of the Mexican-Spanish homesteads was replaced by the East Coast villa style whose ornamental gardens were unsuited to the aridity of the area (Fig. 2.47). A plan published by John McLaren, Superintendent of Golden Gate Park,

Fig. 2.46   Ranch establishment in California, about 1858 (see also Fig. 2.8).

Fig. 2.47 "Victorian" house and garden, Sacramento, California (late 19th Century).

is very reminiscent of Downing's work.[5] A large front lawn preserving a social distance from the street was an important element of the layout. Kitchen gardens and orchards were also included (Fig. 2.48).

Frederick Law Olmsted criticized the inability of Californians to adapt to the specific climatic conditions of the West and expressed disapproval of the widespread tendency to ignore the advantages of health and comfort which the close relationship between house and garden would provide. His scheme for the Stanford campus (1880) illustrated what he considered appropriate architectural forms; arcades and courtyards similar to those seen in Spain and North Africa, which would compensate for the effects of heat and wind (Fig. 2.49). There were no

lawns to be irrigated and the original planting was completed with drought-tolerant species suited to the climate.

A revival of interest in Classical architecture at the end of the nineteenth century resulted in the building of numerous "Mediterranean" villas and "Spanish colonial" houses in California and elsewhere (Figs. 2.50 and 2.51). The gardens, which were an integral part of the style, were imbued with formality and order. Bruce Porter (1915), a San Francisco artist and garden designer, commended this return to direct design and criticized the picturesque curve and gravel drive of the landscape garden which John McLaren advocated and which he felt should be relegated "to a more leisurely, romantic and lingering generation."[6] Further, he found satisfaction in the

way the house extended into the garden and, irrespective of the relative artistic merits, this aspect of the eclectic forms inherent in the originals of Italy and Spain on which they were based undoubtedly provided a more direct relationship between indoors and out. In addition, the architectural style was more easily adaptable to the smaller garden.

The use of loggias similar to that at the Villa Medici (Fig. 2.18) permitted a more direct link between the house and garden than existed in the "Victorian" type of house, which was usually set up off the ground with porches related to the rooms of the house but not the garden. In other examples of the new style, the placing of the front entrance at the side of the house facilitated a different relationship between the living room and the garden. In the earlier prototypes the living rooms would have been at the front facing the street.

In the early 1900s there was an active campaign to attract new settlers to California. A Union Pacific brochure of the time, *California Calls You*, shows an attractive young lady sitting on a grassy bank studded with California poppies, under the shade of a California live oak with a lake and snow-capped mountain in the background. Real estate operators flooded the East Coast and the midwest with brochures describing subdivisions and cities in California waiting to be lived in. They used seductive language. Another brochure described Oakland as the "Athens of the Pacific—the beauty spot of the earth." Physicians wrote of the health benefits to be obtained by living in California.

5. John McLaren, *Gardening in California, Landscape and Flower* (San Francisco: A. M. Robertson, 1924).
6. Garnett Porter, *Stately Homes of California*. With an introduction by Bruce Porter (Boston: Little, Brown, 1915).

Fig. 2.49   Portion of the Stanford campus (1880).

Fig. 2.48   Plan for a villa garden (1900) by John McLaren, superintendant of Golden Gate Park. Note the similarities with A. J. Downing plan (Fig. 2.44). 1. vegetable garden 2. orchard, 3. front lawn, 4. garage.

A significant development in the early 1900s related to these enticements was the "invention" of the California bungalow as a convenient house type for an increasing population of families with modest incomes (Fig. 2.52). Typically consisting of six to nine rooms, these single-story houses with many windows, ample porches, and wide eaves were built on small lots in a variety of architectural styles. The Gamble house by the Green Brothers in Pasadena, although not a bungalow, initiated the concept. It has many porches related to the rooms of the house, permitting outdoor living. The bungalow became a prevalent house type and did recognize, as Olmsted put it, the advantages of health and comfort which could be provided by a direct relationship with the outdoors. The back porch was an important element. Overlooking a small garden, its use was extended to the serving of meals and family activity somewhat as the Spanish-Mexican patio had served.

The quality of life afforded by the California bungalow was described by C. F. Saunders as "informal but not necessarily bohemian" and "simple without being sloppy."[7] A popular gardening book of the day by Eugene Murmann[8] illustrated many de-

7. Charles Francis Saunders, *Under the Sky in California* (New York: McBride, Nast, 1913).
8. Eugene O. Murmann, *Typical California Bungalows* (Los Angeles: E. O. Murmann, 1913).

Fig. 2.50 The eclectic revival in California and elsewhere produced formal gardens and houses with more intimate connections between indoors and out. Key: L. living room, K. kitchen, S. service yard, 1. gazebo, 2. fountain pool, 3. parterre, 4. terrace.

Fig. 2.51 A "Mediterranean" villa in California (1920).

signs for small bungalow gardens in a variety of styles including "Japanese," "landscape," and "flower." The significant features of these bungalows were the large proportions of space devoted to the front lawn, the major entrance and porch facing the street, and the garage in the rear where the coach house would have been traditionally, requiring a long driveway up the side of the lot (Fig. 2.53). All these traditional and space-consuming characteristics were clearly derived from landscape garden layout concepts suited for a much larger scale or plot of land. As yet, the small garden was not regarded as a special design problem.

In the 1930s, after the Depression, the urban areas of California continued to expand. Smaller building lots and the presence of the ubiquitous automobile resulted in the reduction of usable garden space for the average homeowner. There was a growing shortage of gardeners and a lack of time and enthusiasm for gardening. At the same time there was an increasing change in attitude toward gardens and a realization of their potential for providing additional living space in a mild and agreeable climate.

This change in attitude seems to have been intensified during the war, when gasoline and tire rationing limited weekend auto excursions. Californians

Fig. 2.52 California bungalow.

Fig. 2.53 Plan of a California bungalow and garden. 1. porch, 2. veranda, 3. vegetables, 4. lawn, 5. summer house, 6. garage.

began to find that staying at home was not so bad after all and *Sunset Magazine* encouraged the development of a life style in which the garden and all its components—terrace, barbecue, and swimming pool—combined into a home environment with the ambiance of a resort.

A new breed of college-educated landscape architects emerged in the late 1930s and in larger numbers after the war. Perhaps the chief innovator, or at least the elder statesman of garden design in California, is Thomas Church, who studied at Berkeley (and also Harvard). He set up his practice in 1930. His work was extremely influential on the profession of landscape architecture and also helped, through *House and Home* and *Sunset Magazine*, to shape public opinion about the form and use of the domestic garden, small or large, in California and elsewhere.

Developments in art and architecture in Europe, cubism and abstract expressionism, functional architecture, and the modern movement, had their impact first on the East Coast but also in California. Modern architecture needed modern landscape architecture. Church and later Eckbo on the West Coast, James Rose on the East, and Christopher Tunnard and others in England became the avant garde of modern landscape architecture in the late 1930s. The landscape garden and the eclectic neoclassical garden were rejected.

The career of Thomas Church is considered here in detail for three reasons. First, he was an innovator like the other great designers in history whose works have already been discussed. He evolved an approach to design suited to the environment and social context in which he practiced. Second, his practice was almost exclusively in private gardens, which is the subject of this chapter. And third, his interest lay in the small garden.

The first ten years of Church's professional career were spent searching for new garden forms that would satisfy the changing needs of society and through which he could express the new aesthetic. With adventurous clients and young architects such as William Wurster, Gardner Daily, and Ernest Born, he found opportunities to experiment. He adopted a theory which followed that of the new architecture. This recognized three sources of form. The first consisted of human needs and the specific personal requirements and characteristics of the client. The second comprised the technology of materials, construction, and plants, including maintenance and a whole range of form determinants derived from the site conditions and quality. The third was a concern for the spatial expression, which would go beyond the mere satisfaction of requirements and into the realms of fine art.

At first the garden forms he used were traditional with clipped hedges and eclectic motifs (Fig. 2.54). He designed small town gardens and wrote about the challenge they presented. He said that the small garden could not be "natural" if it was to serve as an extension to the house. Their scale and use called for hard surfaces, screens to separate areas, and design forms that would increase their apparent size (Fig. 2.55). Church recognized that many people had small gardens, especially in urban settings where they have vital function as an outdoor room or to serve as a giardino segretto such as his own small

garden behind a wall in San Francisco. Like it or not, he said, the function of the house had spilled out into the garden and must be provided for. The landscape architect no longer had a choice between the functional and the aesthetic approaches.

The increasing use of garden space was encouraged by modern architecture which provided direct access between house and garden. The use of the garden for outdoor entertaining, games, and children's play combined with the need to reduce maintenance resulted in the widespread introduction of paving materials and groundcover plants designed

as simple shapes. Church recommended that the spatially wasteful front lawn should be dispensed with and showed the advantages of this in several examples in which the street was screened off by walls or fences, providing usable private space (Fig. 2.56).

In 1937 the San Francisco Museum of Art held an exhibition called Contemporary Landscape Architecture. The work illustrated was chiefly garden design but also included the important work of the U.S. Forest Service and the National Parks service. One model illustrated a "formistic" garden layout by

Fig. 2.54 California garden of the 1930's, by Thomas D. Church. House by William W. Wurster.

Fig. 2.55 Small garden in San Francisco, by Thomas D. Church (1940).

Thomas Church for a house by William Wurster in San Mateo (Fig. 2.54). The description stated that the garden was on both sides with direct access to the living room. Wurster and Church also combined on a fantasy pavilion. In this we see the beginnings of new curvilinear forms in the garden.

Church developed a theory based on cubism, that a garden should have no beginning and no end and that it should be pleasing when seen from any angle, not only from the house. Asymmetric lines were used to create greater apparent dimensions. Simplicity of form, line, and shape were regarded as more restful to look at and easier to maintain. Form, shape, and pattern in the gardens were provided by pavings, walls, and espaliered or trained plants.

Two small gardens designed for the 1940 Golden Gate Exposition marked the beginning of this new phase (Fig. 2.57). They demonstrated the possibilities for the evolution of new visual forms in the garden while satisfying all practical criteria. The central axis was abandoned in favor of multiplicity of viewpoints, simple planes, and flowing lines. Texture and color, space and form were manipulated in a manner reminiscent of the cubist painters. A variety of curvilinear shapes, textured surfaces, and walls were combined with a sure sense of proportion and the gardens incorporated some new materials such as corrugated asbestos and wooden paving blocks. Stylistically they were a very dramatic advance on all previous garden designs.

The genius of the California garden thus lies in the combination of numerous concepts and traditions and a recognition of local conditions. Landscape architects in Britain, Scandinavia, Germany, and Switzerland produced a European synthesis with equally distinctive results. The East Coast struggled with its obsession with the landscape tra-

dition and Burle Marx in Brazil developed an approach to design that is based on modern painting and botany.

San Francisco became the home of many of the best-known landscape offices in the country. In addition to Church and Eckbo (Fig. 2.58), Royston, Williams, Halprin, Osmundson, and others designed gardens in the Bay Area in the 1940s and 1950s. A second exhibition in 1948 at the San Francisco Museum of Art showed the development in style and form and also the wider range of projects being handled by landscape architects in California.

In the domestic work we see an expression of af-

Fig. 2.56 Treatment of front garden by Thomas D. Church.

Fig. 2.57 Exhibition garden by Thomas D. Church, 1940.

Fig. 2.58 Modern garden design by Garrett Eckbo (1945) shows uses allocated for all parts of a small lot and sculptural structuring of space. Key: 1. play area 2. childrens' yard 3. flower area 4. grass 5. decomposed granite 6. service yard 7. fruit trees 8. shrub hedges B. Bedroom L. Living room K. Kitchen G. Garage

Fig. 2.59 Donnell Garden, California (1948), Thomas D. Church.

fluence and a delight with indoor/outdoor living. Church's beach house at Aptos and the Donnell garden at Sonoma (Figs. 2.59 and 8.33) show this and also show further sophistication in his approach and in the manipulation of form. They represent in my view the peak of his career. The beach garden at Aptos introduces the idea of wood as a paving surface, relatively cheap in a timber zone and relatively maintenance free. One of the most beautiful modern gardens in the world, ranking with Villa Lante, is the Donnell garden at Sonoma. The form of the swimming pool, quite simple in plan, is more complex and elegant seen in perspective. The outline is derived from the meandering of the Sonoma River in the flatlands seen below. The aesthetic connection between pool shape and forms in nature is dynamic. Contrasting with the flowing forms of the pool is a rectangular grid of concrete paving and wood decking. The decking is used in one place so that some existing live oaks could grow through and the ground remain undisturbed (Fig. 8.33). The garden shows concern for the existing and surrounding environment.

Although most of the gardens in the exhibition emphasized outdoor living, they were shown in photographs without people. Many used redwood for practically everything: steps, planters, and fences. It became a trademark of the California garden.

Ten years later there was another exhibition. Gardens were still included, although none was by Thomas Church. Some of those shown displayed a high degree of self-conscious overdesign and represented an extreme and rather foolish concern with abstract form and detail. However, the attention of most landscape architects was now being given to more significant large scale work on housing, recreation, and urban development.

In one hundred years the garden in California went through a series of transitions. First it was regarded as a necessity, as at Camulos. Here fruit and vegetables were grown and the patio served as a workplace. Next the garden became a status symbol as it came under the influence of the East Coast and the landscape garden tradition. The eclectic movement was equally demanding stylistically, and equally pretentious. In the 1960s it came to be regarded as a useful outdoor space for activities previously confined to the house, and beyond this, with the addition of swimming pools, games areas, sun decks, barbecue, children's sandbox and play equipment, the private domain took on the qualities of a recreation area. It expressed a more luxurious life style and also perhaps a withdrawing of the individual back inside the walls of the garden to compensate for the increasing publicness and tension of daily life.

The California garden is only one type, but its **evolution is characteristic**. The form is related to the Islamic, Hellenic, and Oriental traditions which preceded it and based on the people, climate, and landscape of the region.

FUTURE OF THE GARDEN

It is difficult to say what future there is for the private garden. There seems to be a revival of interest in gardening and in organic vegetables. In most California gardens irrigation has been required because many "exotic" plants were favored over the native or drought-tolerant plants. In a country where water is not plentiful, this seems wasteful. So the future of the garden in California at least must take account of this environmental factor. But the survival of private gardens as a concept is a separate issue. The increasing popularity of condominiums and cluster developments (Fig. 5.12) is fostering, or may be the result of, a change in attitude. It seems that many people do not want to have anything to do with gardens and gardening. They would like to look at grass, tress, and flowers but prefer maintenance crews to take care of it. I think this is an unenlightened theory developed by people who sell real estate. For most people the garden or a symbol of it which they nourish themselves will remain an important part of life.

Most contemporary landscape architects, with a few notable exceptions, have given up designing private gardens. Perhaps this is appropriate. There is certainly a case to be made for more participation in the design process by clients. Professional technology is definitely required, however, especially in fragile environments where the impact of inept construction could be devastating and widespread. Also, the imagination and conceptual thinking of a designer is still a valid input in a process whose purpose is to reveal possibilities and develop unthought-of solutions suited to the specific setting.

Suggested Readings

General Histories of Landscape Architecture and Garden Design

Berral, Julia S., *The Garden: An Illustrated History*.
Clifford, Derek, *A History of Garden Design*.
Crowe, Sylvia, *Garden Design*, pp. 17–77.
Fairbrother, Nan, *Men and Gardens*.
Gotheim, M. Louise, *The History of Garden Art*.
Hadfield, Miles, *Gardens*.
Hyams, Edward, *A History of Gardens and Gardening*.
Newton, Norman T., *Design on the Land*.
Sorensen, Carl Theodore, *The Origin of Garden Art*.
Tobey, George, *A History of Landscape Architecture*.
Wright, Richardson Little, *The Story of Gardening*.

Primitive

Clifford, Derek, *A History of Garden Design*, Ch. 1, "Pliny and the Renaissance Garden."
Crisp, Frank, *Medieval Gardens*.
Tobey, George, *A History of Landscape Architecture*, Chs. 1–9.
Wright, Richardson Little, *The Story of Gardening*, Ch. 2, "How Gardening Began."
Films, music and novels describing or produced in particular periods of history contribute to an understanding of the social and environmental context of the gardens.

Ancient Rome:
The films "Cleopatra" (1963) and "Julius Caesar" (1950).

Egypt:
The opera "Aida" (Verdi).

Middle Ages:
"Gothic" films of Bergman such as "The Seventh Seal" (1956).
The films "The Lion in Winter" (1968) and "Becket" (1964).
Narcissus and Goldmund by Herman Hesse.
Religious and secular music of Medieval Europe by Dunstable, Binchois, and Dufay.

Spain

Crowe, Sylvia, *Garden Design*, Ch. 3, "The Hispano Arabic Garden."
Villiers-Stuart, Constance M., *Spanish Gardens*.
The film "El Cid" (1961).
Thirteenth-century troubador and Trouvere music and de Falla's "Nights in the Gardens of Spain."
Alhambra by Washington Irving (1829).

Italy

Crowe, Sylvia, *Garden Design*, Ch. 4, "The Italian Garden."
Jellicoe, Geoffrey A., *Studies in Landscape Design*, Ch. 1, pp. 1–15, "The Italian Garden of the Renaissance."
Masson, Georgina, *Italian Gardens*, pp. 142–144, "Villa Lante," pp. 136–139, "Villa D'Este."
Shepherd, John C., and Geoffrey A. Jellicoe, *Italian Gardens of the Renaissance*, pp. 1–24.
The films "Romeo and Juliet" (Zeffirelli production), and "Taming of the Shrew" (Zeffirelli production with Taylor and Burton).
Masses and madrigals by Monteverdi, Palestrina, and Gabrielli.

France

Clifford, Derek, *A History of Garden Design*, Ch. 3., "France."
Crowe, Sylvia, *Garden Design*, Ch. 5, "The French Tradition."
Fox, Helen, *André le Nôtre*.
Giedion, Sigfried, *Space, Time and Architecture*, pp. 133–160, "Organization of Outer Space."
Hazlehurst, Franklin H., *Jacques Boyceau and the French Formal Garden*.
The films "La prise du pouvoir par Louis XIV," "The Rise of Louis XIV" (1965) and "L'année dernière à Marienbad," "Last Year at Marienbad" (1961).

Sun King by Nancy Mitford.
The Three Musketeers by Alexander Dumas.
Operatic, religious, dance, and ballet music by Charpentier, de Lalande, and Lully (Court musician to Louis XIV).

England

Chadwick, George F., *The Works of Sir Joseph Paxton*, pp. 19–43.
Clark, H. F., *The English Landscape Garden*, esp. pp. 1–35, 37–38, Chiswick.
Crowe, Sylvia, *Garden Design*, Ch. 6, "The English Landscape Garden."
Dutton, Ralph, *The English Garden*.
Green, David, *Gardener to Queen Anne*, "Henry Wise and the Formal Garden."
Hussey, Christopher, *The Picturesque*.
Hyams, Edward S., *The English Garden*.
Jourdain, Margaret, *The Work of William Kent*, pp. 15–26, Introduction by Christopher Hussey.
Massingham, Betty, *Miss Jekyll*.
Pevsner, Nikolaas, "The Genesis of the Picturesque," *Architectural Review*, Vol. 96, November 1944, pp. 139–166.
Stroud, Dorothy, *Capability Brown*, pp. 13–20, Introduction by Christopher Hussey.
Stroud, Dorothy, *Humphry Repton*.
Taylor, Geoffrey, *The Victorian Flower Garden*.
The film "Tom Jones" (1963).
Oliver Goldsmith's restoration comedy "She Stoops to Conquer."
Stage, religious, string, and keyboard music, madrigals, masses, lute songs, etc., by Tallis (for Henry VIII at Hampton Court). Morley, Byrd, Purcell, Boyce, Haydn, and Handel (Royal Firework Music for open air concert, 1749).

Japan, China and India

Berral, Julia S., *The Garden: An Illustrated History*, pp. 327-364.
Graham, Dorothy, *Chinese Gardens*.

Horiguchi, Sutami, *Tradition of Japanese Gardens*.
International Federation of Landscape Architects, *Landscape Architecture in Japan*, 9th Congress, 1964.
Morse, Edward S., *Japanese Homes and Their Surroundings*.
Newsom, S., *A Thousand Years of Japanese Gardens*.
Siren, Oswald, *Gardens of China*.
Tamura, Tsuyoshi, *Art of Landscape Gardens in Japan*.
Villiers-Stuart, Constance M., *Gardens of the Great Moghuls*.
The film "Chushingura."

United States

American Society of Landscape Architects, *Colonial Gardens*.
Cleveland, Horace W. S., *Landscape Architecture* (1873), Ch. 2, pp. 6–9.
Downing, Andrew Jackson, *Landscape Gardening: Adapted to North America*.
Eaton, Leonard K., *Landscape Artist in America: The Life and Work of Jens Jensen*, pp. 81–211, "The Private Work."
Fabos, Julius, et al., *Frederick Law Olmsted, Sr.*
Laurie, Michael, "The California Garden," *Landscape Architecture*, October 1965, pp. 23–27.
Laurie, Michael, "The California Influence on Contemporary Landscape Architecture," *Landscape Architecture*, July 1966, pp. 292–298.
Lockwood, Alice G. B., for Garden Club of America, *Gardens of Colony and State*.
Newton, Norman T., *Design on the Land*, Ch. XVIII, "Early American Backgrounds," Ch. XXIII, "Eclecticism," Ch. XXX, "The Country Place Era."
Tobey, George, *A History of Landscape Architecture*, Ch. 15, "Conquerors of Wilderness," Ch. 16, "United States, 1800-1850," Ch. 18, "The Arcadian Myth," Ch. 21, "Form Follows Function."
The film "Mon Oncle" (Jacques Tati) pokes fun at modern garden design.
Sinclair Lewis' novels *Babbitt* and *Main Street*.
F. Scott Fitzgerald's novel *The Great Gatsby*.

3. LANDSCAPE AND NATURAL RESOURCES

Two themes from the historical review of landscape and resources are important in the study of landscape architecture. The first comprises the events or movements that led up to government action or intervention in the conservation of resources such as forests, wildlife, soil, and water, and the establishment of such agencies as the U. S. Forest Service, the Geological Survey, Soil Conservation, and the Bureau of Land Management at the Federal level, and departments of fisheries and wildlife in states. The second theme involves the events that led up to governmental support for the conservation of natural scenic landscape for public use and enjoyment resulting in the U.S. National Parks Service and the state parks movement. These themes are intertwined yet separate. They deal with the attitudes of people and changes in those attitudes toward landscape and resources in the nineteenth century. It seems important to understand the background of these agencies and the reasons for their establishment. Many employ landscape architects. Others provide information useful in land use planning and design. The work of some is changing in response to concepts of multiple use and the increasing demand for recreation.

SETTLEMENT OF THE AMERICAN LANDSCAPE

In 1620 when the Mayflower landed on the East Coast of America, the Indians who populated the land had been present on the continent for countless generations. The Indians held beliefs about landscape different from those of the West European. The land ethic of the American Indian was an I-thou ethic (as defined by Gutkind), involving a reverence for the life-sustaining landscape, its plants and animals. The Indian related to a particular landscape region by ties of kinship and nature rather than by an understanding of property ownership. There was a close relationship between settlement and resources; the amount of food available determined the population and its distribution.

By contrast, the European thought in terms of estates and land parcels he could own, cultivate, and use as he wished. His concept of land ownership involving exclusive possession of land was supported by legal documents and deeds. The landscape was thus divided into rectangles. William Penn's plan for Philadelphia (1683) and the land survey of 1878, which sectioned the entire American landscape west of the Appalachians, are clear expressions of that attitude (Fig. 3.1).

The first task of forest-bound colonists was to develop woodsmanship; homes and stockades had to be built, land cleared, and firewood cut. Clearings for agriculture could be carved out of the forest only by great effort or the deliberate use of fire. Tree cutting preceded the establishment of agriculture and the worst forest destruction was justified with this reasoning. Either the original vegetation was replaced with a crop which was harvested, or else the land was used for cattle and sheep grazing. The shock was often too great. The crude techniques of lumbering employed in early Colonial times resulted in soil erosion. Cropping without replenishing the soil with nutrients reduced its fertility. Overgrazing resulted in thin grass cover, resulting in poor yield and soil erosion.

Late eighteenth-century illustrations show primitive clearing of fields and space for farmhouse and buildings surrounded or enclosed by the native forest. When the land was exhausted, the farmer would move on to a new site.

Some who unwittingly destroyed land were simply poor farmers ignorant of the processes of nature and techniques of sound agriculture. The homesteaders in the plains states created the dust bowl by not understanding the laws of drought and the importance of grass in an arid land.

The virgin forests of North America were some of the finest in the world. East of the great plains every acre was originally covered by trees and to the west coniferous forests flourished in the Rocky Mountains and along the Pacific Coast. A growing nation needed wood for housing, ship-building, and fuel, and by the 1800s cities began to need lumber in very large quantities. Machines, circular saws, and steam mills were organized to provide it. The invention of the wood pulp process for paper manufacture also led to an increased demand for timber. Thus, in addition to the farmers' desire for cleared land, there were great incentives to cut timber for economic return. Lumbering quickly became America's largest industry. Although there was a great quantity of forest, the wasteful techniques of cutting and the fires that were a side effect resulted in rapid depletion of the resource and by 1900 the myth of superabundance had been revealed as a fallacy (Fig. 3.2).

The wildlife of the country was equally plentiful and varied and was equally plundered. The fashionable beaver hat resulted in the depletion of that species. Hunters shot buffalo from railroad cars (Fig. 3.3). Seals and other animals and birds, including the American eagle, symbol of the nation, were practically eliminated. The passenger pigeon was extinguished completely.

Fig. 3.2 Wasteful clear cutting practices. Photograph by U.S. Forest Service.

Fig. 3.1 Section lines of the land survey (1878) are one mile apart. The American Midwest. Photograph by William A. Garnett.

Fig. 3.3 "A lively scene on an American prairie—a buffalo hunt by steam." From Frank Leslie's illustrated newspaper, 28 November 1868.

Fig. 3.4 Hydraulic mining in California. See also Fig. 1.9. Courtesy of the Bancroft Library, University of California, Berkeley.

Fig. 3.5 Denudation gullies, Kennett, California, 1934. Photograph by U.S. Forest Service.

Resources such as oil, coal, and mineral ores were mined as easily as possible and then, as soon as it became difficult or uneconomical, the process stopped, leaving half-finished workings, dereliction of landscape, and heaps of overburden. This strip and run process was not only wasteful of the sought-after resource but also resulted in severe soil erosion and destruction of the natural system. For example, hydraulic mining in California removed soil and overburden covering gold deposits by a jet of water (Fig. 3.4). The soil was thus washed into rivers, which carried the silt to lower levels where a raising of the river beds caused flooding on farmlands. There was therefore a conflict between agriculture interests and mining. Ultimately hydraulic mining was made illegal by the state legislature. Excessive erosion was also caused by overgrazing by cattle and the growing of annual crops in grassland country. Overfarming and overgrazing were as disastrous in terms of soil loss as were overlogging and mining (Fig. 3.5).

CONSERVATION OF RESOURCES

In 1864 George Perkins Marsh inquired into the balance of nature and the interrelationship of plant and animal communities and said that "The ravages committed by man subvert the relations and destroy the balance which nature has established." He was convinced that the balance could be restored only if man used wisdom in managing resources.[1]

Marsh had considerable influence in the legislature and his efforts and writings contributed to the passing of the Public Lands Bill of 1891, which empowered the President to set aside forest lands as public reservations.

The Forest Reserve Act was passed in 1891. Millions of acres of forest were thus made public reservations by successive presidents. This conserved the country's future lumber supply and also saved scenic lands from being divided haphazardly into homesteads. The U. S. Forest Service was established in 1905 within the Department of Agriculture to manage these lands. The Forest Service leases timber rights to commercial operators and is thereby a self-supporting government agency. Part of the revenue is directed to the needs of local communities and to provision of recreation facilities for the public.

At the same time, soil and moisture conservation became the concern of government. It was estimated that the annual cost of erosion in terms of production was $400 million. In 1935 the Soil Conservation Service was established in the Department of Agriculture. Today the Soil Conservation Service devotes much of its efforts to mapping soils in terms of their quality and best use. These data can now be used in assessing the agricultural capability, susceptibility to erosion, and foundation suitability of soils.

It was the economic depression of the 1930s which precipitated much government action in connection with conservation. The New Deal introduced conservation as an integral part in the war against economic depression. After his election in 1932 President Franklin Roosevelt sponsored conservation of forests, soil, and water and initiated the Civilian Conservation Corps to achieve it. Many of the features—

Fig. 3.6 Tennessee Valley region of 42,000 square miles. The watershed area is unrelated to state boundaries. K. Knoxville, A. Asheville, C. Chattanooga.

buildings, outlooks, trails, roads, and camps—to be found in the state and national parks today resulted from these efforts.

One bill of the New Deal established the Tennessee Valley Authority. Under this legislation, a broad plan was proposed for a physiographic region which included parts of seven states (Fig. 3.6). A semiindependent regional authority was created and given wide powers to promote the economic and social well-being of the people of the entire valley. The Tennessee Valley had been rich in timber and petroleum resources, but its ruthless exploitation resulted in a derelict landscape and a depressed population. In 1933 no region of the United States had lower incomes or more families on relief. The Tennessee River had superior hydraulic power sites, yet it flowed unchecked through counties and states where few farmers had electricity. In addition to the T.V.A. dam building program, the plan included navigation, reforestation, soil conservation, outdoor recreation, the retirement of marginal farmland, and the manufacture of fertilizer. In ten years the river was harnessed, over 700 miles were made navigable, and the dams provided low-cost power and flood controls. Scientific agriculture and contour plowing

1. George Perkins Marsh, *Man and Nature* (New York: Scribner, 1864).

were introduced. Reforestation added to the revitalized landscape, and attractive scenery was created in which lakes provided opportunities for water-oriented recreation (Fig. 3.7).

LANDSCAPE QUALITY

The conservation of scenic landscape for public use and enjoyment has a different source from the movement that led to the conservation of forests, soil, and land as government policy. To understand the background it is necessary to go back again to England in the eighteenth century and to the Ro-

mantic movement, source of the landscape garden and new forms in literature and the arts. It is also related to a changed attitude toward wilderness and large scale scenery which, up until the end of the seventeenth century, had been considered hostile and uncouth.

In England in the eighteenth century, in association with the landscape movement, a taste for "recreational travel" was stimulated by the published accounts of tours through England, Scotland, and Wales by William Gilpin (Fig. 3.8).[2] The concept that the landscape itself was worthy of attention

Fig. 3.8 Sketch in the style of William Gilpin which contributed to the popularity of romantic landscape in England in the 18th Century.

was advanced in essays such as Gilpin's "Picturesque Beauty"[3] and "The Picturesque as Compared with the Sublime and the Beautiful" (by Uvedale Price).[4] William Wordsworth, writing of the year 1750 in his *Guide Through the Lakes*, noted: "Travellers, instead of confining their observations to towns, manufactures or mines, began to wander over the island in search of sequestered spots, distinguished, as they might accidentally have learned, for the sublimity of the forms of nature there to be seen." William Gilpin described the objective of picturesque travel as "Beauty of every kind. . . . This great object(ive)," he wrote, "we pursue through the

Fig. 3.7 The T.V.A., Tims Ford Reservoir.
Photograph Courtesy Tennessee Valley Authority

2. William Gilpin, *Mountains and Lakes of Cumberland and Westmoreland* (London: R. Blamire, 1772).
3. William Gilpin, *Three Essays: On Picturesque Beauty; On Picturesque Travel; and On Sketching Landscape* (London: R. Blamire, 1792).
4. Uvedale Price, *An Essay on the Picturesque as Compared with the Sublime and the Beautiful* (London: J. Robson, 1794).

scenery of nature, and examine it by the rules of painting, we seek it among all the ingredients of landscape—trees, rocks, broken grounds, woods, rivers and lakes, plains, valleys, mountains and distances. These objects themselves produce infinite variety—no two rocks or trees are the same. They are varied, a second time by combination, and almost as much a third time, by different lights and shades and other aerial effects." Thus the landscape was described as though it were a painting. It is also a description of all the qualities which we enjoy in landscape today, particularly diversity and contrast.

English painters of the nineteenth century also stimulated the new generation of native tourists who were eager to see the scenes they depicted on canvas. The best known of these were Turner and Constable. Their work was central to the Romantic movement. The Industrial Revolution also fostered interest in the beauty of natural landscape as a contrast to urban ugliness. The concept of ideal landscape as pictured earlier by Claude and Poussin in the eighteenth century and on which the landscape garden was based became less credible under the impact of the economist Malthus (who argued that there were limits to the population the world could support) and Darwin, whose theory of evolution helped to dispel the notion that some God had given perfection to nature in a moment of original creativity. In the course of the nineteenth century, paintings which were close imitations of nature (not idealized landscapes) became the most popular form of art. Some paintings depicted rocks almost as though the painting were a scientific study, accurate and geologically correct. A peaceful scene with water in the foreground reflecting a luminous sky and set off by dark trees was something which

everyone agreed was beautiful, as in previous ages they had agreed about a naked athlete, a madonna and child, or an idealized Classical landscape by Poussin.

But in spite of Darwin there was still a moralistic overtone to this interest in natural landscape. Constable believed, for example, that nature was the clearest revelation of God's will and thus landscapes painted in the spirit of humble truth could be a means of conveying moral ideas. Both Wordsworth and Constable believed that there was something in trees, flowers, meadows, and mountains that was imbued with divinity and so it was felt that if nature was contemplated with sufficient devotion it would reveal a moral and spiritual quality of its own. In this argument, the landscape was regarded as a symbol of the self and as a symbol of God, rather than as evidence of the divinity.

The publication of picture books and the development of the railroads in England gave impetus to and made possible tourism on a popular scale. In 1841 Thomas Cook started his business of arranging tours for working people from the cities to the coast or the mountains.

Interest in nature and the out-of-doors was further stimulated by the growth of the natural sciences in the nineteenth century. Botany, biology, and geology all involved field trips into natural areas. Geologists who went to the Alps to study the rocks were overwhelmed by the beauty of the landscape and incidentally developed mountaineering as a pastime.

But even in these early days the possibility of destroying the beauty of natural landscape was evident. In his *Guide through the Lakes in the North of England*, written in 1810, William Wordsworth warned about the despoliation of the landscape and the disfigurement of the lakes by new settlers and

their houses. "The author has been induced to speak thus at length by a wish to preserve the native beauty of this delightful district." Then, anticipating a solution and the concept of national parks Wordsworth wrote: "The author will be joined by persons of pure taste throughout the whole island who by their visits (often repeated) to the lakes (in the North of England) testify that they deem the district a sort of national property in which every man has a right and interest."[5]

In the early part of the nineteenth century the United States had its share of naturalists—Bartram, a botanist; Audubon, famous for his bird paintings; Emerson and Thoreau, known for their writings. Bartram's *Travels* was used by Wordsworth and Coleridge in England as a wildland reference book. Audubon's *Birds of America* was published in 1839. His work inspired interest in the wonders and variety of nature. In 1836 Emerson wrote an essay called "Nature," in which he felt strongly that the individual should enjoy an original relation to the universe as opposed to (reading) books and second-hand experience (about nature).[6] Thoreau believed that the order of the week as set out in the Bible should be reversed. The seventh day should be a day of work and sweat and toil; in the remaining six days man should be free to feed his soul with sublime revelations of nature. He was one of the nation's first preservationists, believing that some landscapes should be left unspoiled and that animals should have in-

5. William Wordsworth, *A Guide Through the District of the Lakes in the North of England* (London: R. Hart-Davis, 1951). (First issued anonymously in 1810.)
6. Ralph Waldo Emerson, *Nature* (New York: Scholars Facsimiles and Reprints, 1940). (First published in 1836.)

Fig. 3.9 Yosemite Valley. (See also Figs. 9.16 and 9.17). Photograph by Wilford Hoover.

Fig. 3.10 Travellers arriving in Yosemite Valley (late 19th century). Courtesy of the Bancroft Library, University of California, Berkeley.

violate places of refuge.[7] In 1858 he made a plea for "National Preserves," in which wild animals would be protected not for sport but for "inspiration and our own true recreation."

CONSERVATION OF SCENERY

Frederick Law Olmsted, son of a New England middle-class merchant, farmer, traveler, author (and as already mentioned, inventor of the title "landscape architecture"), came to California in 1863 as a

land manager for the Fremont lands in the foothills of the Sierra Nevada.

Like the poet Wordsworth and the painter Constable in England, and like Emerson and Thoreau in America, Olmsted felt the strong moral appeal in natural landscape beauty and studied the potential of the landscape for the advancement of human morality and happiness. He was also a keen student of the books of William Gilpin. He was a serious and energetic man who, in the course of his own work,

became familiar with the natural qualities of Yosemite Valley and also with the threats to its natural beauty and ecological stability, due to sheep farming and mining (Fig. 3.9).

The valley had already attracted attention for the drama of its physical features. Photographs from as early as 1829 illustrated the awesome statistics, a valley 2,300 feet deep and the Yo-hamite Falls, 1,300

7. Henry David Thoreau, *Walden* (Boston: Ticknor and Fields, 1856).

Fig. 3.11 Tourists in Yosemite (late 19th century). Courtesy of the Bancroft Library, University of California, Berkeley.

Fig. 3.12 Niagara Falls. A scenic wonder which became popular in the 19th century.

feet high. Lithographers and artists also reproduced the scene and in 1868 Bierstadt painted his famous view of the valley. In the short time that he was in California, Olmsted worked for its preservation under the guiding principle that enjoyment of scenery of this kind could have a profound influence on mankind and it should therefore be conserved and made accessible to the public. In 1864 he was appointed one of several commissioners of Yosemite Valley, which by act of the Federal Government was granted to the State of California "for public use, resort and recreation." This act provided through government action the first scenic area for public enjoyment in the United States and, indeed, the world. Olmsted prepared a report and plan of action. It recognized the essential principles of land management in terms of preservation of natural scenery and public access. The philosophy and principles in the report were to become central in the work of the National Parks Service, founded subsequently in 1916.

A few years later, in 1870, members of an expedition exploring the Yellowstone Region of Wyoming were impressed by the natural beauty they saw there: the canyons, hot springs, waterfalls, lakes, and forests. And though they could legally have filed homesteads or mining claims, they decided that the area should be a permanent public preserve and such action was subsequently taken by the government.

The battle lines were drawn in the conflict of in-

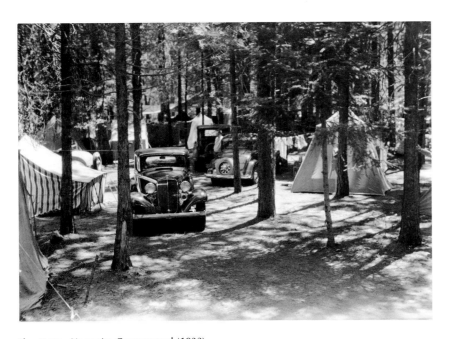

Fig. 3.13 Yosemite Campground (1933).
Photograph courtesy National Park Service, Yosemite.

Fig. 3.14 Yosemite campground (1959).
Photograph courtesy of National Park Service, Yosemite.

terest between the exploiters of resources, the lumbermen, miners, hunters, on the one hand, and, on the other, such figures as naturalist John Muir. Muir and the Sierra Club gathered national support for the preservation of the entire Yosemite region surrounding the relatively small state-managed valley. Muir worked and wrote passionately against the destruction of watersheds, scenic landscape, and forests through overgrazing and exploitative lumbering. In 1890 the government created a forest reservation (including the valley) of more than 1 million acres.

John Muir continued his campaign and was a major force behind the 1916 bill of Senator William Kent establishing the National Parks Service, which has now developed into a large scale manager of land, interpreter of landscape and natural history, and provider of recreation facilities.

Thus John Muir combined his emotional love of wilderness and natural landscape with the scientific teachings of George Perkins Marsh to achieve in stark political reality that which Emerson and others only dreamed of. Together with the Save the Red-

woods League, Muir persuaded the State of California to purchase 12,000 acres of redwood forest at Big Basin and in Humboldt County, which formed the nucleus of a state park system that was established in 1927. The system now includes more than 725,000 acres in parks, beaches, and recreation and historic areas. Similar park systems were developed in most states, with much progress being made in the 1930s.

A role for the landscape architect became defined in bringing people in contact with landscape in such a way that scenic qualities were maintained at the same time that convenience and services were provided. Up to World War II, when the numbers of visitors were relatively small, this could be done with little conflict. However, in recent years the increase in numbers and the satisfaction of their demand for lodging, campgrounds, road access, and so forth, by a parks service eager to please, has finally been found to lead to conditions at odds with the original intent. Yosemite National Park has in excess of 2 million visitors annually. There is overuse and overcrowding in virtually all national and state parks. (Figs. 3.13, 3.14) Reservation of campsites is necessary in many, and various strategies are being devised to maintain the experience of nature.

Some reappraisal of recreation needs as they relate to the setting is necessary. Less spectacular scenery than that found in the national parks may be acceptable for the social kind of vacation that many seek at Yosemite and elsewhere (Fig. 3.15). In Britain the country park concept has been developed to meet this need. These parks are situated closer to urban centers than most national parks or wild areas of landscape, and they are designed for intensive use. They either relate to existing amenities and features or depend on the creation of entirely new recreation environments out of derelict land.

The record of mismanagement and exploitation of land and landscape outlined here is not unique to the United States. It seems to have been the pattern for all Western cultures and industrialized nations. In all cases, government has responded sooner or later with conservation measures of one sort or another.

But the conservation struggle continues. Conflicts occur between the economic interests of corporations and individuals and the long term values of conservation for present and future generations. Conserva-

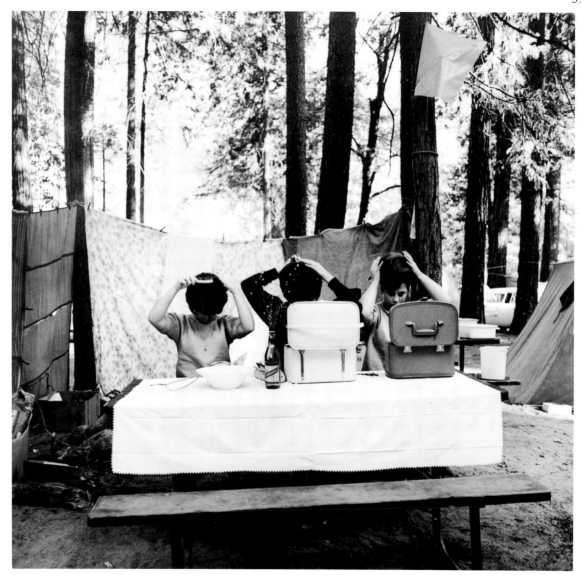

Fig. 3.15 Camping in Yosemite. Photograph by Bruce Davidson.

tion organizations lock horns with corporations and sometimes government agencies in protest over pollution, destruction of natural resources and scenery, and so on. Government often finds itself in the middle. The goals of the environmentalist sometimes seem at odds with those of the working man— ecology versus jobs. But these are simply short term problems that must be seen in broader perspective. Enlightened government must protect resources and environmental quality as part of a viable economic program.

Fig. 3.16   Motorcycle riding, one of many new sports in need of suitable terrain in the hinterland of urban communities. Photograph by Cynthia Anderson.

Suggested Readings

Coyle, Davis C., *Conservation, An American Story of Conflict and Accomplishment.*
Huth, Hans, *Nature and the American.*
Leopold, Aldo, *A Sand County Almanac.*
Marsh, George Perkins, *Man and Nature* (1864).
Muir, John, *Yosemite,* Doubleday Anchor Book.
Mumford, Lewis, *The Brown Decades,* pp. 59–80.
Newton, Norman, *Design on the Land,* Ch. XXXV and XXXVI, "The National Park System," Ch. XXXVII, "The State Park Movement."
Udall, Stewart, *The Quiet Crisis,* Ch. XX, pp. 109–125, "Wild and Park Lands," Ch. XIII, "Conservation and the Future."

Music:
Grand Canyon Suite (1931), Ferde Grofé.
Appalachian Spring (1945), Aaron Copland.
Amid Nature, op. 91, Antonin Dvořák.

4. URBAN PARKS AND RECREATION

EUROPE

In the ancient civilizations of Greece and Rome a number of urban open spaces were traditional: the marketplace (the agora in Greece, the forum in Rome); gymnasia for athletes; and sacred burial groves. Each of these was designed or set aside for a specific purpose. No areas of public landscape or public parks as we understand the term today were provided within the cities for unspecified recreation. Only on special occasions when a private estate was opened to the public did people have an opportunity to enjoy planted gardens.

The Medieval towns of Europe were densely populated but the small scale of the cities meant that the countryside and fresh air were readily available and accessible (Fig. 2.13). There was little room and no particular need for land set aside within the city for recreation. The urban marketplace and the church steps and square were the major open spaces in which the public could gather in crowds. The church plaza was used for the performance of symbolic or mystic plays and the marketplace was, of course, used for the exchange and sale of goods and fresh produce brought in from the surrounding countryside. As in the cities of Greece and Rome, those open spaces that did exist in the Medieval town were set aside for uses other than recreation, although they were in fact used in a variety of un-

Fig. 4.1 St. James Park, London.

planned and recreational ways.

In Renaissance Europe we see the periodic opening of private grounds or palace gardens to the public. In London the large Royal Parks, property of the Crown, were in time completely given over to public use. The same applied in other royal capitals. These cities richly endowed with parks were uniquely favored and were exceptional in the early nineteenth century in having a considerable amount of public park land, albeit unplanned and accidentally placed

in relation to the population. In London a ready-made park system was provided by the opening to the public of St. James, Hyde, and Green parks and, later, Regents Park. Some of the older parks went through transformations related to changes in taste. In the seventeenth century. St. James Park was laid out with a straight-edged canal with parallel avenues of trees. In the eighteenth century the layout was converted into the romantic landscape setting that exists today (Fig. 4.1).

61

In 1810 Regents Park, property of the Crown, was planned by John Nash partly as a public park and partly as a real estate venture (Fig. 4.2). The terraces and crescents that surrounded the park were conceived and built at the same time as the central core, which was a landscape park open to the public. This landscape also served to increase the desirability and value of the property. The park was laid out in the landscape style with meandering lakes and plantations and was like a country gentleman's estate and at the same scale. Each leaseholder of a terrace house and each individual roaming through the landscape could imagine that it was his own. Thus in the heart of the city the feeling and appearance of a large landscape garden were achieved for many people at a fraction of the cost to each.

However, the expanding industrial cities had very little provision of parks; moreover, parks were randomly distributed as a result of individual philanthropy. Frequently there were no parks at all. The expanding urban populations were housed in minimum housing built back to back with virtually no yards and only narrow access alleys between rows (Fig. 4.3). Because of these conditions, the poor were unhealthy and their performance at work was low. This fact became a major concern for industrialists and manufacturers who relied on the work capability of the people for their profits. Dickens' *Oliver Twist* provides a vivid description of these times and conditions. Many died at an early age due to ill health, attributed to crowding, poor buildings and services, polluted air, bad working conditions, and long working hours for men, women, and children. As a result of concern for the health of the workers, various acts of Parliament were passed in England between 1833 and 1843. These allowed for the use of

Fig. 4.2 Regents Park, London (1810).

Fig. 4.3 Typical 19th Century English industrial town with back-to-back housing in close proximity to factories.

public monies or taxes to provide improvements, sewers, and sanitation systems and to provide public parks.

BIRKINHEAD PARK

The city of Birkinhead near Liverpool was the first municipality to use these powers. Joseph Paxton was asked in 1843 to prepare plans for a park and also

a real estate venture conceived by the park commissioners. The act permitting the use of taxes stipulated that 70 acres were to be set aside for the free recreation of the inhabitants. In fact, 226 acres of sterile clay land, unsuitable for agriculture, were purchased. Of these, 125 were appropriated for public use and the remainder was set aside and sold for building sites. The two functions, private housing and public recreation, were planned together as

Fig. 4.4 Birkinhead Park, England (1843). a. plan b. view.

Nash had done earlier at Regents Park. A special attraction of this combination was its financial success. The sale of the surrounding building land at enhanced values due to its situation covered the cost of the park itself. The plan (Fig. 4.4) included meadows for sports such as cricket and archery. There were winding carriage drives and separate pathways meandering through trees and around the edge of irregular lakes or fish ponds. Undulating topography was created with the excavated material from the lakes. Running from one side to the other is a wide road to permit business traffic to cross the park, which otherwise broke the extended grid of the street pattern. Although the house sites were adjacent to and overlooked the park, vehicular access to them was provided by roads outside the park. In 1852 Frederick Law Olmsted, who visited Birkinhead, wrote in his book *Walks and Talks of An American Farmer in England* that he was "Amazed at the manner in which art had been employed to obtain from nature so much beauty." Birkinhead Park was a success and stimulated a period of park building in Britain. Many of the new parks were designed by Paxton.

1. Frederick Law Olmsted, *Walks and Talks of An American Farmer in England* (New York: Putnam, 1852).

UNITED STATES

In the United States there was, of course, no tradition of royal parks. Open space specifically set aside for recreation was rarely embodied in urban developments of the eighteenth century, nor was it needed. However, such functional areas as the New England common, originally for the grazing of stock or for military parades, began to assume the role of public parks in the early nineteenth century.

Some planned cities such as Philadelphia and Savannah included residential squares planted with trees in the manner of Georgian London. These squares were not public parks but usually were reserved for use by residents of the surrounding houses. However, they do represent acceptance of the concept of bringing green areas into the city.

In 1848 Andrew Jackson Downing expressed concern over the lack of public parks in the United States. Despite the earlier traditions of the New England commons, the courthouse square in the south, and the planned towns of the eighteenth century, public parks were essentially unknown in America. Grotesque though it may seem, the closest approximation to a public park was the embellished rural cemetery. Many of these were laid out adjacent to the large cities in the nineteenth century. Laurel Hill in Philadelphia, Mount Auburn in Boston, and Greenwood in New York (Fig. 4.5) all existed in the 1830s. A description of Mount Auburn in 1831 tells that "The avenues are winding in their course and exceedingly beautiful in their gentle circuits adapted picturesquely to the inequalities of the surface of the ground and producing charming landscape effects from this natural arrangement." These areas of naturalistic landscape included monuments and

Fig. 4.5 Greenwood Cemetery, New York, 1852.
Reproduced from the collections of the Library of Congress.

tombstones, buildings and planting, and they were extremely popular with the inhabitants of the large cities. Guidebooks were prepared for visitors, suggesting routes through the grounds which would take in the most impressive monuments and viewpoints. On fine days hundreds of visitors, mostly on

pleasure outings and picnics, would visit the cemeteries. It is said that 30,000 people visited Laurel Hill in Philadelphia between April and December of 1848 and almost twice that number visited Greenwood, New York. Downing argued that the general interest shown in the cemeteries proved that public gardens "established in a liberal and suitable manner near our cities would be successful."

The case for public parks in the nineteenth century was built largely on the same concerns as that for improved housing. There seem to be four basic arguments: one is concerned with public health, the second with the morality of the people, the third is related to the development of the Romantic movement, and the fourth is concerned with economics.

A concern for public health led to reform in housing and improved sanitary sewers and drains. Included in the concept of better health was the availability of parks allowing the circulation of fresh air and providing space for exercise, rest, and refreshment in a sunny landscape setting. The concern for public health also resulted in the building of rural suburbs for the rich, who wished to get as far away from the urban conditions as possible. Thus began the exodus from the city based on the opinion that cities were ugly, unhealthy, and dangerous, a viewpoint which has grown in popularity and resulted in the critical disintegration of contemporary American cities. Now more people live in the suburbs than in the cities, with those in the cities mostly black, those in the suburbs mostly white.

Second, the concern for morality is associated with the idea that nature itself is a source of moral inspiration. The advocates of this concept felt that if the workers had an opportunity to study and contemplate nature, this would improve their mental stability and provide them with beliefs that would transcend day to day drudgery and substitute for the oblivion which the "gin palaces" provided. Parks were thus associated with this concept of morality in nature inasmuch as they would provide landscape for contemplation. Sports facilities and allotments in which vegetables could be cultivated were also considered to serve this moral purpose.

The aesthetic argument was that the visual qualities of the expanding industrial cities were generally considered ugly (although there were some artists who found beauty in blast furnaces and other industrial installations). Essentially, the city was equated with ugliness and public parks as large landscapes inserted into this ugliness would thus serve as an antidote.

The economic argument derives from the first three. These propositions are the basis for a money-making system whereby public parks provide qualities of health, morality, and beauty for the workers, whose productivity is thus improved. At the same time, real estate values are increased by proximity to the romantic landscape in an otherwise drab environment. This in turn produces revenue for the city through higher taxes.

Although the landscape style of gardening was not specifically a response to the depraved urban conditions, it might well have been. The eighteenth-century theories of landscape design based on informality, naturalism, Romanticism, and the picturesque became the logical antithesis to urban conditions of the nineteenth century. Park designs included all of the elements one would expect: curvilinear drives and paths, rustic gates, Gothic architecture, irregular lakes, and informal landscape planting. In fact, the public park was to become the only place of sufficient size where the landscape garden style could be carried out successfully and parks were thus laid out as though they were large private estates with accommodations made for the greater number of people.

Andrew Jackson Downing became a strong advocate of public parks for America in the manner of Birkinhead. He advanced the revolutionary idea that, as in England, parks should be maintained at the expense of the taxpayer. He also recognized the real estate, money-making possibilities for land adjacent to public parks. In addition, he argued the moral case that "such park projects would civilize and refine the national character, foster the love of rural beauty and increase the knowledge of and taste for rare and beautiful trees and plants." He saw the park as a piece of rural scenery in which people could walk, ride, or drive in carriages. It would be a relief from the city streets: "Pedestrians would find quiet and secluded walks when they wished to be solitary and broad alleys filled with happy faces when they would be gay." Downing died in 1852, but his advocacy persuaded the city of New York that it should plan a major public park.

CENTRAL PARK, NEW YORK

As early as 1785, New Yorkers had seen the need for "a proper spot where the city's numerous inhabitants can enjoy, with convenience, the exercise that is necessary for health and amusement." Political difficulties and arguments preceded the selection and purchase of land. Eventually a board of commissioners advertised for designs for the layout and offered prizes for the four best plans submitted.

The competition was won in 1858 by Frederick Law Olmsted and his partner, Calvert Vaux (Fig. 4.6). The statement with the plan justified the largeness of the area (843 acres) with the assumption that the city would some day be built up on all sides and that this park would be, to a large extent, the only chance the inhabitants would have of seeing such a landscape. Olmsted intended that the park be the

Fig. 4.6 Central Park, New York, 1858.

precise center of the population of a city of 2 million, an estimate which was farsighted at the time. (However, by the time of his death in 1903, the population had already reached 4 million.) He predicted the day when the park would be surrounded by an artificial wall twice as high as the great wall of China, composed of urban buildings. The workers who could not spend holidays in the country, he argued, should be supplied with some semblance of it within the park. It was laid out as a piece of rural scenery and a deliberate attempt was made to screen out the anticipated buildings beyond the park boundaries (Fig. 4.7). One formal element was included in the plan, the central mall: "An essential feature of a metropolitan park—level, spacious and thoroughly shaded." This provided for a very human need: a stage for parading and also a place in which to sit and watch other people, which was what Downing had in mind when he talked of broad alleys filled with happy faces.

The circulation system in which traffic types were separated was particularly innovative. Four roads for crosstown traffic connecting the east and west sides of the park were arranged with underpasses, which would avoid any conflict with park uses and remain unseen below grade. People in the park, walking, riding, or driving in carriages, were thus separated from and unaware of the ordinary city traffic. Carriage drives, riding trails, and footpaths were also separated within the park itself.

In the early days the park was too far away from the center to be visited by the majority of New Yorkers except on special occasions, holidays, Saturday afternoons, and Sundays. Nonetheless, in 1871 the number of visitors was estimated at 10 million, or 30,000 average per day (at a time when the city had less than 1 million inhabitants). On days that were not holidays the average was 23,000, of which about 9,000 came on foot and 14,000 in carriages or on horseback. Attendance was greatest on Sundays and band concert days. The number of pedestrians would be as many as 50,000 on the finest

Fig. 4.7 Central Park, New York.

PARKS MOVEMENT

This first major park in the United States, and the public's approval of it, gave momentum to an urban parks movement. Olmsted became the major practitioner and designed parks for Boston, Brooklyn, Buffalo, Detroit, and many other major cities. Other landscape architects including Horace Cleveland and Jens Jensen made contributions in Minneapolis and Chicago. In Boston Charles Eliot worked with Olmsted to combine an engineering solution to flooding and sanitation problems with a greatly needed open space system. The Boston parks system connects the Common to Franklin Park through driveways planted with trees, running in a continuous landscape expanding to 1,500 feet in places and contracting to as little as 200 feet in others (Fig. 4.8).

It is interesting to note that land which was considered useful for more economic purposes was rarely selected for a park. At Birkinhead the land was poor quality; Central Park included the unbuildable granite ridge of Manhattan Island. The Boston parks system was created out of marshes. And in San Francisco, which was not to be left out in the fashion of building large city parks, the land which was purchased in 1870 consisted of 1,000 acres of wind-swept sterile sand dunes well outside the built-up area.

William Hammond Hall was appointed Park Engineer for Golden Gate Park. He started by preparing a plan for the quarter nearest the city, and while this was being constructed a program of planting was begun on the remaining land in a successful attempt to stabilize the shifting sands (Fig. 6.9). Hall corresponded with Olmsted, whose influence was no doubt responsible for some of the park's features, especially the circulation system separating wheeled

days of the season. Use of the park was stimulated by the facilities. Riding and driving in carriages were provided for by winding roads and bridle paths and as the park came into greater use, new habits and customs developed. Skating was one innovation that grew amazingly in popularity.

In addition to these benefits to the people, Central Park was also considered a financial success. In 1872 it was estimated that the annual increase in taxes directly related to the development of the park exceeded the annual interest on the cost of the park lands and improvements by over 4 million dollars.

But careful control was necessary to prevent the park turning into a repository for features that would negate its original intent. In 1863 Olmsted catalogued the "encroachments" that had been proposed for Central Park which had been "warded off" in the previous five years. These included "Towers, houses, telescopes, mineral water fountains, cottages, Aeolian harps, gymnasiums, observations and weighing scales, steam engines, snow shows and ice boats, and the use of the ice for fancy dress carnivals, the sale of vegetables, velocipedes, perambulators, Indian work, tobacco, and cigars." His journal records without alarm, however, the introduction of seven pairs of English sparrows.

Fig. 4.8 Boston Park System. Key: 1. Boston Common 2. Commonwealth Avenue 3. Back Bay Fens 4. Muddy River 5. Olmsted Park 6. Jamaica Pond 7. Arnold Arboretum 8. Franklin Park 9. Forest Hills Cemetery A. State House B. Fine Arts Museum C. Colleges D. Brookline E. M.I.T.

traffic from pedestrians with bridges at critical intersections (Fig. 4.10). In 1887 John McLaren became superintendent of the park and through his horticultural expertise brought the park to maturity and completed the transformation of barren sand dunes into today's Golden Gate Park: 1,000 acres of well-watered forests, glades, and lakes connected with drives, paths, and riding trails (Fig. 4.11).

Although there is no consistent pattern, it seems that derelict land or land in some other way unattractive or unsuitable for other uses will always be the land most likely to be available for parks and recreation. The disused canals and railroad tracks of England have in some cases been cleaned up and turned into public amenities. Worked-out coal mines, waste disposal areas, and old gravel pits have also found new use as recreation areas. This pattern in history suggests other possibilities for today. Power line rights of way (Fig. 4.12), river flood plains, and other land unsuited for anything else may be linked up in recreation systems.

It is another fact of changing times that the real estate benefits of location next to a public park do not necessarily apply in all cases. It may still be true of Central Park and Regents Park, but there are other instances in which the once expensive housing situated near a park is now a slum. The building of new parks, which in the eyes of local residents might attract illicit behavior, is sometimes seen as a threat, especially where nearby homes already have private gardens. The commonly agreed lack of safety by day as well as by night in the larger city parks, although not always supported by statistics, is also a new social factor to be contended with.

Fig. 4.9 Golden Gate Park (1872). Original state of site. Courtesy of Bancroft Library, University of California, Berkeley.

Fig. 4.11 Golden Gate Park.

Fig. 4.10 Golden Gate Park. Plan for eastern portion of the park, published in 1872. Key: A. dressed ground or lawn B. flower garden C. conservatory D. the Manor House E. croquet or children's playground F. plateau—carriage concourse G. botanical garden L. lakes M. the meadow P. parade, cricket or baseball ground S. Strawberry Hill H. space for large pavillion a) small observatory b) bridges f) fountains k) rustic pavillion p) the lodge r) traffic road.

PARKS AND RECREATION STANDARDS

Since the nineteenth century "parks and recreation" have become a major industry with a large civil service in cities, counties, states, and regional districts. In an attempt to measure the effectiveness of a city's provision of parks, organizations such as the National Recreation Association formulated standards in terms of acres per unit of population. By these standards there was never enough. Although they are generalities, which must be weighed with the variables of the specific place, it is still true that cities and other agencies tend to think of recreation facilities in terms of such standards.

The standards and acreages cited below are based on a combination of several sources. It should be noted, however, that the recommendations in the California guide for recreation and parks vary according to the climatic zones of the state. Thus larger acreages are recommended in the warmer zones to permit more extensive tree planting.[2]

In the conventional system, recreation units are classified in terms of their scale and distribution. The play lot, or block playground for use by preschool-age children, is the smallest unit and should, according to the standards, be within walking distance of a majority of homes, located perhaps in the interior of a city block. They should be between 1/8 and 1/4 acre in size and are especially important where the density is high. The recent "mini-park" building program in run-down sections of cities indicates the value of play lots in such areas; low-density suburban housing may have less need.

The next category is at the neighborhood level: the neighborhood park, playground, or recreation center, or a combination of all three. In this case the neighborhood is usually described as the area served by an elementary school. (Busing of children between neighborhoods to achieve racial balance in the schools may conflict with this concept.) The facility should provide indoor and outdoor recreation for children between 5 and 14 years of age. Preschool children and family groups should also be provided for and a landscape area of at least 2 acres is desirable. Ideally the neighborhood playground would be situated within 1/2 mile of each home. Recent standards argue that it is logical to combine the park with the elementary school and its yard. The standards suggest that if the school is 10 acres, then the related park should be 6 acres. If separate, 16 acres would be needed. Another standard sug-

2. *Guide for Planning Recreation Parks in California* (Sacramento: State Printing Office, 1956).

Fig. 4.12   Park on a power line right of way. Oakland, California (1969).

gests that there should be 1 acre of neighborhood park for every 800 of population. But the facilities and parks should reflect the population. Old people who do not drive may have realistic needs for open space equivalent to the tot lot close to home.

The standards also call for community recreation areas, or playfields. A community is defined as a number of neighborhoods, or a section or district of a city. It is suggested that these facilities should provide a wider range of recreation possibilities than

Fig. 4.13 Hyde Park, London. A city wide recreation area within the city but large enough to be insulated from it.

those at the neighborhood level, including fields, courts, and swimming pool, and a center in which arts and crafts, clubs, and social activities may take place. The recommended size is 32 acres or 20 acres if connected to a school, and they should be located between ½ and 1 mile of every home. Another measure is that 1 acre of community park should be provided for every 800 population.

Finally, city-wide recreation areas are described as large parks providing the city dweller a chance to get away from the noise of the city, its dirt and traffic. If the automobile was permanently prohibited from the large nineteenth-century parks this would be possible. They should provide the variety of activities and possibilities to be found in Central and Golden Gate parks. The desired effect can hardly be provided in less than 100 acres. There should be sports centers and facilities for golf, boating, and so on. The 1956 standards for California suggest that a city of 100,000 should have 883 acres of city park, of which 21 would be needed for parking. Beyond these park standards lie special items. Every city should have golf courses, outdoor theater, zoos, botanic gardens, or similar facilities.

These standards are, of course, abstractions, created by the parks and recreation industry. They may not take into account the extent to which recreation patterns have changed in recent years, but in general they make sense.

To what extent have recreation patterns changed since the nineteenth century? Shorter working hours and automation tend to result in boredom rather than exhaustion for the blue-collar worker. At the adult level, Wayne Williams has observed that the traditional leisure triangle has been reversed.[3] Those with the most leisure time today tend to be the unskilled, the semiskilled, and the skilled, in that order. Thus it is perhaps obvious that the need is for diversion rather than for recuperation and that the majority of people need and will seek challenging and active recreation and meaningful involvement. For children, Williams believes that the whole city should be considered a playground, a park, and a classroom and that ways should be found to incorporate the public and especially children into the various workshops of the city—bakeries, auto repair shops, and so on. In this concept, recreation is regarded as an integral part of living, as it should be.

3. Wayne R. Williams, *Recreation Places* (New York: Reinhold, 1958).

Suggested Readings

Butler, George D., *Introduction to Community Recreation,* Ch. 5, "History of Municipal Recreation in the United States," Ch. 11, "City Planning for Recreation."

Chadwick, George F., *The Park and the Town,* Ch. 1, pp. 19–36, "The English Landscape Movement and the Public Park," Ch. 4, pp. 66–93, "Sir Joseph Paxton," Ch. 9, pp. 163–220, "The American Park Movement."

Chadwick, George, *The Works of Sir Joseph Paxton,* Ch. 3, pp. 44–71, "Paxton and the Wider Landscape."

Cleveland, Horace W. S., *Landscape Architecture* (1872).

Creese, Walter, *The Search for Environment: The Garden City Before and After.*

Fabos, Julius, et al., *Frederick Law Olmsted.*

Fein, Albert, *Landscape into Cityscape.*

Fein, Albert, *Frederick Law Olmsted and the American Environmental Tradition.*

Giedeon, Sigfried, *Space, Time and Architecture,* pp. 618–626, "The Dominance of Greenery in London Squares," pp. 641–666, "The Transformation of Paris, 1853–68."

Meyerson, Martin, *Face of the Metropolis,* pp. 11–37, "The Changing Cityscale."

Mumford, Lewis, *The Brown Decades,* pp. 80–96.

Reps, John W., *The Making of Urban America,* Ch. 12, "Cemeteries, Parks and Suburbs."

Tunnard, Christopher, *American Skyline.*

Udall, Stewart, *The Quiet Crisis,* pp. 159–172, "Cities in Trouble."

5. HOUSING

The house becomes housing when it is thought of in multiples either as a set of separate entities on individual plots of land or as row housing, condominiums, or apartment complexes. This chapter deals with the relationship of open space for public or private use to the individual domestic unit in a variety of housing systems. We will see the historical transformation from situations in which the garden is held within the form of the house itself, as at Pompeii (Fig. 2.10), to others in which the dwellings are set in a larger landscape, as in cluster developments of new towns (Fig. 5.1). We must ask ourselves the meaning of this reversal in concept and the implications in social and ecological terms.

The Medieval city may be thought of as large multiple dwellings somewhat similar to Soleri's Arcologies.[1] They were built piecemeal and slowly. Open landscape and farmland surrounded the urban organism, whose texture included small courtyards, public streets, and squares intimately related to the dwelling units (Fig. 2.13).

It is not until the seventeenth century in France that we find the conscious planning and design of multiple housing on a large scale influencing the form of the city. In Paris residential squares were favored by a rising middle class who had aspirations

1. Paolo Soleri, *Arcology: The City in the Image of Man* (Cambridge: MIT Press, 1969).

Fig. 5.1 Cluster development (1960).

they could not afford. The aspiration in seventeenth-century France was to live in a palace like Versailles (Fig. 2.25). This being impossible, housing was built around urban squares in which the sides of the squares were designed to look like modest-sized palaces. In fact, each side contained six or eight individual row houses of four or five stories.

THE LONDON SQUARE

This concept was developed especially well in England in the eighteenth and nineteenth centuries. In London, squares were built in which the sides were designed as one architectural facade (Fig. 5.2). At the back of each row house was a private garden at the bottom of which were stables with access from a mews, or alley. Formal access to the houses was from the roadway surrounding the square. In the middle of this was a fenced garden enclosure for the exclusive use of the residents whose houses faced it; each resident had a key to the gates. In the seventeenth century these gardens were quite urban, paved and perhaps having a pool in the center and a formal arrangement of trees. It was a symbol of the countryside carefully framed by the fence and surrounding pavement representing a cautious acceptance of nature in the city. The urban form that was developed at Bloomsbury in London included several degrees of privacy, from the total privacy of the house, to the open but private back garden, to the public street, and then to the semiprivacy of the central garden in which other residents but not the general public would be encountered. Variations included one in which the central area of a city block was developed as a garden for the residents of surrounding terraces, who reached it through a very small private garden at the back of the house, the

Fig. 5.2 A London square (18th Century).

other side of which faced onto the street. Such systems of housing achieved quite high density since the units were often only about 20 feet wide. At the same time private gardens were provided for each house and community gardens for the entire block.

The gardens in the squares of the eighteenth century were laid out in the newly fashionable landscape style providing a refreshing view from the windows of the houses. The square itself was usually designed with shrubbery, large trees, and ground shaping in an attempt to screen out the urban surroundings. This paradise was separated by a fence from physical intrusions by the masses, and it was an arrangement of privilege.

The extension of the idea that such pieces of nature were desirable elements of city life can be seen in the development of crescents or terraces of houses which looked onto larger or more extensive landscapes than the small square could provide. The crescents of Regents Park (Fig. 4.2) and Bath confront nature in much the same way as Versailles did. Nature is accepted. There is no longer fear or appre-

Fig. 5.3 Royal Crescent, Bath (1767).

hension associated with the natural world and the city is no longer confined by walls and a limited concept of urbanism. The Royal Crescent at Bath built in 1767 was a product of the eighteenth-century landscape movement (Fig. 5.3). Landsdowne crescent with its undulating naturalistic form is even more responsive to the new spirit or attitude. Both reflect the increasing enjoyment of natural landscape and command views of parkland and the countryside beyond. The terraces surrounding Regents Park were considered sophisticated because of their landscape outlook and consequently commanded higher values. The residential square had burst its bounds and grown into a public park.

In the United States the concept of the London square was incorporated to some extent into the urban developments on the East Coast. Penn's plan for Philadelphia incorporated five squares, four of them for the exclusive use of the residents around them. The plan of Savannah was also based on the residential square. In Baltimore, New York, and Boston there were squares and terraces, but in general the "London" square does not appear to be a typical element in American cities of the nineteenth century.

THE ROMANTIC SUBURB

The first American contribution to urban form was the romantic suburb of the nineteenth century. This served as an escape from the conditions of the industrial cities and was conceived visually and aesthetically as a contrast to the typical grid pattern of streets in expanding urban areas. In the second half of the nineteenth century landscape architects and others became critical of this grid pattern, which was described as tedious and monotonous on flat land and hideous when set on undulating ground. It was said that natural beauty was thus sacrificed for speculative convenience. San Francisco must be the classic exception to this argument. Olmsted, Downing, and others developed a new concept of residential site planning which became known as the romantic suburb. In 1852 Alexander Davis laid out a suburb at Llewellyn Park, New Jersey. Its entrance gate was Gothic, the roads were winding, and the sites for housing were set in a framework of trees and shrubs. In addition there was a central landscape park.

Another example is Riverside in Chicago, laid out by Frederick Law Olmsted in 1869 (Figs. 5.4 and 5.5). Curvilinear roads and irregular-shaped parcels of land were held together by a linear park which followed a river. This was the social meeting place for the community. There were no continuous rows of buildings forming architectural units as in the London squares and in Regents Park. There was very little architectural definition. The buildings or villas were separated from a close association with the street and were embosomed within a green land-

Fig. 5.4 Riverside, Chicago (1869).

Fig. 5.5 Riverside, Chicago (1869).

scape and deliberately absorbed by it. Once the planting reached maturity the houses would be secondary in the view from the streets.

This kind of planning called for variations in the size and shape of the traditional residential block. It represents a new concept of a continuous city/park/ garden resulting in what Chadwick calls the urban-rural continuum.[2] Infrared aerial photography reveals the extent and degree to which a green matrix does exist in the current suburban and also central city environments. If the romantic suburb repre-

sented the best kind of residential setting in 1852, there seems to have been very little change between then and now. The highest priced residential areas in the United States, with the exception of a few stylish downtown sectors, seem to have a similar appearance with perhaps the addition of a high security fence. Although these suburbs were intended for wealthy merchants, the ideas of the romantic suburb could be, and later were, easily applied to garden cities, industrial communities, and new towns.

THE COMPANY TOWN

The concept of company towns in which housing was built by industrialists next to their factories was developed in Europe and in New England in the nineteenth century. Originally the arrangement was one of convenience, with most of the advantages on the side of the capitalist, but in time productivity was seen to be related to the health and welfare of

2. George F. Chadwick, *The Park and the Town* (London: Architectural Press, 1966).

Fig. 5.6 A row of workers' houses, Port Sunlight (1887).

the workers. Thus toward the end of the century industrial communities responded to this point of view. It was believed that the effects of mass production procedures on the workers could be counteracted with attractive homes and gardens and community facilities and open space. The earliest significant examples were built in England.

At Port Sunlight, Lever built a town to house the workers for his soap factory. The location he chose had all the attributes of a good industrial site: cheap land, water frontage, transportation, and an avail-

able labor supply. Of the 52 acres Lever acquired, the factory occupied 24 and the remainder was devoted to the model village. It was Lever's dream that the workers would no longer have to walk out to the country to experience the beautiful world but that natural beauty would constantly surround them. Port Sunlight at Birkinhead was a vivid contrast to the back-to-back slum housing in Liverpool. It incorporated the concept of the romantic suburb with curvilinear roads, private gardens, and a central park. The houses were attached and designed as

clusters of ten or more units to look like large manor houses. The visual quality appears as a collection of mansions set in a park instead of the collection of modest workers' dwellings which it actually was (Fig. 5.6). The factory was present in the background and easily reached on foot.

In 1879 the Cadbury brothers moved their chocolate factory from Birmingham to open fields four miles away and established a garden village at Bourneville. The goal was to prevent speculative building as well as to provide housing for key workers. Bourneville is thus unlike Port Sunlight, not strictly a company town. The most influential concept at Bourneville was the Cadburys' belief that the workers would benefit physically and psychologically from the most natural and healthful of all recreations, gardening. Gardens would also help to lower the density, which in itself would be an improvement on the industrial city. One hundred and twenty acres of land around the factory were developed. Sixteen acres were set aside for public open spaces, which included a village green, two parks, and two playgrounds, one of which provided supervision and care for children under 12. Streets were laid out and planted with trees. The houses built in groups were architecturally attractive and provided with ¼-acre gardens at the back. These were laid out, dug, and planted for the tenant in advance. Planted in each garden were eight fruit trees (pears, apples, and one plum) and twelve gooseberry bushes. Significant quantities of food were grown. Once the town was established, figures indicate that the death rate in Bourneville was half that of the rest of the country and that the stature of the children was greater on average than that of Birmingham children.

The industrial or company towns built in America after these experiments reflected some of the new ideas but were, with a few exceptions, less philanthropic and usually laid out with the economic grid pattern of streets. Pullman, Illinois (1885), was one such planned community in which housing was built in groups and public buildings, schools, and a park with a lake were provided. Gary, Indiana (1907), a steel town, depended on private initiative for infilling the grid layout of streets within which land for two public parks and various public buildings was set aside by the company.

THE GARDEN CITY

There is a direct line from these towns planned by philanthropic industrialists to improve living conditions for their own workers to the garden city movement. This was a very influential concept in the early twentieth century. Its origins also lie in the romantic suburb. The garden city idea was formulated by a law court clerk named Ebenezer Howard in 1898.[3] The economic essence of the theory was that the community should own the land, but this was not necessarily what happened in practice. Howard sought the abolition of the evils of the industrial revolution. Like Lever and the Cadburys, he was a reformer and wished to see the elimination of slums, overcrowding, and urban squalor. He conceived the city as a series of concentric circles, the inner core of which would be a civic center in a common or park. The outermost ring would be set aside as a green belt for agriculture and institutional use. Between these would be housing and a section for industry. The diagram was an abstraction to be applied according to the specific conditions of topography and transportation of the selected site.

This concept was attempted twice in England, at Letchworth (1908) and Wellwyn Garden City (1924) (Fig. 5.7). Letchworth was supposed to have a population of 30,000 but failed to attract it after 25 years. It was not an economic success. Wellwyn was more successful because by 1924 the garden city idea had parliamentary approval as a method of improving urban housing, and in 1921 legislation was passed enabling the government to give financial assistance for the building of the new city. As a result of the failure of Letchworth, changes were made. The company set out to design a town of definite size to accommodate between 40,000 and 50,000 inhabitants on 24,000 acres. The location was chosen 20 miles from London so it was near but definitely separate from the big city. After 12 years there were 9,000 inhabitants, 2,500 houses, and 40 industries, and Wellwyn was well on its way to fulfillment. The romantic suburb concept transformed to a popular scale in the industrial villages or company towns was now expanded into full-scale garden cities. Landscape and greenery as a background for life became the popular taste, available to a broader segment of society than before. Improvements in transportation, rail, streetcars, and automobiles, contributed significantly to its success.

In the 1920s the garden city concept was seen as a possible solution to better housing in the United States. The architects Clarence Stein and Henry Wright were two of its champions. Under their guidance the City Housing Corporation of New York built some tentative new forms in 1924. Common green spaces were provided in the interiors of otherwise fairly conventional blocks. More radical innovations came at Radburn, New Jersey (Figs. 5.8 and 5.9). The community was planned in 1929 but un-

Fig. 5.7 Welwyn Garden City (1924).

3. Ebenezer Howard, *Garden Cities of Tomorrow* (London: S. Sonnenschein, 1902). (First published as *Tomorrow; A Peaceful Path to Real Reform*, 1898.)

fortunately coincided with the economic depression and was never fully completed. Radburn, as built, was not a garden city by definition, although Stein and Wright did believe strongly in Howard's ideals of green belts and towns of limited size planned for work as well as living. At Radburn they recognized the limitations of the conventional block system and developed what they called the superblock.

In spite of only partial fulfillment of the original plan, Radburn is significant for demonstrating some new forms for community development suited to the early twentieth-century life style. The houses were designed for middle-income white-collar families. The floor plan reversed the usual relationship of living rooms to the street, new kinds of circulation were provided, and safety for children was given special importance. The typical super-block was about 40 acres. The hierarchy of roads begins with the expressway linking the town to the outside world. Main through roads connect the neighborhoods to each other and to the expressway and then secondary connector roads encircle the superblocks. Finally, culs-de-sac serve as access roads to clusters of twelve to fifteen houses (some semidetached). The average density is four families per gross acre. Pedestrian circulation connects the private gardens at the back and runs between them leading to a central park area. Paths lead through this area and underpass the secondary connector roads, allowing children traffic-free routes to other superblocks and to an elementary school which serves several blocks lying within a half-mile radius which comprises a neighborhood.

The plan reflects the preoccupation with the automobile both from the point of view of circulation and ease of driving access, but it also recognizes that the automobile has its place and that it is desirable

Fig. 5.8 Radburn, New Jersey (1929). A neighborhood of six super blocks.

Fig. 5.9 Radburn, New Jersey (1929). Relationship of cul-de-sacs to central green.

to be free of it. The street or cul-de-sac is considered a service function and the living rooms face onto the garden at the other side. There has always been a tendency for children to find the service side more interesting (auto repairs, hard surface for cycles, and so on), but at least the cul-de-sac is not filled with fast-moving traffic. The park contains community facilities, swimming pool, and play areas. The form of housing was found to be satisfactory. A housing association to which all homeowners belonged and contributed took care of maintenance in the park and provision and running of the recreation facilities.

Other communities were built on similar patterns at Pittsburgh (Chatham Village), Greenbelt, Maryland, and elsewhere, often in wartime housing and government projects. But in spite of the apparent advantages and environmental quality the system provided for people, the layout was not widely adopted. Real estate developers preferred the single family conventional subdivision, which was easier to handle, and the public had little choice in the matter.

The Radburn idea was adapted to a rental apartment development at Baldwin Hills in Los Angeles in 1941. One large superblock of 80 acres includes 627 dwelling units. The density is thus 7.8 families per gross acre. The automobiles are restricted to garage courts separated from the buildings and connected to them by walkways. The parking ratio is three spaces per house, much higher than at Radburn. The units have small patios with access to a central "village green," ½ mile long and varying between 50 and 250 feet wide. In this way, many people are brought together with amenities at fairly high density. It is an ideal plan for children but also well suited for older or retired people who want seclusion and quiet.

NEW TOWNS

In Britain after the war there was an urgent need for new housing and reconstruction. The government supported an extensive public housing program through which, as in the rest of Europe, the current thinking in housing was expressed in physical form and in large quantities. There were two basic sources of inspiration: the *Ville Radieuse concept* of Le Corbusier,[4] in which high-rise buildings stood in a landscape park (Fig. 5.13), and the Radburn plan, in which compact planning allowed the provision of public open space within the framework of the housing. One way or another, the new towns had a great deal of open space. By comparison with the urban areas from which the people came, the density, at ten families per gross acre, was low. "Prairie planning," as it was called by cynics, meant long distances to walk to schools and shops. The environments were alien to people who had grown up in the warm closeness of the East End of London, and thus to some extent the physical form of the new towns destroyed or prevented social interaction of the type they had been accustomed to.

A second group of new towns built in the 1950s tried to adjust to some of the criticisms. At Cumbernauld, for example, a more dense town was planned, with average densities twice that of the earlier attempts (Fig. 5.10). Even at the higher densities, however, considerable open space was included, but it was distributed differently. The larger areas,

4. Charles Edouard Jeanneret-Gris, *The Radiant City* (New York: Orion Press, 1967). (First published in 1933 as *La Ville Radieuse.)*

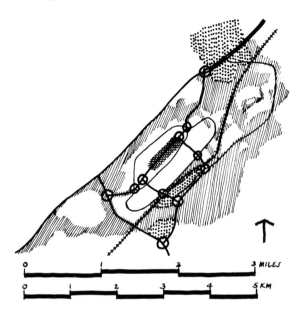

Fig. 5.10 Cumbernauld New Town, U.K. (1958).

Fig. 5.11 Columbia New Town, Maryland (1964).

sports fields and parks, were situated around the built-up area, not within it as at Stevenage. Cumbernauld closely fits Howard's conceptual plan for a garden city. In the middle is the town center, within ten minutes' walk of the farthest house (theoretically, and weather permitting). The circulation system, derived from the Radburn superblock principle, is arranged so that no traffic lights or traffic policemen are needed. Pedestrians are separated from automobiles, which are frequently stored in auto courts, as at Baldwin Hills. Even though the density is high, the housing areas are predominantly low rise and have private gardens or accessible small scale open space within the layouts and connected to the green belt. Although the new towns in Britain consisted of low-rent public housing so that the houses are relatively small for economic reasons, the layouts are innovative and have application in other circumstances (Figs. 7.13 to 7.20).

New town building in America has been carried out only on a limited scale and on a privately financed basis. Reston, West Virginia, Columbia, Maryland, and Irvine in Southern California are three examples. These private enterprise towns are planned as garden cities with housing, industry, and green belts.

Reston was planned for 75,000 people with a variety of housing types at various densities, oriented toward village centers. In addition, the town seemed to be planned around sporting interests. Riding, water sports, swimming, fishing, canoeing, and golf are available. An advertising brochure states that "In all cases the resident of Reston can locate for leisure with his favorite recreation activities waiting for him just beyond his doorstep." Thus in this case open space in housing takes on specific recreational uses as well as providing aesthetic beauty. This justifies the incorporation of so much landscape in the plan. Walking and cycling paths, separated from the roads, run through the open spaces and connect the schools and village centers.

Although all this open landscape may sound like an ideal environment in which to raise a family, social life at Reston still depends on at least two cars in the garage. Another problem is illustrated by the disruption caused in the community when a child was drowned in the lake. The amenities were then seen to some to represent social problems and physical hazards to health and safety.

Columbia, near Washington, D.C., is a similar kind of new town planned for 105,000 people by 1980 (Fig. 5.11). Much of it is already built on an area 5 by 9 miles. It has a hierarchy of neighbor-

Fig. 5.12 Woodlake, California. An apartment complex with a large central park and recreation facility. Wurster, Bernardi and Emmons, architects. Lawrence Halprin, Landscape Architect.

Fig. 5.13 High rise concept. La Ville Radieuse (1933).

Fig. 5.14 Radburn type housing layout in Denmark provides privacy as well as common open space at densities similar to or less than conventional subdivision.

hoods, villages, and a town center:

"As we drive through, some other qualities start to come into focus, striking qualities, new ones. The first sensation comes abruptly. There is no urban geometry here, no precise roadway grid, no ninety degree intersection every 400 feet. The streets are all curved gently. Most of the houses are built on oval culs-de-sac. There is no overhead lattice of utility lines and poles. All that is underground. There is no tin forest of T.V. aerials. Gone, in short, are the straight lines, the hard edges that rigidify and segment the typical residential neighborhood. And that absence leaves, in the scene of swaying willows, old oaks and spreading greensward, a softness, an openess, a newness."

This description in *The New York Times* recalls the quality of the romantic suburb of the 1850s. And although it seems that most people who live there consider it the "American dream," there are unexpected social problems. For example, such open-plan communities with lakes, restaurants, and facilities present ambiguities about who may use what and how.

In condominium developments the surrounding landscape and facilities are usually provided and taken care of by a homeowners' association (Fig. 5.12). Even the houses are maintained this way. Although some similarity may exist between their plan forms and the Radburn superblock, there is often very little similarity in life styles. In Radburn the inhabitants wanted to lead conventional family lives with a community of like-minded people. In condominiums, children often are not allowed. People frequently leave at weekends and there is very little sense of community. Such homes often are thought of as investments.

This review has shown a complete change in concept from the Roman house, tightly enclosing its symbols of nature, through the intermediate stages of the urban square and romantic suburbs, to the new towns and cluster developments in which land-scape surrounds and permeates the dwellings.

Two techniques in housing have been used to provide substantial areas of open space in close proximity to the dwellings. One is the high-rise apartment block which frees the land that would otherwise have been covered by conventional houses and gardens. Mother finds herself on the tenth floor with her two children, looking down at the sur-rounding open space, wondering if it's going to rain or not, and wondering if she should go down in the elevator, which may, in any case, be out of order (Fig. 5.13).

Another new technique is the cluster concept, which concentrates building in high-density groups allowing views out into a landscape that would otherwise be subdivided if the same number of houses were spread out at an overall low density (Fig. 5.1). This system provides attractive views and open space which may be used for community facili-ties as in a condominium, or for pedestrian cycle and riding trials as in a new town, or for unstructured children's play. Whichever way, the land has to be maintained and managed at someone's expense. Both schemes are wasteful of land. Neither seems to understand the different kinds of open space that are needed or the real values to be gained by more com-

Fig. 5.15 Minimum garden: balcony and window boxes.

pact planning, which should be part of a larger ur-ban policy in which conservation zones for water catchment and flood control are assembled as a sys-tem related to and incorporating the open space component of residential areas.

In Scandinavia, where land is perhaps more highly valued, one finds numerous examples of housing with private gardens and common greens (Fig. 5.14). They are essentially Radburn-type layouts. The minimum garden opens onto a public lawn. Privacy is provided with hedges and fences

and there is a free flow between public and private areas, the family and the community. Planning is compact and densities are high.

Continuing down in scale, the patio house enclos-ing its garden and providing extreme privacy in the Roman manner is in fact an economic and socially appropriate solution where land is scarce and society is complex—and where is it not? A private terrace or balcony sheltered from wind is the minimum out-door unit where plants can be grown in pots and window boxes, and where one can relax in the sun (Fig. 5.15). All dwellings should have at least this possibility.

Suggested Readings

Chermayeff, Serge and Christopher Alexander, *Community and Privacy.*
Breckenfeld, Gurney, *Columbia and the New Cities.*
Creese, Walter L., *The Search for Environment: The Garden City Before and After*, pp. 108–143, "Neat and Clean at Port Sunlight and Bourneville," pp. 203–218, "The First Garden City of Letchworth," pp. 315–344, "The New Towns."
Howard, Ebenezer, *Garden Cities of Tomorrow.*
Reps, John W., *The Making of Urban America*, Ch. 15, "The Towns the Companies Built."
Stein, Clarence, *Towards New Towns for America*, pp. 37–74, Radburn.

6. LANDSCAPE PLANNING

In recent years there has been a marked change in public sensitivity and interest in the environment. Ecology and planning have become household words. Air and water pollution, nuclear power plants, highways, and billboards are a few of the issues that have been determined largely according to conservation and environmental quality considerations. Literature on the subject has come forth steadily, and public figures, elected and hereditary, have given their prestigious support to the cause. Commissions, agencies, and programs have been established with varying powers to regulate, control, and beautify the environment. The extent to which it has become a public concern may be measured to some degree by increased television coverage and the use of conservation and ecological terminology in the advertising industry. This broad interest in the environment is, of course, not enough. Experts such as Meier and Darling, who believe in the future of mankind, do so only with severe provisos. Political policies at local and international levels have to be implemented to control pollution and population and to generate renewable resources.

Two things are needed. First, the public must commit itself to the survival of the species homo sapiens and the environment on which this depends. Second, the planners must develop techniques to facilitate the goal. We should realize that the problems of the environment, pollution, and waste of re-

sources are the result of the stated goals currently given primacy in our society: to produce for profit and to utilize one's land in any reasonable way one wishes. The geographer Philip Wagner states the problem: "Until we are willing to pay for aesthetic and ecological improvement, until we are willing to sacrifice some degree of economic benefits, our environmental problems are going to persist and get worse."[1]

Having directed a share of the responsibility where it belongs, let us now proceed to a brief discussion of the scope and nature of the problem as it relates to landscape architecture and then move on to a discussion of techniques.

ENVIRONMENTAL CRISIS

The environmental context in which we are operating today in the United States and in the world is one in which we are faced with the impact of an immense increase in population associated in some places with rising standards of living. We can expect the 3 to 6 thousand million people in the world today to almost double in the next 30 years. Some authorities estimate that the earth's population could eventually level off at 15 billion and that these people could be supported by the earth's resources provided we go about it in the right way. The problem facing mankind in the immediate future is how to house and feed these people.

Fig. 6.1 Competing uses, housing and agriculture on the richest agricultural soil in the world. Davis, California.

The implications of these population projections tend to vary, depending on one's viewpoint and geographical location. In the United States, with vast resources and a relatively slow population increase compared with the Asian countries, the American consumes 130 times more than the average Indian. In a world view this represents a peculiar imbalance. Locally, however, the environmental problems of the advanced technological societies have their own de-

1. Philip L. Wagner, *Constraints Necessary to Achieve the Quality of Life: The Geographer's Viewpoint*. Man and His Total Environment (Los Angeles: University of California Water Resources Center, 1967).

gree of importance when seen out of global context.

In spite of the fact that we all inhabit the same earth, each society naturally tries to solve its own problems within its own socioeconomic framework and with the resources available to it. This is a practical but short term view. Although it is easy to accept the trends of society and to deal as they arise with environmental problems such as water and air pollution, depletion of agricultural soil, energy shortages, and higher food prices, we might also begin to think in terms of dealing with the trends before they are generated. If a widespread understanding of the ecological facts of life together with a concern for the common good and the long term survival of mankind were to permeate the lawmakers' chambers, the advertising agencies, and the industrialists' design studios, many potential problems might never arise. Planning under these circumstances would be a positive rather than a negative procedure. Having said this, we now turn to some specific conflicts.

The effect of expanded populations can be expressed and made comprehensible in a variety of ways. For example, it is predicted that by 1990 more than half the population of the world will be living in cities of 100,000 or more. Herman Kahn suggests that perhaps 80 to 90 percent of the developed world will be urbanized by the end of the century and cities of the less developed nations will double their population every 15 years.[2] In California it is estimated that 5 million new homes will have to be built to accommodate a projected doubling of the state's population from 15 to 30 million. If two-thirds of the projected increase in the population of the United States by the year 2000 were to be

2. Herman Kahn, *The Year 2000* (New York: Macmillan, 1967).

Fig. 6.2   a) Arlington, Virginia, suburb of Washington, D. C. consumes woodland landscape (1957). b) West Covina, Southern California. Orange groves being replaced with subdivisions (1952).
Photographs by William A. Garnett.

Fig. 6.3 Lakewood, California (1950). "17,500 houses in 18 months."

Photographs by William A. Garnett.

housed in new metropolises, two 90,000-person cities would have to be built every month.

Kahn predicts the evolution of a "San-San Pacific Megalopolis," a continuous urban area centered around Los Angeles stretching from San Diego to Santa Barbara and ultimately to San Francisco. The same is expected on the East Coast between Boston and Washington. Reston and Columbia are manifestations of this infilling process. In Europe the concentration of population centered in the southeast of England around London is seen as developing into a conurbation stretching from Manchester to Milan. However, because of the implied concentration, the projected population of the United States in the year 2000 will occupy only 2 percent of the land and the population of England and Wales will take up only 16 percent. Currently half the population of the United States lives within 50 miles or one hour's drive of the oceans, the Gulf of Mexico, or the Great Lakes. The fact quite simply is that certain areas of countries and regions throughout the world are more attractive for settlement than others for a variety of reasons—economic, political, geographical, and so on—and these locations, already urbanized, are likely to continue to attract the major portion of population increase, even if its rate of growth is reduced. New York, Los Angeles, San Francisco, London, Tokyo, and Paris will continue to be attractors. The water's edge is particularly attractive.

Increasing urbanization, together with ultimate limitations on convenient territorial expansion of cities, poses the question of population densities. Currently there is a wide range. For example, the greater Los Angeles area, comprising some 4,000 square miles, is at present occupied by 9 million people, at an overall average density of 2,250 per square mile. By contrast, the 7 million people in Calcutta occupy 400 square miles at an average density of 50,000 per square mile. Manhattan Island is even higher with 68,000, and between the extremes there is every conceivable rate. There is no conclusive evidence that the higher densities are bad and the lower are better. Density cannot be equated with quality of environment without further qualification in terms of dwelling type, accessibility, and distribution of open space. Evidence suggests, however, that certain ill-defined aspects of the urban environment do lead to a high incidence of neuroses and social pathologies such as delinquency and mental and physical ill health.

The consequences of urban expansion are enormous in terms of additional housing, schools, recreation facilities, industry, retail centers, and transportation systems. The problems of water supply and sewage and waste disposal are also critical and these involve the relationship of the expanding metropolis to the hinterland. In addition, it is no accident that the highest concentration of population tends to coincide with or adjoin the areas of the most productive soils in the world (Figs. 6.1 and 6.2). The loss of such land due to urbanization is of major concern and its impact must be evaluated in the larger terms of world food production, supply, and consumption. The statistics can be expressed in a variety of dramatic ways. For example, it is estimated that the United States has lost as much as 1 million acres of its best farmland in a year. Britain has been losing it at the rate of 10 acres a day.

Whatever planning concepts are employed in the accommodation and distribution of increased population, there seem to be two major implications. First, land not hitherto urbanized will be required for new development. Second, the interaction between expanded urban populations and the surrounding hinterland will be greatly increased and intensified in terms of recreation and the supply of resources. Also implied is the redevelopment and environmental improvement of existing urban centers and a questioning of the widely held belief that high-density living is undesirable.

The crisislike proportions of the population and resources problem, which can now be clearly seen, and a worldwide historical record of squandered resources and environmental chaos, make a comprehensive approach to planning the environment imperative for survival if for no other reason.

Some problems are, of course, much larger than a matter of physical planning and design. Clearly designers cannot themselves create the social and economic stability necessary for a healthy and great society. Yet it is the planner's and designer's role to create the environment of society, and in doing this he must be aware of the possibilities inherent in the arrangement of the environment for the encouragement, permission, or frustration of human aspirations and human needs, for social and cultural interaction and fulfillment, and for economic stability, efficiency, health, comfort, and human happiness. The environment and its design and planning cannot be separated from these fundamental social factors.

LANDSCAPE ASSESSMENT AND LAND USE PLANNING

Regardless of whether socioeconomic considerations suggest the establishment of new towns, the continued physical expansion of existing cities to accommodate population increase, or some other solution, the selection of land suitable for urbanization should depend on an assessment of its fragility and

Fig. 6.4 Soil erosion.

Fig. 6.5 A flood diversion channel.

Fig. 6.7 Productive agricultural soil, a scarce resource of value to society.

Fig. 6.6 The same channel about a year later silted up as a result of erosion caused by subdivision development.

Clearly the ability to make decisions based on these criteria of fragility and value depends on an understanding of the evolution of the landscape, the essential elements of environment, and the basic natural processes and ecological interrelationships within which we operate. It is then necessary to find a way to evaluate the variables of the natural system so that they can become powerful and manageable determinants of land use policy and of form in project planning and design.

This is the essence of what is defined here as landscape planning. It is perhaps worthwhile to look a little deeper into what is meant by the term and how it differs from social and economic planning. Hackett sees the role of the landscape planner as the locating and welding together of various land uses in a process based on a technical knowledge of the physiology of landscape and an aesthetic understanding of its appearance. The result would be another stage in the evolution of the landscape.[3] Crowe suggests that landscape planning is a wider concept than land use planning, because it includes appearance as well as use, pleasure as well as fertility. She sees the function of landscape planning as guiding the intricate intermeshing of functions and habitats, as separating the incompatible, reconciling diverse uses, and relating each specialized use to the overall landscape seen as setting for life.[4] McHarg asks that we view man-made changes to the landscape in terms of creativity. He argues that man as

its value for other uses. The fragility of a landscape is a function of geology, soil, slope, climate, vegetation, wildlife, and scenic quality, and the extent to which landscape degradation would result from its disturbance. Symptoms of landscape degradation are excessive soil erosion, silting of streams, landslides, flooding, and loss of wildlife (Figs. 6.4 to 6.6). Moreover, assessment of alternative uses or higher

values depends on a concept in which landscape and its social content are regarded as a resource. Thus clean rivers and aquifers, rare vegetation and wildlife, high-quality agricultural soil, and areas of historic interest and scenic quality would be considered for conservation on the basis of their uniqueness, scarcity, or irreplaceability and therefore their value to society (Fig. 6.7).

3. Brian Hackett, *Landscape Planning* (Newcastle: Oriel Press, 1971).
4. Sylvia Crowe, The Need for Landscape Planning, in *Towards a New Relationship of Man and Nature in Temperate Lands* (Morges: IUCN, 1967).

Fig. 6.8 Landscape type: mountains/wilderness. Absaroka Range, Wyoming. Shoshone National Forest.
Photograph by R. Burton Litton, Jr.

Fig. 6.9 Landscape type: Coastline. Tomales Bay, California. North and leeward exposure supporting live oak and California Bay.
Photograph by R. Burton Litton, Jr.

part of nature is required to be creative in the evolutionary process and that changes should be judged in terms of the laws of nature and evolution. His system of landscape planning is based on the proposition that nature is process and value exhibiting both opportunities and constraints for human use.[5]

These views describe the intentions of landscape planning. Its process can be divided into four stages: (1) survey and analysis; (2) evaluation; (3) policy or design solution; and (4) implementation. The landscape survey is an assessment of the facts and forces that have formed the landscape. The landscape plan sets out the framework and lines of action by which the landscape is to be adjusted in accordance with ecological principles to meet the needs of changed circumstances. Landscape planning consists of a scientific aspect concerned with research and a shaping aspect based on the research; the two parts result in the production of a policy statement.

Three classes of information comprise the survey: the landscape-ecological factors; the human, socioeconomic, and cultural factors; and the visual appearance representing the interaction of these two. The survey is concerned first with the identification of landscape types. These can be defined on the basis of ecology and visual quality. Land in whatever state of cultivation or wilderness is clearly not a uniform commodity. Every landscape is unique as a result of the variables involved in its formation and its basic structure and geographical location. Each land-

5. Jan McHarg, *Design with Nature* (New York: Natural History Press, 1969).

Fig. 6.10 Landscape type: Riparian meadow. Taylor Creek, Eldorado National Forest, Lake Tahoe. Photograph by R. Burton Litton, Jr.

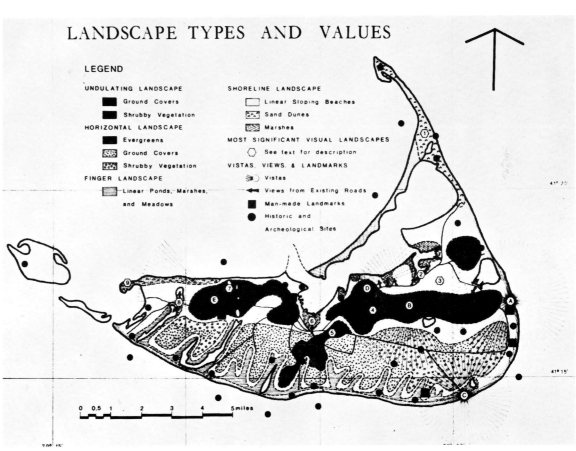

Fig. 6.11 Landscape types and values mapped for Nantucket Island (Zube, 1966).

scape type or ecosystem is thus a dynamic reflection of the facts and forces of its evolution. Thus deserts are different from coastal strands, mountains are different from marshlands, and so on (Figs. 6.8 to 6.10, and 11.7). Within each basic type lie microenvironments related to differences in geology, soil, exposure, slope vegetation, and use by man (Fig. 6.11).

The level of detail required in the analysis depends on its purpose. Where the study is of a broad nature dealing with intrinsic suitabilities of land for some use, then a comprehensive evaluation of all natural factors is essential.

The landscape-ecological factors survey must include a description of the historical geological processes responsible for the basic form of the landscape and the distribution and outcropping of various geological formations. These strata must be located and described in terms of permeability and water-holding capacity, stability, and other variables (Fig. 6.12). Fault lines, landslides, river cutting, and other dynamic aspects must also be recorded and mapped. The soil is an extension of geology, although not always located where it was formed. The composition of the soil varies according to its geological parentage and its method of formation and the subsequent weathering process and use by man. Soils are classified and named on the basis of these and other variables and are described in terms of stability, erodability, shrink-swell factor, fertility, and so on.

Water is not only an important factor in giving form to the landscape, but all life depends on it. Its presence is a major ecological determinant. In addition, water is the link between all dynamic aspects of the environment. Our analyses must therefore show where it comes from, where it runs to, and where it is stored above and below ground. The climate is responsible for the amount of water that is precipitated on land. Temperature and winds, together with water, make up the components of erosion which have shaped the landscape over millions of years. The variables—temperature, water, soil—determine the distribution of vegetation. The variety

Fig. 6.12 Building suitability map based on a combination of geological factors. It will be noted that the distribution of population does not correspond to the areas of least hazard. Study by students of Landscape Architecture, University of California, Berkeley (1972). (Robin Chiang and Robin Nelson).

of vegetation and its location in a natural landscape is an indicator of these variables. The topography of the landscape represents other determinants in the distribution of vegetation (elevation and slope orientation) and the stability of geological formations and soils (steepness of slope). Wildlife is dependent on the quantity and distribution of the vegetation. All these data must be assembled and mapped in such a way that the variables can be related to each other and to the purpose of the study.

The human, socioeconomic, and cultural factors included in the survey will, of course, vary, depend-

Fig. 6.15 Visual analysis. The Virgin Islands (Zube, 1968).

iography are themselves potential resources that may be evaluated according to their uniqueness and the principles of the artist. Photographs and sketches taken from likely viewpoints and zones of landscape which are part of important views constitute the raw data. Prominent landmarks and all elements fundamental to visual quality can be mapped in the same way as the other survey information (Figs. 6.13, 6.14, and 6.15). Now we are ready for the analysis leading to evaluation.

Wagner suggests in a general way that we should assess the landscape in terms of economic, aesthetic, and ecological values.[6] Our management of the land should aim toward the optimization of ecological fitness and health, visual beauty, and employment. Put another way, the evaluation stage should be concerned with a balance between the natural potential and the economic and technical requirements of the human society. The survey information collected thus must be interpreted and evaluated in terms of the existing natural processes, intrinsic suitability of the land, and pressures for change to that land. Features must be evaluated in terms of their scarcity value, their limitations for development, and their opportunities for various land uses, in terms of their impact or lack of impact on the natural system.

The evaluation is made in terms of potential land uses and the degree to which the natural system can sustain disturbance. We can therefore look at the landscape in terms of potential uses and the optimum criteria of those uses and thus find areas where they can best be fulfilled within the allowable level of disturbance. We are concerned with two basic questions: first finding the optimum landscape criteria for those uses that are adequately defined, and

6. Wagner, *op. cit.*

second determining the impact of various land uses on different types of landscape. We can arrive at degrees of suitability for a particular land use based on these factors. The point at which a degree of suitability becomes unacceptable is a function of the values of society. The reliability of the data is of course critical, and the development of new technology might render some criteria obsolete or reduce the estimated environmental damage. "Capability" usually refers to a scientific evaluation of land in terms of its capacity for change, whereas "suitability" is related to the criteria for specific uses and social values in relation to capability (Fig. 6.16).

The issues of criteria and impact are clearly interrelated, but for the moment let us look at them separately. The criteria for land uses vary to some extent depending on the geographical and cultural context. The specification for each is written from two points of view, that of the operator or user and that of the public. The criteria fall into three categories: (1) economics, (2) health and safety, and (3) ecological and visual relationships. Thus optimum agricultural use will have criteria for soil, slope, drainage, aspect, and access. High-speed highways will have criteria for curves and gradients. Housing will have criteria for geological stability, sewage disposal, and microclimate. Flood plains and land subject to subsidence or slippage are obviously unsuitable for housing or schools. In addition, earthquake fault zones and filled land in earthquake-prone areas should be regarded as unsuitable. Even though residents of such areas frequently are unconcerned or fatalistic about the danger, there can be great cost to society (Fig. 6.17). When disaster strikes, it is usually the public that pays for repair of roads and services and special loans to the victims. In other words, there is a loss to society. Nuclear power

Fig. 6.16 Lake Tahoe Basin, Land Capabilities. A portion of the map prepared by the U.S. Forest Service in cooperation with the Tahoe Regional Planning Agency (1971). The map shows seven land capability classes designated by number in order of increasing tolerance for use without sustaining permanent damage. Land capability involves consideration of (1) risks of land damage from erosion and other causes and (2) the subsequent impact of such damage on vegetation, sedimentation, flooding, wild life and water quality.

The land capabilities are determined according to the frequency and magnitude of the hazards encountered: floods, landslides, high water tables, poorly drained soils, fragile flora and fauna and easily erodible soils. Class 1 represents areas that exhibit the greatest frequency or highest magnitude of hazardous conditions, or both. Class 7 represents areas where existence of hazardous conditions is negligible.

The map can be used to judge the risk of land damage and to assign use activities and intensities within hydrologic and topographic limitations. The study does not suggest that development should occur on the locations shown.

The land rated lowest has the least tolerance for use, the steepest slopes (over 30%), the greatest potential for erosion and the highest run off potential, or the poorest drainage and flora and fauna.

Fig. 6.17   (a) and (b) The San Andreas fault runs through the lake at the top right hand corner and out to the Pacific Ocean in the foreground. Evidence of land failure can be seen and the highway has been closed indefinitely. Oblivious to the dangers, subdivisions, schools and other construction has taken place within the fault zone with effects such as that shown even without a significant earthquake. Photograph 17(a) by William A. Garnett (1958). Photograph 17(b) by Jean Stein (1973).

plants are a special case where stability of foundations is of widespread concern.

Houses can be located in terms of achieving the best microclimate for people. The warming effect of lakes in winter, the cooling effect of winds, and the presence of vegetation can be taken advantage of to achieve the best outdoor living conditions and the least cost of heating and cooling. Conversely, zones of land in temperate climates which by virtue of

their slope or orientation receive little direct sunlight throughout the year, and particularly in winter, should, from the points of view of health, heating costs, and energy conservation, be regarded as relatively unsuitable for human occupation. From an economic point of view land that will increase building costs is unlikely to be attractive to developers unless there is some compensating factor, such as location or view. The location of housing in relation

to areas of visual quality requires some special criteria which will ensure that quality.

Suitability is simply indicated by the concurrence of a number or a majority of positive factors in any one area. Multiple use is, of course, possible and compatible; alternatives are likely to occur as part of the evaluation process.

The impact question is concerned with the possible effect of a change in land use on the environment in general and also on nonrenewable resources such as fertile soil, pure water, economic minerals, and outstanding landscape beauty, however difficult that may be to define. The impact may simply be the loss of such resources. In addition, this definition of resources that may be damaged should include habitats: the soil and vegetation supporting the food chains of ecological communities whose presence is often associated with the control of insects which cause damage to agricultural crops. Thus, as Fraser Darling points out, chunks of underdeveloped landscape and woods are in themselves, without any other use at all, extremely important and productive elements of the environment not to be given up lightly.[7] Some elements of the landscape which do not appear to have any use actually do, if an overall view is taken of the environment and its processes. It is generally true that when man alters natural ecosystems by design or ignorance, they are usually simplified (as in agriculture) or made less complete, and they lose something of their holistic quality of resistance to invasion by foreign species. There is a potential conflict between economic food production and the natural ecology of the area, especially if fields are large and of one main crop. Complexity and richness are essential attributes of an ecologically sound landscape.

Soil erosion is one of the major likely impacts of home building, highway construction, and forestry. Steep slope, lack of vegetative cover, and highly erodable soil types are the causal variables. Construction techniques and machinery are the socioeconomic variables. Excessive erosion caused by the interaction of these factors results in the loss of soil and vegetation and causes flooding at lower levels by silting up streams.

The disposal of sewage by septic tanks can cause pollution to rivers and groundwater. Water quality is thus related to sewage disposal systems whose capacities and service areas may limit the growth of communities.

Extensive paving and roofing covering the natural surface of the land increases the rate of runoff and may result in flooding if the storm sewer system is inadequate or nonexistent. Or if rainwater is removed in storm sewers or otherwise prevented from seeping into the soil, the water table may be lowered with resulting impact on the trees and vegetative cover, some of which may die as the availability of water decreases. The excessive removal of water by wells from aquifers may also have a similar effect. The microclimate can be altered by the filling or creation of lakes and by new topography giving rise to variations in temperature and wind. For example, if San Francisco Bay were filled to the extent to which it could until recently legally have been filled, the temperatures in San Jose would have increased significantly to the extent that buildings would need air conditioners as an essential rather than as a luxury. This may in itself sound as though only money would be involved, but the additional power needed would lead to an increase in the chain of events involved in the production of that power. Many links of this chain have their own detrimental ecological repercussions on resources and environment elsewhere in the region.

There is always an impact. Its extent or degree of destructiveness varies according to the closeness of the fit between the use and the suitability of the land for that use in ecological and social terms. The evaluation phase of landscape planning is involved, then, with matching the uses to the landscape so that the criteria for the uses are fulfilled with the least possible impact.

The results of the evaluation should then become the basis for regional policy or determinants in design and planning at a smaller scale. Implementation of policy requires legal measures democratically approved and enforced in such forms as zoning, performance standards, building codes and ordinances, and means of compensation for reduction of potential for development in the common interest.

The example that follows is a gross oversimplification of the landscape planning process, which is, in reality, highly complex. The East Lothian Study is a theoretical caricature of the method just outlined. The value judgments and the criteria by which decisions were made were not those approved by any legislative body, although they may someday be. They are assumed to be reasonable for the benefit of present and future populations within the context of environmental quality and conservation of resources.

CASE STUDY 1. EAST LOTHIAN

East Lothian is a county of Scotland comprising about 416 square miles. The area lies to the east of the city of Edinburgh with ½ million inhabitants. This may sound small if you live in New York or Los Angeles, but Edinburgh, in the overall scale of the country, represents a considerable center of population and is associated with an industrial belt stretching west to Glasgow. The study area was based on the watershed of the Tyne River running from the highlands in the south to the North Sea.

Note on Figs. 6.18 to 6.33:

The East Lothian Study was done by graduate students in Landscape Architecture at the University of Edinburgh in 1969–70. They were Messrs. Bauld, Filor, Hasting, Desau, Rice, Shihabi, and Smith, and Miss James.

7. Fraser Darling, *New Scientist*, (April 16, 1970).

Fig. 6.18 East Lothian Study: Visual Analysis. 1. Coastal Zone 2. Coastal Plain 3. Tranent ridge 4. Tyne Valley 5. Foothills 6. Moorland a. Berwick Law (volcanic plug) b. Hopeton monument c. Church Tower d. Traprain Law (volcanic plug) e. Lammer Law

The boundary of the watershed does not quite coincide with the county boundaries. Thus the planning unit includes a portion of an adjacent county and not all of East Lothian. In addition, the coastal area, which did not lie within the watershed, was included because of its obvious geographical relationship and its popularity for seaside recreation.

In addition to evaluating the land in terms of its suitability for a variety of probable uses, one chief objective of the study was specifically to locate areas that could be designated as country parks for recreation. These were to provide places where people from Edinburgh and as far away as Glasgow could go for active recreation and social vacations. The country park concept was conceived as having an attractive landscape setting with buildings for group facilities and provision for sports, sailing, and even auto repair work; some place close to but away from the everyday environment, that is, within the hinterland of population centers.

The uses considered likely, in addition to recreation, were housing of three different types (densities); industry (since there was a source of labor as agricultural employment declined); forestry (in relation to a national policy to increase the production of home-grown timber); motorway or freeway route alignment (in relation to the major transportation connection to the south, which, by virtue of the topography, had to pass through the region); and agriculture (which was traditionally a major use of the land due to the excellent soil and a climate suited to the growing of wheat and potatoes). Six possible land uses were thus selected: agriculture, housing, industry, forestry, motorway, and recreation.

The study did not result in a plan for the future of the county or watershed. The objective was rather to examine all the alternative uses, to look at the landscape types in the area, and to recommend the best possible use for that land. This provides quantities of land suited for one use or another if a demand for it should arise. The recommendations are based on a desire to optimize the potential. Thus if at some stage a policy for promoting more industry is established, then the land most suited for this according to optimum criteria is already pinpointed and can be examined in detail for its availability, dimensions, and so forth, related to the specifics of the case. The demand for any land use can be evaluated in terms of an assessment of the land's capability and suitability as already described. Alternative futures can thus be presented to legislators and the public. Decisions can then be made openly in the knowledge of what will be lost if land most suited for one use is used for another.

It is not unnatural that the survey and analysis should begin with visual impressions. The area was divided into six basic landscape units on the basis of their variations in topography, land use, and vegetation patterns and because of their separateness or unique identity: (1) the coastal zone; (2) the coastal plain; (3) a ridge area separating the former from (4) the valley itself; (5) the rolling foothill country; and (6) high moorland landscape (Fig. 6.18). The coastal zone, attractive and popular for recreation, was itself varied according to its form: beach, rocks, marshes, and so on (Fig. 6.19). The coastal plain was flat and extensive, with rich soil; because of its flatness it was suitable for arable farming and also suitable, topographically at least, for building and trailer parks (Fig. 6.20). The ridge area was wooded, providing views to the coast and to the moors (Fig. 6.21). The valley included several historical monuments, battlefields, and country houses, all valuable recreation resources (Fig. 6.22). The foothills, rather

Fig. 6.19 Landscape type 1. Coast.

Fig. 6.20 Landscape type 2. Coastal Plain.

Fig. 6.21 Landscape type 3. Ridge.

Fig. 6.22 Landscape type 4. Valley.

Fig. 6.23 Landscape type 5. Foothills.

Fig. 6.24 Landscape type 6. Moorlands.

more rolling, commanding fine views to the north, were predominantly used for sheep farming (Fig. 6.23). The moorland was bleak and cold, almost at the timberline, and generally without any major tree cover (Fig. 6.24).

Within this framework several conspicuous landmarks were identified: volcanic plugs, distinctive land forms which can be seen for miles around; a monument on a hill; a church spire in the county town. These were selected for their prominence and a map was prepared which showed the visibility of the landmarks. Zones from which all of the landmarks could be seen at once were plotted (Fig. 6.18). Clearly the views from such areas would be panoramic and this information was considered useful in the selection of scenic routes and the location of country parks and picnic areas.

The visual analysis indicated that the quality of the landscape was to a large extent the product of numerous skylines. Skyline zones were thus plotted as areas that should be protected from land uses such as housing, which would severely alter their character (Fig. 6.26).

The sociocultural factors were easily obtainable from maps. Land use information was supplemented with a record made by schoolchildren of the specific use of each field in a particular year. An overall picture was compiled showing woodland, pasture, and wheat and potato farming. A comparison of historical maps showed the changes in the amount of woodland that had occurred, much being added in the eighteenth and nineteenth centuries and some removed later in the trend toward larger fields. The existing landscape includes windbreak plantings, hedgerows, and plantations associated with country estates. The diversity and quantity of these was considered an ecological asset as well as an important component of the visual quality.

The landscape is intensively used for various forms of agriculture with associated small market towns and villages. In addition, there is a considerable quantity of historic and archeological sites scattered throughout the area, representing hundreds of years of settlement and use and a considerable potential for recreation. It is a humanized landscape, attractive in its contrasts and combinations of town and countryside. It is not untypical of well-used landscapes anywhere in the world. People from the cities like to visit the villages, fish in the rivers, have picnics at the seaside, and hike in the hills.

Fig. 6.25 East Lothian study. Overview of landscape types from foothills to coast and showing one of the prominent topographic landmarks.

Meanwhile, the landscape is a working concern, growing food and fiber. The coexistence of these two perceptions of the landscape is vital to both town and country.

The natural factors analysis began with an examination of the geology. The faults associated with the basic divisions of the landscape were no longer active. Minerals of economic value in the area were unimportant. Coal mining which had taken place in one district was no longer operational but left zones of land liable to subsidence for a period of years. A large limestone deposit located adjacent to the study area was being actively extracted and was supposed to satisfy all the predicted future needs of the cement industry. This indicated that the limestone deposits lying within the area need not be considered as potentially valuable. Road stone might be the only material to be extracted from the area and in fact its quarrying was slowly destroying one of the volcanic plugs. The geological analysis in this case was not a significant determinant of land use and the formations were all considered relatively stable.

A study of slopes, however, proved more significant (Fig. 6.27). Slopes over 25% were considered too steep for any building use. Mapping of slopes was carried out in relation to criteria for housing and building in general. These involved building costs and the likelihood of excessive erosion caused by construction. Thus by our selected standards, high-density housing and industry should be located on the flattest land under 2.5%. Medium-density housing could occur on land up to 10%. Single houses at low density could occur on land up to 25%. Mapping of these slope categories showed considerable constraints on the location of high- and medium-density housing and industry.

Climatic studies showed the amount of rainfall and the variation in its distribution within the region. As the land increased in height so the rainfall increased (to 40 inches). At the coast, the rainfall was considerably less (25 inches) and the number of hours of sunshine in the year was one of the highest

Fig. 6.26 East Lothian Study: Skyline zones.

Fig. 6.27 East Lothian Study: Slope analysis.

in the country. Cold easterly winds and sea fog also contributed to the pattern of climate. The rainfall information with other data became particularly important in the assessment of different areas of land for various forestry species.

The soil study rated the soils according to their capability for agriculture. This involves not only the soil type but other related values including the slope of the land, exposure, wind, and rainfall. Agricultural value then was rated from class 1 (best) to 7 (urbanization). The position was adopted that since good agricultural land was an invaluable resource, as much as possible should be reserved for that purpose. The Ministry of Agriculture usually was prepared to fight court battles to preserve classes 1 and 2, and on the basis of this all class 1 and 2 land was allocated for agriculture as a primary value to which all else would take second place. In this way the agriculture suitability map was derived (Fig. 6.28).

The suitability of land for economic forestry depends on the slope of the land (to facilitate operations), rainfall (different species have different optimums), soil (different species thrive best on different soil types), and elevation (colder temperatures affect the growth of certain species). All the data maps showing slope, elevation, rainfall, and soil were thus used in the production of suitability maps for several forest species considered economic in the area: beech, larch, Scots pine, and Norway spruce (Fig. 6.29).

Criteria for the motorway alignment were established. From an economic standpoint, the motorway should not interact with slopes over 2.5%. It should also avoid streams and flood plains. From a conservation viewpoint the motorway should not cross A1 or A2 agricultural land. It should not go through existing settlements and should avoid scenic areas and

Fig. 6.28 East Lothian Study: Agricultural Suitability. 1. class I land 2. class II land 5. class V land 6. class VI land.

Fig. 6.29 East Lothian Study: Forestry suitability.

Fig. 6.30 East Lothian Study: Motorway alignment.

Fig. 6.31 East Lothian Study: Housing and Industry suitability.

historic monuments. Many of the criteria applied were based on reducing the cost of construction. In selecting the route short areas of higher value had to be sacrificed for the sake of distance. The system of overlaying constraints indicates that the route should follow the line of least resistance (Fig. 6.30). We find, however, that if the constraints are valued equally, this may mean the loss of high-quality agricultural land and disruption of farms. When this is the only constraint, longer or more costly alternatives may be proposed on the grounds that the loss of nonrenewable resources may be of longer term importance than short term cost in cash.

A hydrology map indicated the watershed areas, water catchment and reservoirs, and flood plains of streams and rivers. Degrees of pollution were also noted. These data were useful in the recreation suitability study and also in the motorway alignment. The natural habitats were identified. The vegetation and habitat changed according to the land use and the differentiation in topography and natural environment. The various plants and animals to be found in the area were related to these habitats: marshland, sea coast, estuarine, riverine, fields, grassland, uplands, moorland, and others. This variety in habitat contributed to a richness in vegetation and wildlife.

All land with the exception of A1 and A2 agricultural land and skyline zones was considered in the housing and industry suitability studies (Fig. 6.31). The higher density, equivalent to town expansion and public housing (twenty units per acre), was permitted on remaining land with a slope of less than 2.5% but not where woodland occurred. The same land areas were also considered suitable for industry but with the added condition of proximity to major road and rail transportation routes. Areas with a slope of less than 10%, not on good agricultural land, woodland, or skylines, was considered suitable for medium density housing (four to six units per acre). Low-density housing suitability covers virtually all the land except the skylines. A1 and A2 land was included to permit the building of farmhouses or farm workers' dwellings. The housing could go anywhere except on the skylines and slopes over 25%. In many cases the housing would be best situated within woodland and "absorbed" by it. Although it may appear possible from the map that the countryside could be covered with low-density housing, building would be permitted only in relation to farms or on large acreages.

A composite map for housing and industry showed the areas most suited for each use within the criteria established, and it showed areas where there were competing or alternative uses for the same land. From a visual standpoint, one area rated suitable for industry was tested to see how visible it would be from the surrounding landscape, and it was found to be relatively unseen (Fig. 6.31).

The landscape was rated in terms of recreation suitability by giving a value to squares in a kilometer grid according to the number of recreation components they contained (Fig. 6.32). These were identified as woodlands, water, architectural or historical features, and existing recreation facilities; in addition, the lower agriculture values were considered an added positive value in the rating. The squares with the most components were considered at least worthy of consideration for recreation. A further refinement of the system weighted the factors in relation to the amount of each component in the square. This produced a more sensitive and positive map with clearer definition of areas endowed with good recreation opportunities.

**Legend (left map):**
IIIII 0-3 Components
///// 3-6 Components
≡≡≡ 6-9 Components
▓▓▓ 9-12 Components

**Legend (right map):**
⊡- - scenic routes
⊞ Country park site
⊡ picnic area
IIIII Viewshed of industry or housing
≡≡≡ Area from which all 5 Landmarks can be seen

Fig. 6.32 East Lothian Study: Recreation suitability.

Fig. 6.33 East Lothian Study: Map of recreation possibilities including country parks, scenic routes, and picnic sites.

A composite of all the suitabilities was prepared by overlapping all the suitability maps. There were some areas where uses competed, providing alternatives, for example, recreation and mixed farming; low-density housing, recreation, and forestry. However, the criteria selected and the values decided upon actually resulted in very little conflict. Changes in criteria and values would, of course, produce different maps and possibly more conflict. The composite map is in itself not important. It should be understood that this kind of study is not a plan for the future. It is an assessment of the land and some potential uses of that land to be used as a basis for planning. It exposes some values that are not always understood and makes available to planners and the public alike a picture of what is to be lost or gained when any particular planning decision is made. The criteria adopted for any land use may vary. Interpretation of the natural factors data may also vary, but the system shows what could happen if criteria and interpretations were applied consistently and how the public sector might benefit from this procedure.

The recreation study was geared toward the selection of areas suitable for country parks. A map delineated recreation nodes. These occurred within the areas from which views of the landmarks could be obtained and coincided with the coming together of features such as rivers, footpaths, and historic sites. The location of country parks was recommended within the multiple view areas, within the low-density housing suitability areas (to permit structures), and in relation to the highest scoring recreation squares (Fig. 6.33). This is a generalized system of focusing quickly on the most likely areas. The decision to designate one or more sites for country parks depends on the demand, the policy of

the county, and the availability of funds for the purpose. These areas or nodes must, of course, be analyzed in detail for final site selection, but the search need not go outside the areas of highest potential. In other cases, derelict or reclaimed land might be selected on the assumption that landscape quality would be created by design and planting.

Selection of scenic routes was suggested by bringing together the existing road map, areas of good views, and the location of historic monuments. "Conservation corridors" were also proposed. These consisted of woodlands, hedgerows, and rivers connected as reserves for wildlife whose seasonal migration and food gathering involves movement within the countryside pattern.

A discussion of planning large regions of landscape in private ownership may seem idealistic. The political process involved is far from established. The process whereby land owners are persuaded that their land should be used in a certain way for the common good and the long term advantage of society, and then are compensated at public expense for any loss incurred is, as yet, not well worked out or popular. The planning laws of Great Britain and other European countries are perhaps more suited for this strategy than are those of the United States, but the costs are high and the definition of public good often is hazy at best.

LANDSCAPE PLANNING IN THE UNITED STATES

In the United States many plans and planning studies have attempted to relate the principles of landscape planning to the realities of land speculation and ad hoc development practices. Some are concerned with the future expansion of cities (Minneapolis,[8] Baltimore,[9] Santa Cruz Mountains[10]),

others with the control of housing and recreation development in resort areas of scenic value (Lake Tahoe[11]), others with islands (Hawaii,[12] the Virgins,[13] Nantucket[14]), and others with the conservation of recreation sources (Wisconsin[15]). The principles are essentially the same in all cases: resources and landscape types are surveyed and evaluated in terms of uniqueness and impact. Some stop short at capabilities whereas others combine capabilities with socioeconomic pressures and propose optimum form for counties and urban expansion.

There are two difficulties in implementing these plans. The first is to match the administrative unit with the natural regional planning unit. The second is the question of imminent domain, always an unpopular concept, and compensation for landowners whose aspirations are in conflict with the long term common good. Such a system in which potential

8. Wallace, McHarg, Roberts, and Todd, *An Ecological Study for the Twin Cities Metropolitan Area* (Metropolitan Council of the Twin Cities, 1969).
9. Wallace McHarg Associates, *Plan for the Valleys* (Philadelphia, 1963).
10. Tito Patri, David Streatfield, and Tom Ingmire, *Early Warning System* (Berkeley: University of California, Department of Landscape Architecture, 1970).
11. U.S. Forest Service (in cooperation with the Tahoe Regional Planning Agency), *Land Capabilities and Land Use Plan* (U.S. Department of Agriculture, 1970).
12. Eckbo, Dean, Austin, and Williams, and Muroda, Tanaka and Itagaki, Inc., *A General Plan for the Island Kauai* (Honolulu: State of Hawaii, 1970).
13. Ervin H. Zube, *The Islands* (Amherst: University of Massachusetts, Department of Landscape Architecture, 1968).
14. Ervin H. Zube, *An Inventory and Interpretation of Selected Resources of the Island of Nantucket* (Cambridge: University of Massachusetts, 1966).
15. Philip H. Lewis, *The Outdoor Recreation Plan* (Wisconsin Department of Resource Development).

land users are guided as to where they should or should not develop in terms of the larger overview of the common good appears to require sociopolitical changes and enlightenment. More difficult to accept, yet desirable even now, is the idea that in certain cases the removal of development along coasts and lakes would be in the public interest and worth the cost.

CASE STUDY 2. SEA RANCH

Sea Ranch is on the north coast of California within 3½ driving hours from San Francisco, lying in its recreation hinterland. In 1965 a developer proposed a second-home community along 16 miles of the coast and associated coast range. The building program called for an economic density to satisfy the existing demand for vacation houses. At the same time, the landscape had to be maintained visually and ecologically. Lawrence Halprin and Associates made planning recommendations for the use of the land and suitable building forms on the basis of an ecological study. It was felt that these recommendations would enhance rather than destroy the landscape, which would inevitably have been destroyed if uncontrolled growth had been permitted as seen elsewhere on the coast.

A survey and analysis were completed. An understanding of what would be changed with the imposition of new uses plus an understanding of the nature of a second home and especially in this case an understanding of the climate led to criteria for density, location of buildings, and principles of land use and conservation.

The landscape consisted of three zones: the beach and rocky shoreline or cliffs, the ocean terrace or raised beach, and the forested hillside behind (Fig. 6.34). Windbreaks of Monterey cypress existed on

Fig. 6.34 Sea Ranch: view showing the basic components of the landscape, beach, ocean terrace and wooded slopes.

the terrace, having been planted fifty years earlier for agricultural purposes. Grazing practices had kept the terraces in grassland but in places overgrazing had taken place. The hillsides were covered in mixed coniferous forests (primarily Bishop pine) within which a thick underbrush had grown as a result of strict fire control over the previous fifty years, thus increasing the fire hazard.

The soil and geology study was not particularly relevant in this case, since foundations for large structures were not considered. A few minor restrictions were revealed. There were some areas of soil erosion and some marshy places which were considered unsuitable for building.

The climatic studies had a major impact on the form and distribution of the development. On the Northern California coast, one intuitively expects fog in the summer and persistent strong winds, a certain unreliability about the weather, and considerable rainfall in winter. The study set out to determine how bad the climate really was. Would it deter people from buying land there? And if the climate

was a liability, could it be ameliorated or compensated for by design and planning? Analysis revealed that this part of the coast did not in fact have as much fog as elsewhere. Aerial surveillance over a year showed the overall fog pattern tended to reach Sea Ranch last as it moved in from the ocean. This was at least a favorable finding.

The temperatures were influenced by the combined effect of sun, fog, and wind. A radiation chart expressed the heat that was available throughout the year. In spring and fall there was found to be high solar radiation. Even in the summer temperatures were relatively high. Architecturally, the designers interpreted this fact as suggesting the need for skylights and large windows which would capture as much heat as possible. This would save heating costs and ensure warmth in the house, even though it would be used only on weekends.

The existing shelter belts provided areas of shelter. On the lee side, zones of land were found to have wind speed reductions of up to 50 percent (Fig. 6.35). Study of the direction of the winds, their force

Fig. 6.35 Sea Ranch: diagram of shelter provided by wind breaks on ocean terrace (see also Fig. 10.10).

Fig. 6.36 Sea Ranch: Demonstration houses by Joseph Esherick.

and the possibility of providing shelter indicated that for 60 percent of the year the winds came from the northwest and were in excess of 12 miles per hour, a speed in which walking was difficult. Shelter was considered essential for any dwelling on the ocean terrace area. It was proposed that houses be oriented toward the south, with outdoor areas and parking spaces situated on the leeward side of the building. The wind-clipped cypress trees provided inspiration for the form of the demonstration houses by Esherick. Mono-pitched roofs, which would deflect the wind, and fences with air foils were recommended to provide sheltered open spaces and gardens (Fig. 6.36).

Olgay's Bioclimatic Chart was used to produce a table of bioclimate needs.[16] The prevailing temperature, humidity, and sun hours at Sea Ranch were compared with the ideal climate of Olgay's chart; temperatures in the 50-80 degree Fahrenheit range and humidity in the 40–70 percent range. The differences at any time of day or year were translated into the amount of cooling or heating that would be required to maintain such ideal conditions for human comfort. Additional heating to maintain comfort (warmth) was further described in terms of clothing for better understanding of the climate and what it would be like sitting out in it. The range runs from shirtsleeves and shorts to overcoats in relation to the months of the year and the times of the day. It is a vivid way to describe the climate. The conclusion was that the climate was reasonable (although not excessively warm) and would permit outdoor activity and passivity with reasonable comfort, plenty of fresh air, and absolutely no smog—an ideal climate for a vacation home. Wind and solar radiation were the two aspects of the climate of greatest importance; protection from the one and capture of the other were indicated.

The plan was prepared in 1965 (Figs. 6.37 and 6.38). The goals were to achieve a relatively high population density consistent with a habitable environment and a vacation type of life style. The program included sites for condominiums: groups of units joined together into a larger structure, covering less land than separate homes. This allowed large expanses of open space consistent with an economic number of dwellings. This was one technique used

16. Victor Olgay, *Design with Climate* (Princeton, N.J.: Princeton University Press, 1963).

C   Condominium

   Housing area

   Commons open space

R/C   Recreation commercial

Fig. 6.37 Sea Ranch: original plan. Lawrence Halprin and Associates.

Fig. 6.38 Sea Ranch: Detail of development showing meadows and access to the beach.

to maintain the landscape. The program also called for single-family house lots because this was the major demand. Included were a restaurant, village center and hotel, recreation center, golf course, and air strip. It was designed as a village or community and more than just a subdivision of the land. Having regard for the requirement of conserving the quality of the landscape and coping with the natural elements, the plan proposed limited housing situated along existing hedgerows so that dwellings would be sheltered and also relatively inconspicuous. But the meadows between these strips were designated as open space. New planting was included to create other zones of shelter. Most of the housing was proposed within the coniferous forest (with brush cleared). Views from the hillside were spectacular and the density and building codes were such that the forest cover would essentially remain intact.

The demonstration houses by Esherick and the condominium by Moore/Turnbull demonstrated the kind of architecture that was considered appropriate for the landscape and the weather. The recreation center was also designed to counteract the ill effects of the wind. Berms of earth were created and the pool and tennis courts were sunk into the ground to protect them from the wind (Fig. 6.39). The beach was reached by stairs from the upper terrace.

Sea Ranch is an example of an ecological study undertaken for a large area of land in single ownership. The results were used architecturally and the landscape itself was influential on the distribution of building sites. The specifically ecological implications are not certain.

There are different levels of ownership. First there is total ownership (private property)—home and land within a fence. A second level is private restricted land which is owned by the individual outside house and fenced garden, but its use is restricted to natural vegetation. Third, there is common land which is owned by all the property owners in the development and is managed at their expense. Architectural quality is controlled by a design review committee.

Whether or not the intent of the plan is fulfilled depends on its administration. The interpretation of the plan and policy may change as personnel changes. Thus we may expect and see variations in the original concept. This occurrence is characteristic of landscape architecture in general. Landscape plans are always plans for the future by definition, and as such require a certain continuity of administration and management if the objectives are to be achieved.

Fig. 6.39 Sea Ranch. Recreation complex incorporating protective land forms. Moore, Lyndon, Turnbull and Whitacker.

Before the Sea Ranch project was begun, debate over whether this coast land should be in private or public ownership might have been valuable. At a time when only 300 miles of California's 1,300 miles of coastline were open to the public, a strong case could have been made for public acquisition. It is probable that if an overall study of the coast had existed in 1965, as it will under the Coast Planning Act of 1972, these lands might have been considered a scenic and ecological resource to be managed for public use and enjoyment, recreation, conservation, or scenic easement. Be that as it may, this project is interesting because of the way in which the planning and design decisions were made in relation to the natural processes and especially the climate.

CASE STUDY 3. THE VALLEYS

Plan for the Valleys, an area consisting of 60 square miles of Baltimore county lying in the development-prone hinterland of the expanding city, is described in *Design With Nature*.[17] A group of landowners who had a long-standing attachment to the landscape decided that they should attempt to control growth and change so that the inevitable demand for housing could be satisfied without the destruction of a beautiful landscape heritage. The study area was politically defined and included two streams and their valleys and a high plateau area between them.

Ian McHarg and David Wallace, who did the work, sensed the beauty of the landscape and pictured the changes that would occur under the normal subdivision procedures. It was accepted that housing should and could be situated in the landscape as part of the regional goals of the county, but it was agreed that development should be controlled to avoid loss of amenity. It was believed that guidance from the principles of soil and water conservation would indicate the most suitable way to develop the land and ensure a measure of natural beauty. It was also suggested that planned growth would be as profitable as uncontrolled growth. The realization of the plan was seen as a joint venture between the public and private sectors. That is, the good will of the landowner would need to be backed up with legal county ordinance and zoning regulations.

Much of the study involves measures of change, housing costs, and the appropriate population target for the area. The proposition that observation of conservation principles can avert destruction to the landscape and ensure enhancement is perhaps the most important from the landscape planning technique point of view.

The geology and the physiographic features—slopes, vegetation, flood plains, rivers and streams, soil types, and topography—were studied. The highest values were given to two resources, water and soil, and their conservation. Wherever development and construction on the land would adversely affect these resources either through pollution or excessive erosion, these areas were eliminated from consideration for housing. An extensive groundwater resource (or aquifer) was found to be associated with a permeable limestone geological formation underlying the valleys. This meant that the streams and their flood plains were intimately connected with this underground resource, which provided drinking water from wells and which was also related to the river system that fed reservoirs outside of the study area. Because of the potential pollution of this water from septic tanks, and even sewers which leak to some extent, the flood plains and valley bottoms and strips of land 200 feet wide on each side of the streams running into them were considered unsuitable for any housing development. Thus the groundwater recharge area was eliminated in order to maintain water quality.

The higher plateau land between the two valleys was of less permeable geological nature and was therefore suitable for development from this and other points of view. The slopes between the valleys and plateaus presented a variety of conditions with implications for soil erosion. The slopes or valley sides tended to be largely covered with forest or deciduous woodland. The slopes varied in steepness, the steepest tending to face north. Slopes greater than 25% with or without forest cover were considered vulnerable to soil erosion and were eliminated from use altogether (on the recommendation of the Soil Conservation Service). The forest cover is important in conserving soil by preventing the full erosional impact of rainfall and by holding the land together with root systems. Therefore it was decided that slopes of less than 25% with forest cover could have a housing density limit of one house per 3 acres. This would ensure that the construction of houses and access roads would have a limited impact on the forest and thus on erosion. Slopes under 25% without forest vegetation would be prohibited for development, at least until such areas were planted with forest and the trees reached a degree of maturity. Portions of the plateau were forested. In these areas the density was limited to one house per acre. This ensured the maintenance of a thinned forest. Elsewhere on the plateau land, any density would be permitted provided it was marketable; even high-rise apartment towers with low ground-cover were situated at several strategic sites.

A density or residential zoning plan was developed from the application of these principles and criteria of water quality and soil conservation (Figs. 6.40 and 6.41). From this a development plan was made with shopping and cultural nodes at hamlets, villages, and a town center. Two lakes were recommended as part of a water and soil conservation program. The valleys were essentially left alone for agricultural, recreational, and institutional use. It can be seen that the important visual features which gave the area its unique and attractive quality were in the process more or less conserved. The housing program was accommodated using 4,500 fewer acres of land than would be needed under the conventional land subdivision standards and techniques. At the same time, the essential landscape character was

17. McHarg, *op. cit.*

Institutional

1 du/3 acres

1 du/1 acre

2 or more du/acre

Valley floor
no development

Fig. 6.40 Plan for the Valleys: zoning.
Wallace McHarg Associates. (1963)

1 du/3 acres

1 du/1 acre

2 or more du/acre

Special

Flood plain

Valley floor

Fig. 6.41 Plan for the Valleys. Application of zoning principle at the scale of a project. Based on a study by Lindsay Robertson and Narendra Juneja.

maintained. It was projected that by the year 2000 27,000 new houses would be accommodated (according to the plan) on 17,000 acres. Cluster housing was recommended. The densities of the upper land would range from one house per acre to an average of four houses per acre. This is perhaps twice the density expected in the uncontrolled growth pattern. Variations in housing types and densities were recommended not only as a means to accommodate the program but also as a desirable mixture permitting a heterogeneous community.

A nonprofit corporation was recommended to control the development and to distribute the cash return from the land so that those whose land was limited in use would not lose. Some new zoning was needed at a county level: for example, 3-acre zoning for the wooded slopes, 25-acre zoning for the valleys, and natural resource zoning (providing for 200 feet on each side of every stream to be free of construction). These large scale zoning implications also had direct input to the operations of a developer of property. The physiographic features and the criteria for housing density associated with them could provide a zoning plan at any scale. Analysis of the landscape or site would reveal the optimum building program and identify areas to be reserved for conservation.

This plan represents a long term approach to economic development and planning. A number of landowners are involved but they are mostly owners of large holdings who have a common goal: to try to maintain the natural beauty of the area. They probably intend to stay on during and after development. It is thus a unique situation. But it is a case study which reveals very clearly the form that results from planning based on an understanding of the natural processes and an interest in conservation.

LANDSCAPE PLANNING AND ENVIRONMENTAL IMPACT

Landscape planning can be seen as a positive process to fit certain land uses to the most suitable land for the purpose and as a negative process designed to prevent ecological loss or waste of natural resources such as good agricultural soil or clean water. Its implementation would appear to be best suited at government levels (local, county, and state) in the development of a land use policy supported by local powers and by the resources for compensation where necessary.

Whether or not there is an operational system of planning which guides development and land use, it is always important that the specific impact of any project be assessed in terms of its site and detailed ecological relationships. Such project impact assessment is conducted by means of a finer grain of data than those by which land use policy is set. It is possible therefore that even within areas designated as appropriate, a project may result in unforeseen and unacceptable side effects. These may require special design or technical solutions or, if the impact is deemed unacceptable, the project may have to be abandoned or placed elsewhere. This process of assessment is an essential component of good site planning, which may also be required by law.

The National Environmental Policy Act (1970) requires all Federal agencies and certain industries which are licensed by the Federal government to submit a detailed statement on the environmental impact of each new project or recommendation. The act directs these agencies to "utilize a systematic interdisciplinary approach which will ensure the integrated use of the natural and social sciences and the environmental design arts in planning and decision making which may have an impact on man's environment." They are also enjoined to develop methods whereby the currently unquantifiable environmental amenities and values may be included with technical considerations in the assessment of impact.

In addition to addressing itself to the general question of environmental impact, each report is required to specify any adverse environmental effects that are unavoidable should the proposal be implemented. It must also explore alternatives to the proposed action, including the alternative of no project. It must show the extent to which resources will be lost, and is required to show the relationship between local short term uses of the environment and the maintenance and enhancement of long term productivity.

The State of California extended the purpose and intent of the national legislation to the state level with the California Environmental Quality Act (1970). This required all state agencies to prepare environmental impact statements and, most significantly, as a result of a California Supreme Court ruling in the Friends of Mammoth case, required private developers of projects with significant effect to do the same. These were included, it was argued, because by virtue of local building permits they were, in fact, authorized by the government.

The purpose and requirements of the two acts are essentially the same. However, the California act includes an additional requirement to assess the extent to which the project will induce population growth.

A major difficulty lies in the methods by which the impact is assessed. Guidelines have been prepared in the form of a matrix which includes a list of environmental activities that might occur as part of or as the result of the proposed project and a list of existing environmental factors and conditions that might be affected by the activities.

The activities list is lengthy, including activities involved in construction as well as the end product. Ten categories enumerate every possible form of impact: those resulting from waste disposal, chemical treatment, accidents, transportation systems, resource renewal, processing industries, resource extraction, land alteration, construction, and modifications to the existing ecosystem.

The existing factors inventory is divided into three sectors: natural qualities, cultural qualities, and ecological relationships. The first is concerned with a listing of all earth, water, atmospheric, and biological resources and the natural processes of landscape evolution; the second with land use, ownership, and taxation, population distribution, and agricultural productivity. Transportation, pressures for change, and social factors such as life style, comfort, enjoyment, and privacy are also included. Finally, the ecological relationships are concerned with food chains, plant succession, eutrophication, and wildlife habitats.

The matrix relates the two sets of information. The environmental activities involved in the project are checked and the existing factors on which the activities will have an impact are cross checked. The

third stage is the assessment of the magnitude of the impact. This is to be described as low, moderate, or significant.

Once the impact statement is completed, it accompanies the project through the usual agency review procedures. In the case of a private development, it would be reviewed by the appropriate planning commission. In addition, there is provision for public hearings on the report before the final decisions are made.

In principle, the concept of environmental impact statements is excellent. Questions of content and the organization of the content remain to be clarified. So, too, the question of who prepares the reports requires examination. The agency making the proposal is required to prepare the report or cause it to be prepared. Finally, the individual project impact statement procedure can in no way preempt long term planning in which the cumulative effect of a series of projects is seen in a regional context. The two are complementary and are both essential in fulfilling the goals of the National Environmental Policy Act: "To create and maintain conditions under which man and nature can exist in harmony and fulfill the social, economic and other requirements of present and future generations of Americans."

Fig. 6.42 Photograph by William A. Garnett (1966). An oil tank farm, a steel plant, subdivision and shopping center in ill–planned juxtaposition with each other and with the natural resources of the shoreline and saltwater marsh. The tree–covered peninsula was scheduled to be transformed into harbor facilities for the steel works. Only a change in world markets saved it from this fate and a conservationists' struggle saved it from some equally unsuitable commercial venture. It is now part of a regional park system. The objective of landscape planning is to take the chance out of land use decisions and to match uses with the land most suitable for that use without loss of unique and valuable amenities and resources.

Suggested Readings

Bates, Marston, *The Forest and the Sea*, esp. pp. 246–262, "Man's Place in Nature."

Bates, Marston, *Man in Nature*, esp. pp. 94–104, "Ecology and Economics."

Belknap, Raymond, and John Furtado, *Three Approaches to Environmental Resource Analysis.*

Colvin, Brenda, *Land and Landscape*, Ch. 17, pp. 254–258, "The Living Landscape."

Crowe, Sylvia, *Landscape of Power.*

Crowe, Sylvia, *Landscape of Roads.*

Crowe, Sylvia, *Tomorrow's Landscape.*

Darling, F. Fraser, *Wilderness and Plenty.*

Darling, F. Fraser and John P. Milton, eds., *Future Environments for North America.*

Dasmann, Raymond, *Environmental Conservation.*

Dickert, Thomas, ed., *Environmental Impact Assessment.*

Fabos, Julius, et al., *Model for Landscape Resource Assessment.*

Fairbrother, Nan, *New Lives, New Landscapes.*

Hackett, Brian, *Landscape Planning.*

International Union for Conservation of Nature and Natural Resources, *Towards a New Relationship Between Man and Nature in Temperate Lands* (1967).

Lewis, Philip H., *Regional Design for Human Impact.*

Litton, R. Burton, *Forest Landscape Description and Inventories—A Basis for Land Planning and Design.*

Litton, R. Burton, "Landscape and Aesthetic Quality."

Lovejoy, Derek, ed., *Land Use and Landscape Planning.*

McHarg, Ian, "Ecological Determinism."

McHarg, Ian, *Design with Nature*, pp. 7–17, "Sea and Survival," pp. 79–93, "A Response to Values," pp. 127–151, "The River Basin."

Odum, Eugene P., *Fundamentals of Ecology*, pp. 419–447, "Applied Ecology,"

Patri, Tito, David C. Streatfield, and Thomas J. Ingmire, *Early Warning System.*

Progressive Architecture, May 1966, "Sea Ranch."

Sears, Paul B., *Where There is Life*, esp. pp. 214–216, "Reading the Landscape."

Sears, Paul B., *Life and Environment.*

Thomas, William L., ed., *Man's Role in Changing the Face of the Earth*, pp. 453–469, "Environmental Changes through Forces Independent of Man," by Richard J. Russell; pp. 471—481, "The Process of Environmental Change by Man," by Paul B. Sears.

Twiss, Robert, David Streatfield, and Marin County Planning Department. *Nicassio: Hidden Valley in Transition.* San Rafael, Calif., 1969.

Way, Douglas S., *Terrain Analysis.*

Whyte, William H., *The Last Landscape.*

Zube, Ervin H. *The Islands: Selected Resources of the United States Virgin Islands*, 1968.

Zube, Ervin H., ed., *An Inventory and Interpretation of Selected Resources of the Island of Nantucket.*

a

b

c

d

The site planning process is one in which a program for development is fitted on to an area of land of adequate size in such a way that it works efficiently and the characteristics of the site are expressed. These diagrams expressing four stages in the process are based on schematic drawings for a university campus for 5,000 students provided by David Gates. a. The site—conditions, features and relationships. b. Evaluation of the site in terms of developable land. c. Program requirements placed on the site with provision for expansion. 1. 1st phase 2. 2nd phase P. Parking S. Service. d. The site plan.

7. SITE ANALYSIS AND SITE PLANNING

An understanding of landscape at the regional scale is an essential prerequisite to smaller scale site planning and detailed landscape design. Chapter Six considered the relationship between the site and the larger ecosystem and the importance of evaluating the environmental impact which a development will bring to it. Conversely, many of the criteria for land use in regional land use planning should be based on an understanding of construction and grading techniques used in site planning.

SITE ANALYSIS AND INTERPRETATION

To the real estate operator, a site is a parcel of land, a building lot with legal dimensions and boundaries, slopes, and sometimes very obvious distinctive features. Yet, although parcels of land may look similar on a map or subdivision plot plan, each has in fact differences (Fig. 7.1). Such differences in location, topography, and amenities are recognized and make land more or less valuable as a result. Buildable land closely associated to major transportation routes and sources of labor is clearly suited for industrial development. An island in a river commanding riverscape vistas and having access to water and water sports differs considerably from a lot in the urban flatlands of an average city and will be priced accordingly. Subdivisions and communities are named for amenities—Thousand

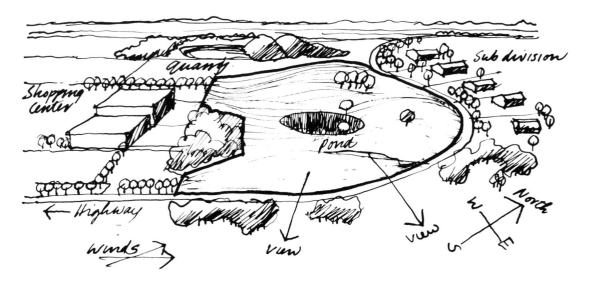

Fig. 7.1 A site has distinctive characteristics and relationships.

Oaks, Lone Pine, Redwood Shores, and so on—and the sensitive developer is careful not to destroy the amenity, which is reflected in the cost of the houses and lots.

The matching of a given program for a project (school, subdivision, or other project) with a suitable site is a function of site analysis. Site selection may be determined by a comparative analysis of several available sites for the same predetermined

program. Factors of importance include the location of the site within the region, its accessibility, its relationship to shops, industry, transportation, and so on, depending on the proposed use. Others will be concerned with the ability of the land to accommodate the proposed program. Which site can best satisfy the requirements?

Occasionally site analysis is carried out to determine what a parcel of land is best suited for. In this case the program is a direct reflection of the site's amenities and potential within its regional, social, and ecological context.

Whichever way the site and its program are brought together, further analysis precedes planning and design. The level of detail depends on the nature of the program (simple or complex) and the type of site (urban or rural). An inventory and interpretation of the site's characteristics and its relationship with adjoining land will provide determinants of form, constraints, and opportunities for the location of buildings and the conservation of amenities.

In site analysis there are two important sets of factors: those established through reference to regional characteristics and those that are unique to the specific site. Regional factors include climate, vegetation zone, social organization and tradition, local government regulations, historical background, the neighborhood provision of parks and playgrounds, and the availability of sewage, water, and other services. All of these have an influence on a site and what can or should be done with it.

In the site analysis of a specific site there are two phases. A research phase, in which all relevant site data, maps, and other information are assembled and drawn to the same scale. Second is a site assessment phase in which visual values and relationships, feelings, and moods are recorded. With the establishment of a detailed program indicating building sites required and the dimension and requirements of other land uses to be included, the site planning process can begin. Most of the considerations in site planning have economic significance. In terms of development costs, the site plan should be efficient without sacrificing unique features of the landscape. The analysis and evaluation is directed to these considerations.

The categories of data in site analysis are similar to those for a landscape survey. The information is more specific, however, and its interpretation is related to the proposed project. Geology and soil, topography and slopes, drainage, vegetation, wildlife, microclimate, man-made features and existing use, visual qualities and relationships, legal regulations, and historical associations are common headings for data collection.

Subsurface geological formations are responsible for the visible land form, the topography. In terms of building foundations, the bearing strength of near-surface geology can vary considerably over the area of a site and between sites. Hard sound rock may have a maximum bearing strength of 60 tons per square foot, whereas that of loose saturated sand-clay soil will have a capacity of 1 ton per square foot. Thus the location and depth of the various geological and soil conditions occurring on a site need to be known before large buildings are arranged and sited.

The ease with which subsurface material can be excavated is related to development costs and may be influential in plan arrangement. Surface drainage is also connected with the underground geology. The presence of aquifers will restrict the use of septic tanks and require the prevention of surface water pollution from other sources. The stability of the geological formation is also important. Geological description is important in assessing the stability of land. The dip slope and type of rock, the topographic slope, and its relationship to other strata may render an area subject to slides or slumping. Such areas are unsuited to construction.

The soil map is a mosaic of different soils, each with properties of importance in site planning. Soil is an extension of the geological formations. A soil is frequently but not always a direct product of the underlying rocks. Soil is an important factor in site planning in relation to stability of the land, foundation suitability, excavation, erosion hazard, drainage, and plant growth.

The stability of sloping land is a factor of soil type and its relation to geological strata. The bearing capacity of soil depends on its type and is a factor in the location of light buildings. The shrink/swell factor of certain clay soils in specific climates is another consideration of importance to the foundations of buildings and their siting.

An economic factor may be the workability of the soil and the ease with which it can be graded. Sandy soil is heavier and less easy to work than loam. Some soils are more prone to erosion than others. This factor is determined by the texture of the soil and the slope of the land and the vegetative cover. Knowledge of the erodability of soils will determine whether or not the stable surfaces should be disturbed and if they are, what measures or controls will be needed to prevent excessive erosion. Soils vary in yet another way. The variables of texture and structure make some soils better drained than others. In a rainstorm, sandy soil will have sharp drainage whereas clay soils will quickly become waterlogged so that the rain will tend to run off the land instead of being absorbed. Thus runoff that can be expected from the surface of land will vary according to the soil. Drainage provision is therefore related to soil type.

Finally, the soil type will determine the plants that will be able to grow well and those that will not. Willows and poplars will thrive on wet clay coils, ericaceous plants on acid, and so on. The topsoil is the most important from the point of view of plant growth. It contains organic material and will have a more open structure conducive to root development, water and mineral uptake, and respiration. It has probably taken thousands of years to reach this condition of texture and fertility. Good soil is a resource that can be very easily and quickly destroyed.

The line below which the spaces between the soil particles are full of water is called the water table. It comes nearest to the surface in low-lying lands. It fluctuates seasonally and if the water table is high, basements will require special waterproofing and construction. A high water table that is connected to the sea and is saline is especially critical in the effect it will have on the growth of plants. Most plant roots will not grow in salt water (except salt marsh types). Filled land developments at the coast or in saltwater estuaries and bays frequently encounter this problem. In this situation trees may be planted only in raised planters or watertight containers.

On the surface of the site, the topography is perhaps the most important factor to be assessed. We have already seen that the underlying geology and the slow processes of natural erosion are responsible for the form of the land and its slopes, valleys, ridges, and knolls. These topographic features may be quite influential in determining the organization of the site plan if we are to be in any way sensitive to the existing landscape characteristics. Visually, the topography and land form are important in the quality of the landscape. Site plans that intend to emphasize this quality must obviously understand the land's structure and pattern so that whatever changes are made can be done in the spirit of the original. In addition, the topographic survey will reveal badly drained areas and natural drainage channels. It will also show places that have good views and parts of the site which are visible or hidden from any selected point within or outside its boundaries.

The way in which different parts of the land can be used is a function of the land's slope and/or the ease with which it can be altered. The economic arrangement and location of buildings will also be influenced by slope. In general, building costs increase as the slopes become steeper. The existing slopes will indicate the minimum gradients of roads and paths that would be possible without grading. A map of the site with the land categorized according to its slope is a quick way in which the consideration of slope alone will be seen to organize the site plan. The categories of slope used in such a slope map will depend on the land uses being considered and the maximum permissible slopes selected for each use. Slopes under 4% appear quite flat but have positive drainage and are suitable for a variety of uses: building and sports fields, for example. Slopes between 4 and 10% can accommodate roads and pathways with little modification. For economic reasons, 6% might be selected as the maximum slope for housing at high densities. Slopes greater than 10% are considered steep, unfavorable for roads and paths without grading, and suited best for free play area and planting. A slope of 15% is considered a maximum for vehicular routes, and 25% is considered a maximum for lawn areas to be cut by machinery. For erosion control reasons, 25% might be the steepest land that could be changed. Topography also determines natural drainage patterns of the site. These should be kept operational if possible and buildings and structures should avoid natural swales unless the whole site is to be restructured.

The next aspect of site analysis is the vegetation. It is essential to record the plants that exist on the land and their maturity and health, important factors in determining whether to save particular trees and shrubs. Existing vegetation may provide protection from adjacent land uses and its conservation may therefore be important in maintaining a buffer from noise, airborne pollutants, or unpleasing views. The fire hazard nature of vegetation is also an important factor where new construction is planned. The erosion control capability of existing vegetation is vital in maintaining the stability of the land's surface. The type of existing vegetation together with the topography may be very important in the definition of the site quality and spatial relationships. Vegetation also gives a clue to the nature of the soil and the microclimate of the site. On large sites, variations in vegetation may exist between slopes with different orientation; this may be a reflection of available moisture, temperature, solar radiation, wind, and so forth. Those plants that are clearly growing well on the site provide an indication for the selection of new planting in site planning.

In association with vegetation, there is a wildlife population. The position of the site and its vegetation within the larger context of the world of insects, birds, and mammals should be carefully considered, especially in rural situations, before existing vegetation is removed or changed.

Each site has a general climate it shares with the region. These climatic factors have a general influence on architecture, site planning, and design. For example, excessive rainfall or long periods of high temperatures and sunshine suggest the need for covered walkways and shading. Frost and snow conditions indicate that the gradients on streets and sidewalks should be minimal.

The microclimate which is specific to the site is composed of variations to the general climate. It is created by topography, plants and vegetative cover, exposure to winds, elevation above sea level, and the relationship of the site to large water bodies. Microclimate information is not always available. Accurate measurements need to be taken at least over one year. If less time is available, some microclimate effects can be deduced from observation. Plants that show evidence of windblow indicate the direction of prevailing winds and differences in its effect within the site. The exposure and orientation of slopes can be used to infer probable conditions of warmth and sunlight, and the natural distribution of vegetation may substantiate this. Sources of industrial pollution, dust, and sound can be specifically identified.

In addition, shade patterns caused by buildings and trees create microclimatic variations in temperature. Exposure and shelter are conditions of the site that also can be recorded. These factors are important in design, for they may be used to advantage or steps may be required to ameliorate their effects. The microclimate is an important factor in the way and extent to which the outdoor areas can be used. The selection of plant materials and their use to create more favorable microclimates in a generally unfavorable climate is a design response within the realms of site planning. Chapter Ten deals in more detail with the implications of climate in site planning and environmental design.

Frequently sites have existing features or buildings or are already in use. Buildings, roads, sewage systems, underground pipes and cables, the access to the site from public roads, and all other inanimate givens of the site which reflect its past and present use and which may form part of the plan for its future constitute essential data.

Related to this set of details are factors that affect the site but are invisible on it. These include, for example, building codes and development regulations which may vary from city to city or county to county. There may be other legal aspects such as rights of way and easements. To these should be added any historical associations or traditions that might legitimately influence the choice of materials or the design of the land. The site itself may have regional significance.

Finally, there should be a visual analysis to record views and vistas that are attractive and adjacent areas that should be screened out. The color of the soil and the existing vegetation, the typical pattern of light and shade, the sky and clouds, the intensity of the sunshine, and the spatial characteristics of the landscape are factors worthy of note. The most successful design will be that which is sensitive to these qualities. The intention is twofold: to develop the program with visually pleasing relationships within the site itself and, second, to fit the project harmoniously into the surrounding environment.

All these site dimensions and characteristics—the rocks and soil, the topography formed by them, the vegetative cover and associated wildlife, the climate and microclimate, man-made features, legal regulations, the visual quality, and historical association—constitute the site analysis. It is a complex set of information, tangible and intangible, objective and subjective. At the same time, we may have a complex program for the development of the site. It is the bringing together of these two and the resolution of conflicts between them which is the process known as site planning.

SITE PLANNING

Site planning may be thought of as a compromise between the adaptation of the site to fit the program and the adaptation of the program on account of the site. The program and the site may be thought of as two sets of forces: one the site, which strives to express itself, its uniqueness; the other the uses in the

Fig. 7.2   Air Force Academy, Colorado, in which the program was the prime generator of form.

program, which also have a generic form-giving process of their own.

Site planning is the process whereby the requirements of the program are provided, located, and connected to each other and to the outside world with minimum destruction of the site (if it has physical attributes), with imagination, and with sensitivity to the implications of the site analysis. The result must be not only workable but also easily maintained and serviced and (not the least) attractive to look at and be in. The extent to which the program and its physical manifestation eliminate the natural conditions of the site depends largely on whether the site has these conditions in the first place and second on whether the program is too ambitious for the land available. Third may be a philosophical question: should the designer choose to remodel the site completely by giving total emphasis to the generation of form from the program (Fig. 7.2)? On the other hand, should the designer maintain an almost religious attitude to the land, basing the form

Fig. 7.3 House designed by Frank Lloyd Wright, Jr., built around and incorporating an existing tree.

Fig. 7.4 Glass windscreen providing shelter but still maintaining the view.

and layout entirely on the utmost conservation of the original site features (Fig. 7.3)? A middle ground attitude is the most usual and appropriate. The site and the program should be combined and manipulated to produce qualities that neither alone would present. The interaction of the program with the site

will result in a land use plan. This will show that the program can be physically accommodated on the site, that there is a system of circulation connecting the elements, and how the project is related to the surrounding environment.

Each item in the program will have a set of criteria. Playing fields and courts are the most specific. The required area, surface, orientation, and microclimate are objective. The criteria for other outdoor uses such as picnic areas, flower gardens, and public plazas are more flexible. But optimum sizes, configurations, and climates can be stated and then provided. Where these and other features of the program are located is a function of the site characteristics that fulfill the criteria and the relationships that may be called for in the program for efficiency and servicing. As well as connecting elements of the plan, it is also appropriate to think in terms of separating uses that are incompatible. Circulation may be of several types, for example, auto, bicycle, and pedestrian. The directness of such circulation is a matter of function and economics.

In site planning we are involved then with the diagrammatic connections between buildings and outdoor space and with the arrangement of elements and allocation of areas for a variety of space needs and functions, all within the limits of a single comprehensive site and its program for development or change. The basis of this process is the resolution of conflicts. A conflict occurs when two functions, or needs, or uses, or systems are in opposition. Conflicts may already exist in the environment or may result from the imposition of one system on another. It may therefore be said that a design problem exists only when there is a conflict. Interrelationships between specific problems or conflicts occur when the solution of one affects the solution of another.

Problems or conflicts in site planning originate from two main areas of inquiry and the web of interactions which result. First we have the proposed or actual functions of buildings or uses of land, which may be called the social factors. The scale may be that of a family of four or five and their dwelling and garden space, or that of a junior college campus or large comprehensive school with thousands of students and a variety of buildings and space needs. The second area of inquiry is the specific site or landscape, its relationships with adjacent land use, and its unique qualities of slope, soil, vegetation, microclimate, and so forth. These may be called the land factors and they vary from those found in a piece of wild coastline to those characteristic of a few blocks of a particular city.

Conflicts may exist entirely within the area of social factors. For example, a desire by older people for quiet and repose in outdoor space is likely to conflict with teenagers' preference for active sports, loud music, crowds, and spontaneity, in situations where both groups are to be accommodated. Or conflicts may occur between social factors and land factors. For example, the exposure of a site to strong prevailing summer winds could conflict with a level of human comfort associated with outdoor relaxation. Further, conflicts may exist or be initiated entirely within the area of land factors. For example, we may regard excessive soil erosion or landslides as a conflict resulting from the interaction of a series of natural variables: slope, vegetable cover, and rainfall.

Another simple example may indicate the possible interrelationship of problems. The solution to the wind exposure difficulty can be solved to some extent by locating a shelter planting or fence in the appropriate place. But if a superb view also happens to lie in the direction of the prevailing winds, as at Sea Ranch or Carmel, we will have succeeded in negating an important quality in the enjoyment of the place. By grouping this requirement or problem statement with the first, we might well arrive at a solution incorporating glass screens to break the wind, maintaining the view at the same time, although this might not be the only possibility (Fig. 7.4). This is simply a method of organizing the design process in such a way that all aspects will be taken into account in the production of form, which can thereby be emancipated from preconceived and arbitrary notions.

At this stage, site planning and detailed design begin to interact and merge. The site plan, once formulated, must eventually be implemented and it can be seen that the possibility of resolving conflicts at the detailed level affects the form of the site plan. This is the subject of Chapter Eight.

The following examples will show how the site and the program are manipulated in the site planning process and the way in which overall concepts for a project are integrated with the process.

CASE STUDY 1. FOOTHILL COLLEGE

Foothill Junior College is a two-year community college for 3,500 students and also serves as a center for civic and cultural activities. Foothill College was designed in 1959 by the architects Kump Marsten and Hurd working with Sasaki, Walker, Landscape Architects. The designers were confronted with 122 acres situated in the east-facing foothills of the coastal range in Los Altos, California. Topographically, the site included two small hills separated by a ravine. The surrounding landscape consisted of a bowl-shape form that was then in transition from orchard and agricultural use to suburban residential development (Fig. 7.5).

In addition to the building program which specified requirements for classrooms, laboratories. library, theater, gymnasium, sports field, student union, and administration building, the Board of Trustees stated general conceptual design criteria: (1) the scheme should be a solution related to the background and tradition of the area, and (2) the scheme should avoid rigid formality or obvious geometric discipline yet produce an air of quiet dignity and sophistication appropriate to a college.

Within the constraints of site and program a number of basic alternative solutions were possible. The topography could be flattened, the ravine filled, so that the college and its considerable parking facilities could be situated on flat land. On the other hand, parking lots could be situated on the high area in the center with the buildings below and around them, or the reverse. The latter arrangement was chosen. It was described as an "acropolis" scheme. The larger of the two hills was used for the academic and other buildings. The gymnasium was placed on the smaller knoll (Fig. 7.6).

The plan is simple: an entrance loop circulation road connects the four parking lots and a visitor arrival point. Pedestrian access from the parking lots is provided by footpaths up the side of the hill penetrating the outer wall at several points connecting to the internal path system leading to each building or destination. The distances between parking lots and buildings are about equal and not excessive. Minor roads lead to the edge of the "acropolis" for service purposes. The site plan type, with buildings in the center and circulation on the outside, suited the site conditions best. One major conflict between auto and pedestrian traffic was resolved with a bridge connecting the academic area with the gym. Others could have been avoided by placing the loop road on the outer edge of the parking lots.

Since the hills were too small to accommodate the diagrammatic arrangement of the buildings, 300,000 cubic yards of earth were moved in a restructuring operation which provided a more or less flat area of about 30 acres for the structures and the desired open space between them. So successful was the regrading that reviewers of the project remarked on the restraint with which the original land had been treated. One-story buildings to accommodate the academic functions were grouped around a central common or green. Special buildings, such as the library and theater, were larger but similar in design. The one-story buildings related in scale with the residential quality of the surrounding neighborhood. The teaching units were arranged around the small courtyards according to the academic disciplines: science, humanities, the arts, and so on. The student union was located near the visitor entrance at the end of the bridge leading to the gym.

The architecture was wood framed. The roofs were clad with redwood shakes, which, with the outline of the roofs, contributed to the distinctive form and strong identity of the college. The roofs were extended in very wide eaves providing protection from sun and rain to the walkways surrounding all the buildings (Fig. 7.9). The walkways consisted of removable concrete slabs covering service ducts. Long, low brick buildings for faculty offices were located behind the classroom buildings forming the outside wall of the "acropolis."

The location of the buildings was determined not only by functional considerations and factors of convenience but also from the point of view of an aesthetic concept. The architect described the com-

Fig. 7.5 Foothill College: original site.

Fig. 7.6 Foothill College (1959). Designed by Kump, Marsten and Hurd, Architects; Sasaki, Walker Associates, Landscape Architects.

plex as having variety within unity, the unity being in the form of the buildings and the variety being in their informal arrangement.

There was also a landscape concept (Fig. 7.7). This recognized and emphasized five zones. The first was the edge, the boundary area connected with the adjacent land and its uses. Here, in whatever space was available (sometimes not much), planting was proposed to correspond with that which existed: eucalyptus or live oaks or orchard varieties. The second zone associated with the first included the parking areas and loop road. Here orchard-scale planting was proposed to serve as a foil to the large automobile parking capacity a commuter college requires. It was intended that these small-scale trees would help break the view of autos from the campus and help blend the development with its surroundings. Unfortunately, budget cuts and maintenance problems resulted in omission of this important element. The third zone, which is considered pedestrian, comprised the natural grass hillsides inside the loop road and up to the outside edge of the "acropolis." Here it was proposed to maintain the natural quality of the grassland and live oaks of the original site. There would be no irrigation and it was thought that this proposal, too, would relate sympathetically to the larger landscape context of summer brown foothills and sparse vegetation (Fig. 7.8).

The fourth zone was the major open space within the enclosure of the grouped buildings (Figs. 7.9 and 7.10). This to a large extent is separated visually from the immediate surroundings but commands distant views of the coast range to the west. Here the concept called for a rich and green landscape essentially enclosed and unseen from outside and representative of the foothill landscape in a more

Fig. 7.7 Foothill College: Conceptual diagram. Zone 1: Edge Zone 2: parking areas Zone 3: natural hillside Zone 4: central open space Zone 5: courtyards.

Fig. 7.8 Foothill College, Zone 3. The outer edge blends into the surrounding landscape.
Photograph by Peter Kostrikin.

symbolic way than the other three zones. Incorporated in this zone were other program requirements: a circulation system and open space for informal use by students. By contrast to the arid third zone, this central area with undulating topography and planted shade trees is green and rich in quality as an oasis, and has come to be the most memorable landscape aspect of the college. The last zone consisted of the intimate courtyards situated between and within the buildings. They were to be refined in detail and quality using special pavings and ornamental plants to give each an individual identity (Fig. 7.11).

Foothill College is a classic example of site planning. There was a detailed and fixed program of requirements: the numbers of students and classrooms, facilities, and parking places were fixed. The site was selected as suitable in size and location. The community around the site had concerns about the quality of the architecture and the effect that it might have on them and possibly the value of their property. The logical and efficient site plan which was developed expressed the program for the college and at the same time responded to the surrounding environment and social concerns.

Fig. 7.9 (a) Foothill College, Zone 4. Photograph by David Arbegast (1966).

Fig. 7.10 (a) Foothill College, Zone 4. Photograph by David Arbegast (1966).

Fig. 7.11 (a) Foothill College, Zone 5. Photograph by David Arbegast (1966).

(b) Foothill College, Zone 4. Photograph by Peter Kostrikin (1973).

(b) Foothill College, Zone 4. Photograph by Peter Kostrikin (1973).

(b) Foothill College, Zone 5. Photograph by Peter Kostrikin (1973).

CASE STUDY 2. CUMBERNAULD NEW TOWN

The new town of Cumbernauld in Britain comprises 4,000 acres of land. The physical planning of this town demonstrates the site planning process: the allocation of land for different purposes and the connecting of the planning units with a variety of circulation types. The town's purpose was to accommodate the increasing demand for housing due to war damage and an expanding number of young families. The housing was built and owned by the government and rented at subsidized rates. The community includes industry, educational facilities, shopping, and recreation and is essentially a garden city as defined by Ebenezer Howard.

For comparison, in McHarg's plan for the Valleys (discussed in Chapter Six) the area of land was 45,000 acres. At Cumbernauld the area is 4,150 acres. The plan for the Valleys called for 150,000 population by the year 2000. At Cumbernauld the planned population is 70,000. The plan for the Valleys was thus designed to accommodate approximately twice the population of Cumbernauld on ten times the amount of land. Cumbernauld represents a much closer knit type of community and a much more frugal approach to the use of land.

The location of the town was strategic, lying in the middle of the growth center between Glasgow and Edinburgh, and with excellent transportation connections. Climatically, the site could hardly have been worse. On average, the area is subject annually to a month of snow, a month of fog, a seven-month period from the first to last frosts, high humidity, strong westerly winds, and 200 days of rain—a travel agent's nightmare!

The land was generally suitable for building with the exception of a few areas which overlay coal mining areas and were liable to subsidence. Some slopes were too steep for construction, other slopes suggested the use of split level houses. The largest area suitable for building coincided with the hog's back, or central hill area, from which the attractive surrounding landscape could be seen (Fig. 7.12). This area was planned to accommodate 50,000 people. The other 20,000 would be situated in outlying areas in "villages." Thus the constraints of the land available and its topographic form gave rise to a compact plan with higher densities than had been the case in the earlier new towns. The 50,000 population would require 14,000 homes, giving an average density of 80 people per acre.

The town center, which was also designed as a regional shopping center, was located at the center of the housing. Recreation and open space surrounded the housing and also threaded through the neighborhoods. The industrial development was located in association with transportation (Fig. 7.13).

The road network consists of an outer ring road and a central spine through the town center. Radial roads break off from the loop road and head east, west, and south, connecting Cumbernauld to other towns and the region. The housing is reached from the ring road only through feeder or access roads which end up in culs-de-sac, garages, and parking areas and connect to the footpath network, so there is a hierarchy of roads as in Radburn. The land required for roads on the hilltop site is 107 acres. The length of the principal roads is almost nine miles. Since they present a visual as well as an acoustical problem, provision is made for a physical barrier between the roads and housing. Strips of land are set aside for the planting of tree belts, which are intended to modify the scale of the roads and have some impact on the noise. Parking was provided at the standard of one space per house plus a percentage for visitors and 5,000 spaces in the town center. The pedestrian network provided traffic-free access to the schools for the children. "There are no traffic lights, traffic wardens, or policemen on traffic control duty and there never will be any need for them in the future." So reads the official literature.

The town center was connected to the housing neighborhoods by footpaths which flowed under the ring roads. A bus service also provided circulation between neighborhoods and the center. No home within the hilltop area was supposed to be more than ten minutes' walk from the town center.

Whenever possible, the schools were located in association with existing agricultural shelter belts, which had been planted by farmers to modify the effect of the wind. The school playgrounds were sited in the leeward zones of the tree belts. If they did not exist, tree plantings were proposed to provide shelter to the schools' open spaces. The area of land occupied by existing shelter belts and the land required for new planting on the hilltop area together amounted to 128 acres. The shelter belts not only screened the wind but also provided informal "adventure" playgrounds and served a variety of unplanned uses.

A standard of 10 acres of open space per 1,000 acres was adopted and achieved in the plan. This includes parks, playing fields, and school playgrounds. Land use acreages on the hilltop area are as follow: housing, 587 acres; schools, 128 acres; central shopping and commercial area, 50 acres; industry, 337 acres; roads, 107 acres; railroad, 36 acres; open space (including tree planting areas, playing

Fig. 7.12 Cumbernauld New Town (1958).

Fig. 7.13 Cumbernauld New Town: Site and assessment of buildable land.

Fig. 7.14 Cumbernauld New Town. Housing. "Park 1"   **Fig. 7.15** Cumbernauld New Town. Housing. "Park 1." a. Central green b. Parking and service cul de sac.

fields, and a city park of some 100 acres), 582 acres.

In addition to the site conditions, slopes, views, and so forth, a number of control factors enter into the design of group housing. The arrangement depends first on the type and size of dwelling and the size of garden, if one is to be provided. It was the goal at Cumbernauld that the density should be achieved with two-story houses with private gardens as far as possible. Where the slopes became steeper than 8.5%, split level houses without gardens were recommended. Even at 100 people per acre, it is possible to have a considerable proportion of two-story housing with gardens.

A second factor is the method of access, getting in and out and the relationship of the house to the automobile, and allowance for a maximum separation between automobiles and pedestrians. At Cumber-

nauld it was agreed that access to the houses by footpaths was acceptable and even desirable.

A third factor especially important in northern latitudes is orientation and the distance between houses for daylighting. The codes of practice at Cumbernauld demanded that one window in the principal living room of each house should be placed so that sunlight could enter it for at least one hour of the day during not less than ten months of the year from February to November. Fourth, the degree of privacy for rooms and yards suggests arrangements and dimensions in layout. In addition, the density of housing is influential in the evolution of a site plan. At Cumbernauld 60 to 70 people per acre was set as a general average goal for housing areas. All of these factors give form to and serve as constraints in the site plan.

A discussion of three housing layouts at Cumbernauld follows. Although there are differences in site and other conditions, the general factors just described apply to each. The comparison thus shows the variety of solutions possible within a basic conceptual framework.

The first example (Figs. 7.14 and 7.15) is "less equal" than the other two in that it has lower density and larger houses. It is a Radburn-type system which separates vehicles and pedestrians and has a central green. The loop road connects to feeder roads, which in turn connect to culs-de-sac giving access to garages, and a gate leads into each enclosed private garden. This provides access to the house, whose front door in turn opens onto the pedestrian footpath and the common green on the other side. This is the public side, the visitors' en-

Fig. 7.16 Cumbernauld New Town. Housing. "Seafar 1."

Fig. 7.17 Cumbernauld New Town: Housing. "Seafar 1." Enclosed back gardens and pedestrian circulation.

Fig. 7.18 Cumbernauld New Town: Housing. "Seafar 1." Central walk aligned along existing hedgerow connecting the housing to other neighborhoods and the town center.

trance. The green includes a small children's play area. Planting separates the sidewalk from the windows of the houses. The street as a social function is eliminated in the conventional sense since the houses which face each other across the central green use different access roads. The green is reminiscent of a London square with identical houses surrounding it, representing a social unit in the town.

A second example, Seafar 1, is higher density and lower cost. The two-story houses are arranged in terraces and each has a private garden (Figs. 7.16 to 7.18). The vehicular access is from the loop road ending in culs-de-sac or garage courts. There is no through movement of vehicles. Access to the houses is by footpath and is less direct than in our first example. Variety of dwelling type is provided by a four-story block of apartments. At the bottom of this block is a corner shop There is also a light industry, a small building with some clean process such as a garment manufacturer, situated close to the loop road. In addition there is a church, a children's playground, and a dentist's office.

The site plan incorporates an existing hedgerow forming the center of the main pedestrian spine, which ties the project together and is also the main through pedestrian link between the other neighborhoods and the town center. The area of the layout is approximately 8 acres. There are 176 dwellings accommodating 617 people at a residential density of 76.5 people per acre. Seafar 1 has 71 habitable rooms per acre. There is a variety of house types: 103 homes with two bedrooms, 40 with three bedrooms, 3 with four bedrooms, 6 one-bedroom flats, 20 two-bedroom maisonettes, and 4 three-bedroom maisonettes.

The third example, Seafar 2, is a superblock with

Fig. 7.19 Cumbernauld New Town. Housing. "Seafar 2."

Fig. 7.20 Cumbernauld New Town. Housing. "Seafar 2."

autos restricted to the edge (Figs. 7.19 and 7.20). Here 147 split level houses are accommodated on a steep hillside of about a 14% slope. There are no private gardens; however, each house has a semi-private entry space. The pathway system connecting the houses to the auto areas flows through a series of expanding and contracting areas planted with trees and groundcover. There is a local shop near the center.

By keeping the sidewalks as far as possible from the windows, privacy is achieved. The living rooms are placed on the upper split level with large windows for view, although people cannot look in. The bedrooms are on the ground level but have high windows for privacy. Here 478 people are accommodated at a density of 55.6 people per acre.

The scale of housing and the programs for these layouts are of course unique to Britain and the socioeconomic context of time and place. However, the three examples illustrate the principles by which form results from a synthesis of concept, program, and site.

In site planning a number of determinants of form are always present and must always be considered, for example, the social factors manifest in the program. What is required? How much space is needed for it? What are the social functions of the project? This leads to a diagrammatic pattern of land uses, a topological diagram of convenient disposition of functions and relationships. The land represents the second basic set of determinants in site planning. Its qualities and characteristics are revealed and assessed in the site analysis and evaluation process. The surface undulation and vegetative cover, the subsurface features of rock, soil, and water, together with the climate, visual quality, and man-made features, make up the land on which the program is to be accommodated. Finally, there is the synthesis stage in which the two are fitted together. In fitting the site to the program and modifying the program connections in terms of the site, there are many technical factors that give form to the site plan. Just as the surface flows of autos and pedestrians affect the layout, so the position of underground flows in cables and pipes determine to some extent what can happen on top of them, where planting can be done and where it cannot, and where the surface of the land can be changed and by how much. Trees cannot be planted in close relationship to underground pipes. The detailed design of the project, paving, planting, and so forth, should be the direct outcome of the decisions made at the site planning level.

Suggested Readings

Alexander, Christopher, *Notes on the Synthesis of Form*.
Baker, Geoffrey H., and Bruno Funaro, *Parking*, p. 164, "Parking Layout and Dimensions."
Cullen, Gordon, *Townscape*, pp. 121–127, "Legs and Wheels," pp. 17–55, "Serial Vision."
Dober, Richard P., *Campus Planning*.
Eckbo, Garrett, *Landscape for Living*, pp. 71–73, "Approach."
Eckbo, Garrett, *Urban Landscape Design*, pp. 7–33, "Elements of Space Organization."
Halprin, Lawrence, *Notebooks, 1959–71*.

Lynch, Kevin, *Site Planning*, pp. 3–8, "Art of Site Planning," pp. 9–25, "Analysis of Site and Purpose," pp. 26–130.
Ritter, Paul, *Planning for Man and Motor*.
Rubenstein, Harvey, *A Guide to Site and Environmental Planning*.
Simonds, John O., *Landscape Architecture*, pp. 44–53, "Site Analysis," pp. 20–77, "Site Structure Unity," pp. 67–69, "Site Structure Plan Development," pp. 173–183, "Structures in the Landscape," pp. 190–193, "Arrangement of Buildings," Ch. 5, p. 145, "Circulation."
Temko, Allen, *Architectural Forum*, "Foothills Campus is a Community in Itself," February 1962.
Weddle, A. E. (ed.), *Techniques of Landscape Architecture*, pp. 1–32, "Site Planning," by Sylvia Crowe; pp. 43–54, "Site Survey and Appreciation," by Norman Clarke.

Pomona College, California, Ralph Cornell, Landscape Architect.

8. LANDSCAPE DESIGN

Landscape design is an extension of site planning and, as we have seen, is involved in the site planning process. It is concerned with the selection of design components, materials, and plants and their combination as solutions to limited but well-defined problems within the site plan. Whereas the site plan indicates use areas and circulation routes, detailed landscape design deals with surfaces, edges and joints, steps and ramps connecting specific differences in elevation, paving, and drainage, and all the decisions that have to be made before the project can be built and planted.

A knowledge of this level of design is essential in site planning if solutions to the detailed design problems which result are to be realistic. Landscape design is the process through which specific quality is given to the diagrammatic spaces of the site plan and is another level on which landscape architecture may be discussed or criticized. It should be rational but also imaginative. The criterion for success is a sense of inevitability—a look of fitness derived by evolution out of the original environment.

VISUAL RELATIONSHIPS

In addition to the technicalities of the materials, dimensions, and details, landscape design is concerned with visual relationships. The designer has the ability to control and manipulate visual experience as well as tactile and other sensory qualities. Optically, spaces can be made to appear larger. Blue colors, which are visually receding, or small textured plants can be used to increase the sense of distance. Concealing the boundaries of the site and the use of diagonal or curving lines may enhance the sense of space in actually quite limited situations. The small town gardens of Thomas Church show these design devices used expertly and to good effect (Fig. 2.55). Of course it is also possible to do the reverse by manipulating color, texture, and edge, making large spaces appear smaller.

The most important visual relationship is scale. It is a difficult and much misused term. It is concerned with the relative size of things. The skyline of Manhattan is a pleasing visual composition seen from some distant point like Brooklyn or Staten Island. The buildings are generally "in scale" with each other. When experienced from the sidewalk, however, they are "out of scale" with the human figure. The architecture of a London square is more humanistic (Fig. 5.2). The buildings are not excessively tall in relation to the open space they surround, and the doors and windows provide a modulation of the surface which brings it into scale with the human experience and our attraction for detail. The scale of the squatter towns of South America is perhaps even more appropriate or comfortable. The houses are more or less built around the family and are almost

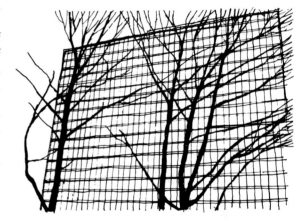

Fig. 8.1 Trees relate to large scale architecture and the individual on the street.

133

exactly scaled to the human figure and a human's basic needs. There is no monumentality.

One frequent task in landscape design is creating transitions from the human experience to large elements around us in the environment. This applies to cities and to natural landscape as well, but it is perhaps more important in cities. For this purpose, trees have a unique attribute in that they are relatively large elements when seen at a distance, yet on closer inspection they break down into a connected system of branches, twigs, leaves, and buds. This quality makes trees an excellent scale transition, being in scale with people and with large structures at the same time. Thus trees planted around tall buildings may be thought of as a scale transition from the multiple building to the individual (Figs. 8.1 and 8.2).

At another level, scale relationships may concern the right fit among dimension, space, and people. In a private garden, where the human scale is set by the dwelling, the danger will be to avoid the excessive breaking up of the space, making the garden seem small and the people feel too big for it. In a children's garden, on the other hand, what might appear cluttered to an adult would seem satisfactory to a child. Thus in design for children we might deliberately reduce the size of everything. The child's eye view is extremely important in the design of playgrounds and tot lots. Disneyland is scaled to two-third size and is especially effective for children because of this.

SOURCES OF PLAN FORM

Just as in landscape planning and site planning, form and shape in landscape design result from the constraints and potentials of the site and a clear definition of the design problem.

Fig. 8.2 (a) and (b) The role of trees in modifying scale relationships.

A fundamental source of form in landscape design is the shape of the site itself, as defined by the boundary lines and the topography (Fig. 7.1). There are also form-giving influences on the site from beyond the boundaries and the plan must show and deal with the modification of the site as it responds to those outside forces, especially climate, views, adjoining buildings, and land uses. The edge zone of the site is thus a double design project. It must relate to the outside while at the same time it has an inside edge that must relate to and be part of the features of the site plan. From an economy of space viewpoint, the alignment and location of playing fields and parking lots, buildings, and roads is likely to be parallel to the site boundaries or major slopes and ridges unless there is a physiographic reason or a strong program requirement to dictate otherwise (Fig. 7.6).

Within this larger framework, we must design spaces or areas to satisfy the program requirements located and connected according to the site plan.

The second source of form in design, then, is from an appraisal of the function or use to be accommodated. Getting at the meaning of the program requirements calls for research. If we are to design a place for quiet sitting, then we must start by analyzing sitting, not just seats (Fig. 8.3). That is to say, we should define and investigate the problem in its unique context. Seats or benches are the solution to a particular interpretation of the need for sitting in a particular situation. It is possible, however, to sit without seats at all. The design of seats and sitting areas is not as simple as it may seem. Steps and the edges of fountains may serve as seats for certain age groups under certain circumstances (Figs. 8.4 and 8.5). A bench without a back is uncomfortable for

Fig. 8.3 "Sitting" is more than seats.
Photograph by Bob Sabbatini.

Fig. 8.5 Edge of a fountain as seats.

Fig. 8.4 Steps as seats.

Fig. 8.6 Seat with something to look at.

most people for any length of time, but such benches have a multidirectional aspect suited for situations where this is needed (Fig. 8.6). Similarly, if we are to design a playground, then we should start by analyzing play, not only playgrounds, and recognize the variables of age and culture (Figs. 8.7 – 8.10). We must ask ourselves to what extent anything we design for children's play is in fact limiting to the child's imagination. The design of playgrounds must clearly emanate from an understanding of being a child with basic needs for security, muscular development and movement, and having drives that are satisfied by discovery and challenge. Whatever the use to be provided and facilitated, there must be enough space for it to take place and the three-dimensional forms and two-dimensional shapes should result from an analysis of the use.

In addition to function, there are other site factors that influence or determine shape and form. These include circulation, topography, architecture, materials, and maintenance. In a park or school layout, the deciding factor determining the shape or the outline of free surfaces or areas may in fact be the circulation routes. Thus circulation, in addition to connecting different places and facilities, may in fact define and separate areas and give shape to some of them. In landscape design pedestrian movement is critical. How do you get from one place to another and under what conditions? When is a straight line best? People in a hurry going between two known fixed points tend to choose the shortest distance. College campuses are one of the best places to see the effect of this (Fig. 8.11).

The width and surface of the circulation routes themselves are determined in terms of the numbers of people who may be expected to move along a particular pathway at any one time. Where many

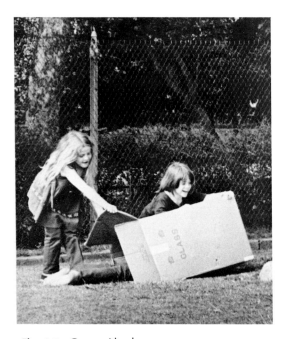

Fig. 8.7 Game with a box.
Photograph by Bob Sabbatini.

Fig. 8.8 Childrens' playground.
Royston, Hanamato, Mayes and Beck (1957).

Fig. 8.9 Captains of the Seven Seas.

Fig. 8.10 Basketball hoop and friends turns sideyard into a park.

people are expected in a flow of movement between two major attractors such as a football stadium and a parking area, or a bus stop and office building entrance, the paths should obviously be wide and straight or at most gently curved so that the movement can be easy and fast. Major desire lines of this sort should be satisfied. If, within the same context, it is desirable to divert the direct route to protect an area for some other use in a city square or park, then some element or "hazard" must be designed into the landscape to give reason and meaning to the diversion as perceived by the hurrying pedestrian (Fig. 8.12). Changes in level, ponds and lakes, and land shaping may be used for this purpose (Fig. 8.13). Apart from directing circulation around use areas, the circulation route may be varied simply for aesthetic reasons or to provide an alternative experience. Thus if the function of the circulation is slow, informal walking and stopping, as in parks or botanic gardens, then the paths can be less direct, less wide, and have expansions in them at places to permit people to pause, sit quietly, or collect in groups.

How wide should a path be? Experiments or observations might be carried out in existing city or campus situations to see at what point paths became inadequate. Beazley suggests that a path 2 feet wide can accommodate a wheelbarrow or baby stroller if the path is unfenced and there are no hazards on either side.[1] But this is very minimal and does not permit two-way traffic. A 7-foot path will allow a baby stroller and a pedestrian side by side. In shopping areas or malls, or where crowds are expected, a minimum of 20 feet is recommended. Shopping street sidewalks should be approximately 12 feet (Figs. 8.14 – 8.16).

1. Elizabeth Beazley, *Design and Detail of the Space between Buildings* (London: Architectural Press, 1960).

Fig. 8.11 Paths worn through planting where important direct route was not provided.
Photograph by Peter Kostrikin.

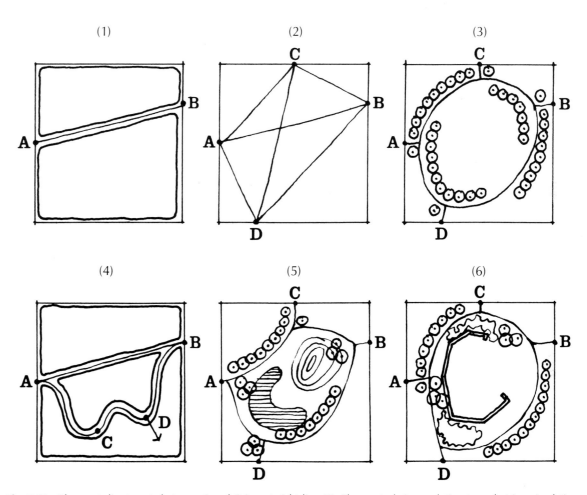

Fig. 8.12 The most direct route between A and B is a straight line (1). The most obvious solution to pedestrian circulation is to connect up all the doors or access points (2). Circulation which is not purposeful as in a park may be circuitous, connecting up view points and places of interest. Distance is no objection and, in fact, becomes desirable (4). Deviation from the straight line approach may be acceptable so long as the route is not excessively roundabout and is most successful when emphasized by planting (3) or made imperative by hazards (5), (6).

Circulation, auto or pedestrian, since it implies movement, is clearly intimately connected with change and the succession of sensual experiences and environments that occur along the route. It is important therefore to recognize the design possibilities in circulation for the sequential experience which can be developed even when the route is straight. We can learn much from the eighteenth-century landscape garden in this respect. The design of a pedestrian route may involve such concepts as place and identity, enclosure, variety, and mystery.

Fig. 8.13 The route of the path is related to the form of the landscape and therefore seems logical.

Land form has intrinsic shape and a logical extent and outline related to that shape and to the angle of repose of the material. Rolling topography at whatever scale logically calls for flowing curves in circulation or the outline of paved areas or use zones (Figs. 7.9 and 7.6). Thus contours of land may indicate appropriate shapes or form. Architecture is also an influence on the shape of areas. Buildings project imaginary lines into the landscape. When these relate to other form-giving forces, they should be adopted. These principles apply whether we are dealing with a natural site or one which is to be completely created in an urban setting.

Another way to define shapes is through the materials they are made of. For example, asphalt, grass, and poured concrete are flowing materials; that is, they take on any shape they are molded into. The surface is uniform, although in the case of concrete, expansion joints do provide a design pattern; the edges are still arbitrary and are determined by considerations other than the material. By contrast, bricks and paving blocks have a fixed unit shape which

Fig. 8.14 Widths of pedestrian routes are related to use.

Fig. 8.15 Path approximately six feet wide.

should not be violated by cutting (although this is often seen). Such precast units differ from cut stone, which is cut to any shape required out of a larger stratum or bed of rock. Bricks and concrete pavers are precast and have an integrity as individual units. The outline of paving using these materials should therefore be rectangular, although curves can be achieved by stepping back with each unit and allowing grass or planting to form the curve.

Finally, maintenance is an important factor in the evolution of specific shapes. Narrow, pointed areas of grass are very difficult to cut with the large scale mowing machinery commonly used in public landscapes. Such narrow strips may simply be trampled out of existence. The edge or shape of grass lawns should therefore be simple. Curvilinear shapes are probably best, but no angular outlines should have points less than about 90°. The narrowest width of grass and the space between tree trunks should be dimensioned to accommodate the mowing machinery to be used.

Fig. 8.16 Shopping street in Copenhagen.

SPATIAL DEFINITION

Landscape design results in three-dimensional space. The way in which that space is defined gives rise to a range of spatial qualities. Space may be defined entirely by natural materials, land form, and plants. A valley or bowl in a treeless landscape has spatial identify, a form that is emphasized by light and shadow and the skyline. Clearings in forests are spaces defined entirely by vegetation. Not only are these spaces defined by nature, they are also the result of natural processes (Figs. 8.17 and 8.18). Similar spatial enclosures can also be man made out of natural materials in a slightly more self-conscious way by design (Figs. 11.14, 11.24, and 11.25). Space can be formed entirely out of man-made inert materials, buildings, paving, and glass. However, landscape design is most likely to involve spaces made out of a combination of natural materials and man-made structures. The important point to realize is that vegetation and land form are as effective in defining space as are buildings and walls (Fig. 8.19).

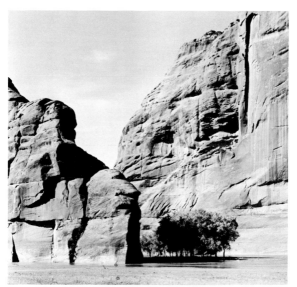

Fig. 8.17 Space defined by natural elements. Canyon de Muerte, New Mexico.
Photograph by R. Burton Litton, Jr.

Fig. 8.18 Three types of natural enclosure of space.

Fig. 8.19 Space defined alternatively by architecture and plants.

SELECTION OF MATERIALS

The way in which the type of paving material may influence the shape of the area to be paved was noted previously. In this chapter we pursue further the differences in surfaces and some considerations for their selection and combination in design. It seems reasonable that there should be some logic for selecting, combining, and changing paving materials. Why should all hard surfaces not be asphalt? Changing surface provides variety, which may be function enough, but the variety should relate to some factor of use or communication about use. Traditionally, surfacing materials have been used in such a way that any change in material reflects a change in use, purpose, or function, or a change in level; that is, a change designed to emphasize something. Old cities are full of such traditions. Steps in which the risers are made out of white marble and the treads out of dark granite emphasize their physical form and clear up visual ambiguity (Fig. 8.20). In old European streets paved with rough cobbles, we can still find two tracks of smooth granite set into the streets for cart wheels. The wheels thus ran smoothly on the tracks while the horses' hoofs had good traction on the cobbles.

Differences in paving materials, especially texture and color, can be used where a warning is needed to indicate danger or hazard (as if to a blind person) at the edges of pools and in other situations such as pedestrian crosswalks and at curbs and to separate incompatible uses (Fig. 8.21). By changing materials for such reasons, variety, pattern, and visual interest are introduced. Where the type of traffic changes, we may expect the surface to change. For example, grass and concrete are two surfaces with entirely different traffic expectations. Asphalt and concrete pav-

Fig. 8.20 Variation in structural material to emphasize form.

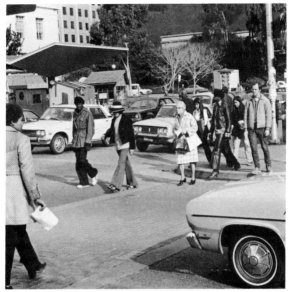

Fig. 8.21 Pedestrian crosswalk indicated by a change in surface.

Fig. 8.23 Directional paving pattern for purposeful circulation, gravel surface for casual use.

ing suggest fast, unimpeded movement, whereas gravel suggests slower, more casual strolling or standing around (Fig. 8.23). The recent practice of paving the crosswalks of pedestrian malls with bricks emphasizes the use of those areas by pedestrians and identifies territories for autos and pedestrians (Fig. 8.21). Changes in surface can also suggest direction of movement, and the texture of the material or the linear arrangement of paving blocks and expansion joints can emphasize direction (Fig. 8.22). Paving patterns can be thought of as information about the environment. Understanding our perception of these clues in the environment is important if the messages we want to communicate are to be clear, yet not overly heavy.

Fig. 8.22 Paving pattern related to the architectural concept.

Paving patterns also may be used as a technique of design to link elements or buildings together, to emphasize some sculpture or object; in doing so they may connect and to some extent conceal such mundane things as drain inlets. Successful paving patterns should emanate from and reinforce the inherent character of the place where it is strong and there is a clear relationship between the buildings and the space between them; alternatively, paving can be used to bring unity to a group of varied buildings. At the Campidoglio in Rome the paving is part of a larger concept and is clearly related to the total composition designed at one time by Michelangelo (Fig. 8.23). By contrast, in the Medieval marketplace of Sienna the paving brings unity to an

Fig. 8.25 Granite blocks, hard wearing material providing fine texture.

Fig. 8.24 Paving pattern brings unity to diverse architecture. Piazza del Campo, Sienna.
Photograph by Charles Rapp.

Fig. 8.26 Poured concrete can form any shape. Expansion joints give pattern.

Fig. 8.27 Bricks grouped into larger units (see also fig. 8.4).
Photograph by Trinidad Juarez.

organic collection of buildings of various heights and styles (Fig. 8.24).

It is also possible to affect scale relationships with paving materials. Paving materials that consist of small but identifiable units provide a fine-textured surface (Fig. 8.25). The unit relates easily to the human dimensions. Alternatively, poured concrete, which does not have small identifiable units, takes on the scale of the unit delineated by the expansion joints (Fig. 8.26). The spacing between these is a function of the thickness of the concrete and whether or not it is reinforced. The thicker and the greater the reinforcing, the larger the unit may be. Thus we can have expanses of paving made up of small units like cobblestones or bricks, or we can have concrete surfaces in which the units are 20 by 20 feet, or asphalt in which there is no discernible unit at all. The patterns the eye perceives then may be large or simple or small-scaled and textured. It is possible to combine the two in such a way that the larger perceived shapes relate to the surrounding buildings while smaller units within the pattern relate to the human experience (Fig. 8.27).

The same unit paving materials can present a different quality of surface depending on the way they are laid. Concrete blocks laid with wide joints seeded with grass present a more rustic and informal surface than the same blocks laid flush with cement joints—a surface more suitable for large pedestrian crowds or wheeled toys (Fig. 8.28; see also Fig. 8.16). The use of a very small but tough material, such as granite blocks laid with open joints or a hollow concrete frame, seeded with grass and treated like a lawn can result in one surface looking like another; thus a lawn can be used as a parking area or take the weight of a fire truck. On the other hand, the reverse is also possible—a surface may

look like lawn but actually be plastic! This seems to have some practicality for sports but is one of those modern innovations that are difficult to accept. The plastic lawn is in fact a solution to a problem related more to economics than to human sensibility.

Standard paving surfaces have many variations and applications. The final selection of materials is determined by the intended use, its maintenance needs and durability factor, cost, and visual quality.

Asphalt is the cheapest hard surface, and one of the most common. It is widely used for roads, paths, playgrounds, courts, and parking lots. It is durable enough to last approximately ten years before resurfacing is needed.[2] Compare this with granite blocks, which essentially last forever but cost a great deal more to obtain and lay in place. Asphalt is a fluid material, which can cover awkward shapes. It is easily laid and can be given a range of supporting capacities for automobiles, trucks, and people.

Gravel is another fluid and relatively cheap material (Fig. 8.23). However, it is not always suitable for general pedestrian movement. This depends on the method of laying and the size of the gravel, which can vary from quarry dust to pea gravel. The former can be compacted into a smooth, hard surface. Pea gravel is difficult to walk on and impossible to use for bicycles and wheeled toys. As a nonwalking surface, large gravel provides relatively low-maintenance groundcover which permits the direct return of rain water to the soil.

Depending on its thickness and quality and the distance it has to be moved to the job, poured concrete costs between two and four times as much as asphalt. It is also a fluid material and can be poured into any shape (Fig. 8.26). The location of the expan-

2. *Ibid.*

sion joints needed to permit volume changes induced by temperature is also a function of thickness and reinforcement, and is planned to prevent cracking of the surface. As the spacing increases, the concrete's thickness and need for reinforcement increases. The weight the surface has to withstand is also a factor that determines the need for reinforcement. The manipulation of all these variables results in visual patterns on the surface. Expansion joints may be made of wood, bitumin, or steel and may be highly visible or almost invisible. The surface of poured concrete may vary according to its finish and aggregate (Fig. 8.29). Exposing the aggregate by

Fig. 8.28 Pre–cast concrete paving slabs with grass joints. (See also Fig. 8.16.)

Fig. 8.29 Concrete paving surface with exposed aggregate. Photograph by Trinidad Juarez.

brushing with acid and washing can reveal texture and color, which are both determined by the nature of the aggregate. On the other hand, the surface may be brush-finished, giving a directional texture. This may be especially suitable in providing a nonslip surface on ramps in cold climates.

Concrete paving blocks are similar in appearance to poured concrete but come precast in specific and relatively small sizes (Fig. 8.16). These may also have texture and color variations and may be laid in a variety of patterns. The joints may be open or closed. They have a unit shape and therefore influence the edge and shape of the areas paved.

Bricks come in a variety of colors depending on their origin and can be laid in several traditional patterns (Figs. 8.30 and 8.31). Their relative cost is between six and eight times the cost of asphalt. They can be laid dry or with cement grouting. If bricks are laid dry, rain water will flow back to the underlying soil and plant roots. If they are laid as a solid surface, the same kind of drainage provision will be needed as for any other hard, impermeable surface. Bricks laid without grouting may even provide ammunition in times of civil disturbance! In cold climates there is a tendency for bricks to "heave" in winter, creating a maintenance problem. Recently a product has become available which is a manufactured, artificial surface that looks like brick paving but is only about an inch thick. This is considerably cheaper than real bricks to purchase and install. At a distance its appearance may be quite satisfactory, but, like plastic grass, on close inspection its true personality is revealed—very synthetic, without variability, and without the ability to age gracefully as bricks do.

Cut stone is very expensive and is used now only in special situations or where tradition demands it

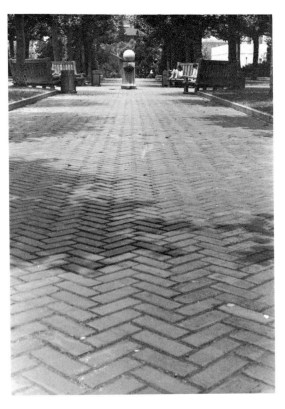

Fig. 8.30 Brick paving, herringbone pattern. Photograph by Trinidad Juarez.

Fig. 8.31 Brick paving. Photograph by Trinidad Juarez.

Fig. 8.32 Stone steps.

(Fig. 8.32). It is likely to cost up to twelve times as much as asphalt. However, its life span is indefinite. It is often thought of as a "gardenesque" material, yet it has paved many an urban plaza and street throughout the world in times when endurance was considered of more importance than short term economics (although, of course, the men who laid the streets were paid very little for their labor).

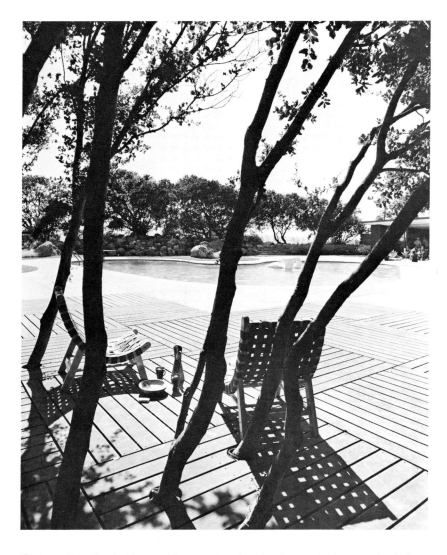

Fig. 8.33 Wooden decking provides extension of level surface on sloping ground and allows existing trees to be retained. Donnell Garden, California. Thomas D. Church, Landscape Architect. Photo by Rondal Partridge.

Wood has become a gardenesque paving material, popular in California because the relatively dry climate favors it and also because wood is easily available (Fig. 8.33). Its use in gardens derives from its functional nautical origins: decks, piers, boardwalks, and so on. The cost of wood as a walking surface is approximately eight or ten times that of asphalt, depending on construction and quantity. As decking, level areas can be extended out from a hillside; on flat sites the wood may be laid on the ground like a dance floor. The connection between wood and ground, however, is a sensitive one. Although preservatives are used in curing wood, it is proper practice to avoid contact between wood and soil. This can be done in a variety of ways using concrete piers in the ground and steel clasps to attach the wood to the concrete. Space between boards allows for drainage. Wooden blocks have also been used like bricks but, although the effect is attractive, their lifespan is limited.

Grass is the cheapest usable surface. Depending on the quantity, the amount of soil preparation, and other operational costs, it is cheaper than asphalt, although it requires more regular maintenance. Its uses are of course determined by the slope of the area, and by maintenance.

Sand is another surface that can be walked on and in which children can play (Fig. 8.8). Its uses are informal and recreational, and it needs containment since it has no capacity to bind together. The edge of sand areas is thus a special design problem.

The edge or joint between materials and surfaces is a very important aspect of design. Joints, which "read" as lines, are usually highly visible and so should complement the design and connect rather than divide; they should integrate the pieces and surfaces of the overall design. The meeting of soft

Fig. 8.34 The joints between surfaces and elements is one of the major aspects of detailed design. Planting and grass.

Fig. 8.35 Building and grass.

and hard surfaces is especially important from a maintenance point of view. The classic solution to the meeting of grass and planting is to separate (or join) them by a paving strip at least 1 foot wide. The grass should be 1 to 2 inches above this mowing strip (Fig. 8.34). These provisions allow for easy cutting of the grass without the destruction of the plants or shrubs, which may branch forward naturally, concealing the edge of the soil. Another critical situation is where grass meets a wall or building. Here again the grass must be separated from the wall by 1 to 2 feet so that the mowing machinery can cut to its edge (Fig. 8.35). If this is not done, a ragged fringe of uncut grass frequently will surround the building. The space between the grass and the building may be paved, providing a solid plane on which the building rests, or else it may be filled with gravel 2 inches below the grass level. If planting is used to make this transition between building and grass, space should be left between the planting and the building to allow for maintenance, window cleaning, and so forth.

The horizontal surfaces make up only one facet of landscape space. In addition to their use in the walls of buildings, which may have a variety of characteristics—glass, brick, concrete, wood—the same architectural materials can be extended or used to make free-standing and retaining walls and fences to form outdoor space.

WATER

One other important landscape material remains to be mentioned: water. This element, combined with paving and plants, provides detail and quality to the spaces of the site plan. It is a basic component of nature and landscape architecture. In nature we see it in mountain streams, tumbling and gushing and

traveling at a speed depending on the gradient of the land and the "newness" of the river (Fig. 8.36). It forms waterfalls and is made white with the interjection of air into it. Its color also varies according to the sky above, its depth, and the nature of the surface below. In lower lands the water runs smoothly, often without sound, sometimes giving ephemeral, but momentarily exact reflections of the surroundings. Instinctively we know water is not solid except when it may be frozen. As a lake, water defines a very exact edge related to the topography and, if the surface is still, it reflects the sky (Fig. 11.6). Wind and tidal forces create waves and ripples in the oceans. Gravity and light result in the numerous forms in which water is found in nature.

Add to the natural phenomena human ingenuity. First by natural pressure and later by artificial means, water has been forced into the air in foaming jets and allowed to return to the ground in a variety of ways, all pleasing to the viewer. This remains a constant preoccupation of man. Historically, water has had symbolic significance and various cultures have appreciated the cooling qualities of water in hot climates. Moorish, Indian, and Persian gardens are examples of this understanding. The reflective quality of water is especially interesting. The water surface must be very still and the bottom of the pool very dark or very deep (Figs. 8.37 and 8.38). Swimming pools are painted or tiled in light colors so that the bottom, and not a reflection, can be seen. The reflection to be seen from any point can be calculated geometrically. Since water reflects the sky, a small pond in a dark, enclosed courtyard may serve to add light. Water is also useful as a cooling agent in hot climates. Water can be jetted into the air to reduce temperatures. Fountains may also be cycled so that the water performance changes, making dif-

Fig. 8.36 Mountain stream.
Photograph by R. Burton Litton, Jr.

Fig. 8.37 Still dark water provides perfect reflections of objects in sunlight.
Photograph by Peter Kostrikin.

Fig. 8.38 Reflections are effected by light and wind.
Photograph by Peter Kostrikin.

Fig. 8.39 Water as a focal point.

Fig. 8.40 Cascade in Portland, Oregon. Lawrence Halprin and Associates, Landscape Architects. Photograph by Paul Ryan.

ferent sound effects as well as visual variation. The sound of falling or running water (like Muzak) may also be relied on to blot out unwanted sounds and create an additional environmental attribute by design. Water for drinking appears in the city and in parks, and there are many ways in which water may be made available to adults and children.

Water has, of course, many recreational uses which can only be touched upon here. Boating and fishing need extensive areas of water (Figs. 4.13 and 8.9). Swimming and skating have special requirements. As we have seen already, to most people—at least when they are dressed—water is something not to get into. It is therefore a ''hazard'' and can be a controller of circulation (Fig. 8.13). Visual continuity can be maintained between two points while access is prevented. A restaurant may be separated from the sidewalk by a pond. Water by its uniqueness, at least in cities, tends to act as a focal point. The foun-

tain in a square becomes a rendezvous (Fig. 8.39). Thus in Portland, Oregon, Halprin's cascades, symbolic of mountain streams yet stylized and urban, attract hundreds of people in the summer. This is a focal point for all segments of the population. It is a landmark and gives distinct quality to part of the city (Figs. 8.40 and 8.41).

Perhaps one of the most critical aspects of designing with water is the edge of the container. In nature water seeks the lowest level and is uncompromisingly horizontal. Thus the edges of an artificial container must be exactly level unless a specific optical illusion is desired, in which water may be made to appear as though it is flowing uphill. But who would want to trifle with that? The edge of the water is always very precise and therefore is visually dominant. The connection of water to land, a very magic zone significant in evolution, attracts us. The

Fig. 8.41 A cascade in the High Sierras, California.
Photograph by R. Burton Litton, Jr.

Fig. 8.42 The meeting of land and water may take various forms depending on the nature of the water and the intended relationship between it and people.

nature of our participation with the water at this edge is crucial to the form it should take and the materials it should be made with (Fig. 8.42).

In summary, landscape design is a very complicated procedure with many alternatives. It is the solution of a series of problems defined by the designer: circulation or movement, surfacing, the location and form of seating, the form and space for any purpose or multiple purposes. It is the giving of form to water and land and the selection of materials. Design is a rational procedure that depends on an experience of life and social behavior. It also depends on an understanding of materials, their technology, and their maintenance. It demands an imaginative design ability to devise new and creative form out of the analysis of the problem and the determinants of form. A design that can be built only on its particular site may be judged successful when affinity with the site and the particular program is evident. Design in these terms is a growth or an evolutionary adaptation of environment. Successful design will express sympathy for the people who will use it, and it will express a feeling and understanding of use. It will exhibit a relationship to all else around, before, and in the future, visually and historically.

Suggested Readings

Beazley, Elizabeth, *Design and Detail of the Space Between Buildings*.

Beazley, Elizabeth, *Designed for Recreation*.

Brookes, John, *Room Outside*.

Church, Thomas D., *Gardens are for People*.

Crowe, Sylvia, *Garden Design*, Part II, "Principles of Design," Part III, "Materials of Design."

Eckbo, Garrett, *Landscape for Living*, Ch. XIII, "Structural Elements Out of Doors."

Halprin, Lawrence, *Cities*.

Jellicoe, Susan, and Geoffrey Jellicoe, *Water*.

Kassler, Elizabeth B., *Modern Gardens and the Landscape*.

Shepheard, Peter, *Gardens*.

Shepheard, Peter, *Modern Gardens*.

Tandy, Clifford, *Handbook of Urban Landscape*.

Tunnard, Christopher, *Gardens in the Modern Landscape*.

Weddle, A. E., ed., *Techniques of Landscape Architecture*, Ch. 5, "Hard Surfaces," by T. Cochrane; Ch. 7, "Outdoor Fittings and Furniture."

9. SOCIAL AND PSYCHOLOGICAL FACTORS IN LANDSCAPE ARCHITECTURE

Elizabeth Kassler suggests that good planning and design will be the product of a process which respects both the nature of man and the nature of nature.[1] Thus far we have emphasized the natural constraints in regional landscape planning and site planning. The criteria for housing, recreation facilities, and use areas have assumed a great deal about the nature of man. In this chapter we consider how social and psychological theory and research may present constraints or positive direction in decision making and the development of form at all scales of landscape architecture. Only recently has there been a concerted effort to relate an understanding of human needs, environmental perception, and attitudes to design and planning in the hope of providing more satisfactory, conflict-free, and socially appropriate environments. Environmental psychology has become almost as popular a subject as ecology.

It seems likely that an understanding of behavior and perception will be helpful in the development of answers to the following and similar questions. What kind of setting is considered suitable for various forms of recreation and leisure time behavior? Which aspects of recreation are derived from a desire to get away from the pressures of the city and which are derived from a need for physical exercise?

1. Elizabeth B. Kassler, *Modern Gardens and the Landscape* (New York: Doubleday, 1964).

How can playgrounds be made responsive to the needs, urges, and feelings of young children when they are designed by adults? What are the appropriate physical relations between teenagers, tots, and parents in such situations? To what extent should the environment be capable of manipulation by people or the "users" to provide change and alternative arrangements? What is the need for public open space in cities and housing areas? What is the need for privacy? To what extent can the environment counteract the effects of tension and ill health encountered in the day-to-day struggle with traffic, a bombardment of information, crowded streets, television, and so forth? How can a designer cope with the fact that everyone does not see and appreciate the environment through *his* eyes or with *his* cultural background and attitudes? The answers to such questions and others are obviously important if design and planning are to be responsive to the social context within which the design must operate and which it serves.

Generally there are two basic ways to become more sensitive to the answers to these and a host of similar questions on every aspect of behavior and environment. One is to learn from observation and direct consultation with members of a community or a specific group in society defined by factors such as age and socioeconomic status. The other way is to become familiar with the general principles or "universals" of behavior and perception.

Fig. 9.1 Child's drawing of an ideal park includes swimming pool, boating lake, baseball diamond, swings, trees, grass and parking.

SOCIAL ANALYSIS

Various methods have been developed to help designers know more about the needs and attitudes of the public client. One method of gathering attitudinal information is the questionnaire or attitude survey. The success of these forms depends on the selection and wording of the questions. Questions such as "what do you think of so and so?" or "what kind of environment would you like?" are inhibiting. Since most members of the public do not know what all the possibilities are, their answers are limited by their past experiences and imaginations, or loaded by the choices they are given in the questions. Although attitude surveys are becoming

increasingly sophisticated, there are so many variables and difficulties that they may only be useful as a
way to substantiate the hypothesis or intuitive guess
of an intelligent designer or planner who is familiar
with the situation (Fig. 9.1).

Factual questionnaire surveys which provide an
indication of the actual use of facilities, parks, and
playgrounds are probably more valuable. Studies of
this nature at least tell us how the existing facilities
are used and the distance people of various ages are
prepared, if not content, to travel for various recreation activities and experiences. The extent to which
particular features of landscape or city have significance or what Lynch[2] calls "imageability" to the majority of the people can also be measured through
interview techniques.

Questionnaires may also be employed in the so-
called feedback or user study. This analysis provides
useful information and opinion about a specific
environment. In this case questions are answered
about an environment in which the respondents live
and about which they are more interested and able and
qualified to answer. Several studies have been made
of reactions and use patterns of tenants in housing
developments in which the findings are contrasted
with the original expectations of the architects,
which are sometimes at odds with the actual use. It
is not possible to make generalizations from these
specific studies, but a series of user feedback studies
may reveal patterns and recurring problems. One of
Alexander's techniques of generating form is based
on the same concept, that of improving the design
by critical analysis of previous solutions to the same
problem.[3]

Direct observation of behavior in particular use or
activity areas reveals another level of information.
For example, Vere Hole's study of children's playgrounds in London,[4] measuring the child's attention time and the variety of environment needed by
children, those occupations and features receiving
most attention, and so forth, provides valuable general information for future design work. Its use is
limited to some extent, however, by the specifics of
the particular case study, since findings related to
children's play behavior in London would not necessarily apply in Los Angeles except in the very basic
physical needs inherent in maturation and body
building. By observing people in parks and public
open spaces in a systematic way, it is possible to get
an impression of the way in which the environment
is used or misused and the way in which the design
and arrangement of elements such as fountains and
benches result in particular behavioral patterns.
Even without the presence of people to observe,
"tell-tale" traces such as litter and worn paths,
graffiti, and other marks can give an indication of
use patterns or dissatisfaction with the environment.

There is one other way by which we can attempt
to match design form with the needs and desires of
the people who will use it. This is the system
whereby people build their own environments,
parks, playgrounds, and even housing or at least
participate in it as in so-called self-help projects
(Figs. 9.2 and 9.3). Here again an ideal concept is
once more limited by the imaginations of the people
and their awareness of the options and alternatives

Fig. 9.2   Direct relationship between the users and the design
in "self help" project.

Fig. 9.3   Community project facilitates group social interaction and group affiliation.

2. Kevin Lynch, *The Image of the City* (Cambridge: MIT
    Press, 1960).
3. Christopher Alexander, *A Pattern Language Which Gen-
    erates Multi-Service Centers* (Berkeley: Center for Envi-
    ronmental Structure, 1968).
4. W. Vere Hole, *Children's Play on Housing Estates* (Lon-
    don: H.M.S.O., 1966).

Social and Psychological Factors in Landscape Architecture   153

Fig. 9.4 The impact of the environment may at times be counteracted by strong social needs and traditional behavior. Photograph courtesy of the Bancroft Library, University of California, Berkeley.

available. The designer's role in such situations is clearly to present alternatives, and ultimately to facilitate the implementation of the plan agreed on. This process, although unique in each case, can also contribute to a better understanding of environmental preferences and suitabilities. That is, the experience of working with the potential users is in itself educational for the designer as well as the partici-

pants. In addition, the project is more likely to reflect the expressed needs and interests of the users as they then are defined. Flexibility in the solution will presumably take care of future users whose needs and preferences may be different.

All these methods are fraught with dangers. The questionnaires may be very parochial, inasmuch as data gathered at one time and under certain circum-

stances may have little relevance a few years later. In addition, we must be cautious of the tremendous adaptability of people to given environmental situations, which can, in fact, lead us to find satisfactory—and even favor—environments that previously or objectively would have been considered unsatisfactory or hostile. Attitudes change, people move, life is ongoing, and there is always the dilemma that what the people seem to want or need at one moment may be in conflict with long term goals or the needs of others. Thus, although the several techniques described here are potentially valuable sources of information in design, they must be used with caution and the conclusions examined with enlightened skepticism.

BEHAVIOR AND ENVIRONMENT

Studies and research into the relationship of social factors and design require a familiarity with general scientific work in behavior and perception. It is necessary to develop an intellectual framework through which design and planning decisions will be related to the basic principles of sociology and human psychology. In attempting to illustrate this relationship we may be able to answer questions of a general nature serving as a common base, or a set of minimum standards and requirements, with which to relate the specifics and variables of site planning and environmental problems.

The interaction between human behavior and the nonhuman environment is a two-way process. On the one hand, the environment has a definite impact on the individual, and our response may be to adapt to the imposed conditions. On the other hand, we are continually manipulating or choosing our physical surroundings in an attempt to make life physically and psychologically more comfortable (Fig. 9.4).

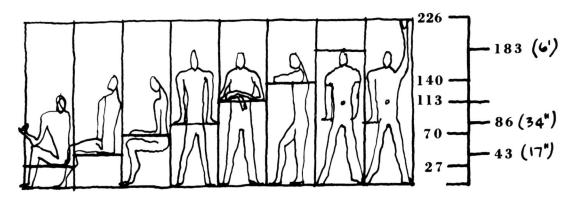

Fig. 9.5 Best average dimensions for a bench, based on "The Measure of Man," by Henry Dreyfuss (1967).

Fig. 9.6 A series of modular dimensions in centimeters developed by Le Corbusier (1948). The measurements derived from the human body are interrelated with the golden rule system of proportions.

Behavior is the result of a complex interaction between two main sets of variables. The first is the environment that surrounds and affects the individual. The second is the inner condition of the individual, which has two parts: physiological, related to the body's biological mechanisms; and psychological, related to the cultural background, motives, and experiences of the individual and his basic needs. Thus in design we are concerned with three categories of human factors: physical, physiological, and psychological.

PHYSICAL FACTORS

The first group is concerned with the rather obvious relationship between physical shape and size of the person and the detailed form of the environment. Analysis of average measurements and postures, movement, and growth results in a set of dimensions for parts of buildings and detailed landscape design. A door must be high enough to allow people to pass through without stooping, seats must be at the right level and inclination to be comfortable, steps must have dimensions evolved from basic movement patterns of the human body (Fig. 9.5). The gradients of ramps and the height of hand rails are further examples of form derived from the physical shape and movement characteristics of the users. Design details derived from purely visual considerations may or may not fulfill the condition of fit for the user. Le Corbusier's modular system derived a set of visually pleasing proportions and dimensions from the human body, thereby theoretically relating beauty and functional satisfaction in his design (Fig. 9.6).[5] Special situations may logically result in deviations from usual dimensions and standards. For example, where young children are involved, the environment must facilitate growth and development of the physical form—muscle development and motor ability—and dimensions of playground features, drinking fountains, and so on, must be appropriate for children. Other variations from the norm can be anticipated for the elderly and disabled. Obviously, then, we can achieve buildings and an outdoor environment for work and leisure which are designed in relation to the form and shape of the user.

5. Charles Edouard Jeanneret-Gris, *The Modular*, 2nd edition (Cambridge: Harvard University Press, 1954).

PHYSIOLOGICAL FACTORS

Human physiological needs are also relatively easy to specify. They result from the interaction of the inner biological condition of an individual with the surrounding environment. People need food, air, water, exercise, and protection from the excesses of heat and cold. A state of health or disease may be regarded as an expression of the success or failure of an organism to respond adaptively to environmental challenges.[6] The process by which the individual maintains its internal environment in an approximately permanent state is called homeostasis. This process is essentially innate and automatic, resulting in the operation of body mechanisms and glands. Perspiring, shivering, and sleeping are examples of the body's response to environmental conditions.

The homeostatic process is facilitated by modifications to the environment. In the evolution of society the building of shelters and the use and control of fire permitted settlement in areas where homeostasis would otherwise have been difficult or impossible to maintain. Homeostasis also may result in migration to places where the conditions are more comfortable.

Thus in theory human physiological needs, like human physical form, can be easily specified. Needs can be fulfilled through the provision of nutritious foods, clean air, adequate and pure water, in addition to the elimination of disease within an effective physical environment which allows for control of cold and heat, provides shelter from weather, and at the same time affords the opportunity for exercise in fresh air and sunlight. A human comfort zone in which maximum and minimum temperatures and humidity are specified has been developed by Olgay, suggesting an optimum environment in terms of the homeostatic process, human comfort, and ease of living.[7]

A semiphysiological need is the need for self-preservation and avoidance of pain. It is a self-protecting device against physical injury and death. The behavioral manifestation is to a large extent instinctive in the sense that we automatically withdraw from excessive heat and take precautionary measures against physical danger. Obviously an environment that is threatening and ambiguous could induce a state of apprehension and ultimately emotional stress harmful to the individual. We therefore seek out and demand a certain level of physical security in the environment. The responsibility of city agencies to provide conditions of safety for citizens has resulted in a series of regulations and design specifications. Fences around swimming pools, and hand rails on bridges and along flights of steps are often legal requirements resulting from safety regulations related to our need for security and fear of injury through falling.

PSYCHOLOGICAL FACTORS

Health is not merely the absence of disease or infirmity. The definition adopted by the World Health Organization describes health as a state of physical, mental, and social well being. Thus we come to the third human component in environmental design: human psychological and social needs, behavioral patterns, and tendencies. It is the most difficult of the three sets of human factors to define and relate to the form of the environment. Yet are we not aware of environments that are not pleasing or useful and do we not desire to modify the environment for the fulfillment of some need? If we hope to plan and design environments that will be sensitive and responsive to the human condition, we must find a way to interpret and take into account our own psychological and emotional needs.

Human psychological needs and perception of the environment differ according to a multitude of variables including age, social class, cultural background, past experience, motives, and daily routine of the individual. These factors influence and differentiate the need structures of individuals and groups. Thus the needs of a child are obviously different from those of an adolescent or an adult. Even if the same needs can be identified, the overt behavior is likely to be different. Despite the complexity of the variables and difficulties in the definition of many needs, it is possible to suggest certain broad categories of inner needs defined on the basis of observed behavior and empirical evidence and social analysis. In reality we have some psychological needs some of the time and other needs at other times; we do not have all needs all of the time. Sometimes some needs are stronger than others, and our need structure changes according to the particular situation.[8]

The basic human inner condition may be classified into five generalized groupings of motivational forces and psychological needs: (1) social, (2) stabilizing, (3) individual, (4) self-expression, and (5) enrichment. There is inevitably overlap and potential conflict among the categories.

The first group, social needs, includes the need of the individual for social interaction, for group affiliation, for companionship, and for love. Together with these go the more subtle need to be needed and to be sustained by others and by implication

6. René Dubos, *Man Adapting* (New Haven: Yale University Press, 1965).
7. Victor Olgay, *Design with Climate* (Princeton, N.J.: Princeton University Press, 1963).
8. Peggy Long Peterson, "The Id and the Image," *Landmark '66* (Berkeley: University of California, Department of Landscape Architecture, 1966).

Fig. 9.7 A grouping of benches in shade facilitates social interaction in Fresno, California. Eckbo, Dean, Austin and Williams, Landscape Architects.

the need for the protection of other people. The family group and the peer group are obvious manifestations of these needs. The whole of society is organized to a large extent around these basic social needs and the behavioral evidence can be seen in the public dance hall, the beach, old people's clubs, veterans' societies, and so on. It is clear, then, that wherever the environment is meant for people or where the purpose of the design is not contrary to the fulfillment of these social needs, it should characteristically have a sociopetal form designed to draw people together, to engender social relationships or at least to make this possible. The Portland cascades attract people and therefore contribute to the fulfillment of this need (Fig. 8.40). So too the self-help or community project, by its very nature, draws people together in participation (Figs. 9.2 and 9.3). At a detailed level, the design and grouping of park benches can engender or inhibit social interaction (Fig. 9.7).

The second set of needs have been called stabilizing needs. We have a need to be free from fear, anxiety, and danger. And we have a need for a clear orientation, a need to develop and to hold a clear philosophy of life, a need to order and to organize the environment, a hope to have a say in its form and content through the democratic process. We have an inherent need to manipulate our environment, not only from the point of view of developing physical conditions responsive to our physiological needs, already mentioned, but also to satisfy some more deeply rooted need to make a mark, to form and shape the environment according to a symbolic, metaphysical urge. The concept of advocacy planning (self-help and self-determination) is to an extent related to this desire for stability through participation in decisions concerning one's own local environment. The concept of self-help projects where derelict, unused land is transformed through the energies, initiative, and artistic expression of local people, who will be the users of the land, gives rise to a form of design activity that not only satisfies the human need for a sense of stability and involvement basic to security but also leads to a completely new type of design process. Other design implications are imageability, the ordering of space so that it is free from ambiguity, and the selection of paving surfaces to provide information about a place and its use. There are many other ways in which design can give a sense of familiarity and security and provide opportunity for participation.

The third group is described as individual needs. Some of these overlap or are similar to needs of self-expression. Here we recognize the need of people at certain moments in their experience and development of self-awareness to be utterly alone for a period of time, that is, the need for privacy. Further, there is a strong need for a certain amount of self-determination, for an identity and sense of personal uniqueness in the environment, and related to this a need to be able to choose or make individual decisions about one's life.

The possibility of privacy in today's urban environment becomes more remote and may be responsible for the influx of campers and backpackers to wilderness or distant landscape areas in search of isolation and a spiritual connection between themselves and nature. The designed environment should make privacy a real possibility. This is most easily achieved within a dwelling itself, although as building economics shrink the size of the house and as other misguided and fashionable concepts lead to more open plans, it becomes a more ephemeral possibility. Privacy also may be attainable by de-

signing the outdoor environment to create areas less accessible to direct use by the urban population yet within minutes of it. Small sitting areas can be located off the beaten path or separated from circulation routes by grade changes (Fig. 12.12). The provision of choice in any environmental situation clearly allows a person to express individuality and identity. Circulation should offer choices. Within reason, we should be able to do what we want. But we must be careful that personal expression will not adversely affect the lives and privacy and equal needs for uniqueness and identity of others in society. It can be seen that there is a potential conflict between need for self-expression and social needs.

There is a variety of component needs making up the self-expression group. They include the need for self-assertion and exhibition, for dominance and power. Some of these needs have been made more specific to the environment in the concept of territory. There is also a need for accomplishment and achievement, for prestige, and to be held in esteem by others. Ardrey calls this the need for status, which is related to the need for territory.[9] The process of "keeping up with the Joneses," so evident in suburbia, is a clear expression of these needs, which, if better understood, could be satisfied in a less wasteful manner (Fig. 9.20).

It has been suggested that the aggressive defense of territory is a form of self-expression fundamental to all animals, including humans. Territoriality can be seen not only in the walls and fences we erect around our houses and gardens (Fig. 9.8), but also in the areas we stake out for ourselves on the public beach or in the camping ground, which indicate territorial rights to be infringed at peril (Fig. 9.9). Much evidence related to human territorial instincts derives from studies of animal behavior.[10] The ex-

Fig. 9.8 Barbed wire and warnings, physical manifestations of territoriality.

tent and location of territory tend to vary with the species, mating activity, seasonal change, and availability of food in the environment. Territoriality ensures proper spacing and thus prevents the overexploitation of the environment the family depends on for sustenance. Thus, by regulating density, territoriality ensures propagation of the species.

Territoriality has been identified as one of the three fundamental human drives, the other two being status and sex.[11] Laying claim to a territory and maintaining a certain distance from one's fellow may be considered a real human biological need, as it appears to be in other animals, although its human expression may be different and culturally

9. Robert Ardrey, *The Territorial Imperative* (New York: Atheneum, 1966).
10. Konrad Lorenz, *Studies in Animal and Human Behavior,* translated by Robert Martin (Cambridge: Harvard University Press, 1970).
11. Ardrey, *op. cit.*

Fig. 9.9 Territoriality in Yosemite National Park.
Photograph by Bruce Davidson.

Fig. 9.10 (a) Beach scene in Venezuela. People possibly spaced closer than they might be in Scandinavia. Photograph by Francis Violich.
(b) Desolate beach on which to be alone.

conditioned.[12] Trespass laws and the legal status of private property are clear manifestations of a territorial urge.[13] We are also only too well aware of the concept of "turf," an area where members of a gang feel safe and where intruders will be regarded with hostility.[14]

There is a clear relationship between space or territory and animal survival. Since we are not highly dependent on our immediate environment, this is not a human concern. However, we must be inter-ested in the relationship between space and behavior. Observations indicate that space limitations or crowding can force people into stressful situations; on the other hand, in certain cases there can be too much space or distance between people, inhibiting conversation and use.[15] A second aspect of importance is the evidence of pronounced variations in spacing mechanisms and personal space exhibited by people of different cultural background and nationality. Sensitivity to this fact may lead to differ-

12. Dubos, *op. cit.*
13. Edward T. Hall, *The Hidden Dimension* (New York: Doubleday, 1966).
14. Robert Sommer, *Personal Space* (Englewood Cliffs, N.J.: Prentice-Hall, 1969).
15. e.g., "West Side Story."

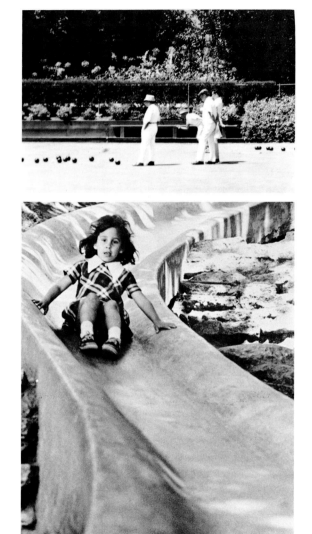

Fig. 9.11 (a)(b) Two contrasting forms of play fulfilling the same need for self-expression.
Photograph (b) by Robert Sabbatini.

ent design criteria for ostensibly the same facility or use area, depending upon regional variation. The crowding limit of a popular public place or beach is subject to a culturally imbued sense of territory and personal space (Fig. 9.10).[16]

Is there a point at which too little personal space may result in psychological breakdown or antisocial behavior? Experiments with rats in an artificial environment in which food was not a territorial factor have shown that severe conditions of overcrowding result in serious physiological effects and unnatural behavior.[17] The virtual impossibility of solitude leads to the disorganization of the society of rats and ultimately to population collapse. Although there are strong arguments that overcrowding in urban slum conditions is equally detrimental to the mental and physical health of its inhabitants, the human population is so profoundly conditioned by cultural and social factors that the question of human overcrowding in cities is more complicated than is the case with animal populations. Thus it is still not conclusive that high densities in cities are undesirable and that we cannot design urban forms that would emphasize benefits of large city life and high concentrations of people, at the same time reducing the ill effects.[18] In other words, it does not follow that suburban form and densities are best. The studies suggesting the prevalence of mental ill health in New York City have not been paralleled by similar studies in suburbia or a midwestern farm community where we may find similar or other problems.

Another form of self-expression is play (Fig. 9.11). We must thus ensure that the environment will provide possibilities for play as a general concept more than simply through the provision of "playgrounds" for organzied games and sports. A city should have built-in variety and possibilities for

imaginative response. The pedestrian circulation system at Cumbernauld was augmented with boulders and other features that could be perceived in any way a child or adult wished—as a mountain, a bench, or a hideout.

The last group of human needs is called enrichment needs. People (and especially children) have a thirst for knowledge. Related to this is a need for self-realization and personal creativity, and, it seems, a strong need for beauty and aesthetic experience. People have very definite creativity urges, although their strength and relative fulfillment take various forms and result in artifacts of various degrees of quality. Thus, although we are all artists, some are greater than others. The popularity of scenic and beautiful landscapes such as the Grand Canyon of Arizona (Fig. 1.13), Yosemite (Fig. 3.9), and Yellowstone, the lake district and western highlands of the United Kingdom, all of the great natural wonders of the world, leads one to think that we do indeed have a very strong need for visual beauty, although obviously the basis of trips to such landscapes is also a response to some of the other needs already discussed. Human enrichment needs, then, seem to require the provision of information about the environment so that our understanding of what we see may be increased in detail. Moreover, the environment should not only be intrinsically beautiful itself, since this seems to be a basic human need,

16. Hall, *op. cit.*
17. John B. Calhoun, "The Role of Space in Animal Sociology," *Journal of Social Issues*, XXII (4) (October 1966).
18. Christopher Alexander, *The City as a Mechanism for Sustaining Human Contact* (Berkeley: University of California, Center for Planning and Development Research, 1966).

0   100   200   500 FT

0   100   200 M

Fig. 9.12 Two plan views of Christopher Alexander's theoretical neighborhood: (a) the private patios as they would relate to the hillside park; (b) the internal road system and houses.

but it also should provide the possibility for creativity in the form of environmental manipulation or simply in the provision of opportunities within some kind of open space or recreation program for personal involvement in the arts, in sculpture, in gardening, or in play and theater.

In design, enrichment may be equated with complexity. The instinctive and continuing human need to decorate the environment can be seen in primitive cave drawings, in the supergraphics of the 1970s, and in all that lies between. Modern architect-

ural theory of the 1930s and subsequent economic constraints have tended to work against our desire for ornament. The "lean-to" architecture of the 1960s and 1970s, the renewed interest in the decoration of earlier eras, and the revival of the traditionally complex cottage garden, in which fruit, vegetables, and flowers are combined, indicate a fresh and intuitive understanding of this need. Here, in parallel with arguments favoring complexity in the natural environment for ecological purposes, are arguments for complexity and variety in the human or built environment also.

Having reviewed the generalities of human needs, we must beware of the danger of becoming oversensitive and self-conscious about these needs, which are part of our general awareness. There is a danger in the development of specific design forms to satisfy or fulfill some of these needs which would lead in all probability to disappointment and conflict. It is not the intention here to suggest that design should be, or indeed can be, specifically oriented toward the fulfillment of any specific aspect of this spectrum of human emotional needs. On the contrary, it is simply suggested that the design process should identify some of the basic demands or needs which a particular component of the environment may reasonably be expected to satisfy and then should ensure that the geometric arrangement of the design does not prevent the fulfillment of those stated needs and desires. And, if possible, the design of any piece of environment—be it building, open space, park, or street—should be formed through an understanding of and sensitivity to the complexity of the human personality. In addition, it should be remembered that the physical environment is only one part of a larger process. It is the setting in which we, the social animal, interact with

other human beings or the social environment.

A theoretical example of residential neighborhood form by Christopher Alexander illustrates the unexpected possibilities that may result when preconceived spatial designations are abandoned and emphasis is given to behavioral factors (Fig. 9.12).[19] This incomplete study, essentially a diagram, concentrates on the human need for frequent intimate social contact, which, according to Alexander, contemporary society tends to inhibit. Its form is designed to allow ease of access by freeway networks for potential visitors in an automobile-oriented suburb. The number of homes in the cluster is based on probability studies which will ensure the presence of enough children of the same age to form play groups. The surface of the hill is a park in which the children can play but are insulated from the roads. Each house maintains its privacy and the idea is to emphasize the advantages of suburban living and counteract the undesirable qualities. The solution may be debatable, but nonetheless it is a good example of a form resulting from a process emphasizing certain social factors, a concept that can be applied with other and more precise data to all aspects of the environment.

ENVIRONMENTAL PERCEPTION AND BEHAVIOR

Behavior, then, results from the interaction of the individual with other individuals (the social environment) and with the surrounding (the physical environment). Consequently, the environmental designer must be interested in the structure of the environment and its effect on the individual. Sec-

19. *Ibid.*

ond, and very much related to this, we must understand the way in which the environment is perceived by the individual; and third, we must be interested in general behavioral reaction to stiuations, social and physical.

Experiments show that variation in physical environmental stimulation is necessary for normal orientation and even for mental balance in the human being. Our sensitivity to the environment and our adaptability or response to environmental conditions can result in specific behavior, although we are actually unconscious of the effect of the environment on us. This possibility underscores the power that is in the hands of the environmental designer. It has been demonstrated that behavior and social interaction can be influenced by the arrangement of furniture in a room.[20] It has also been suggested that architectural arrangements can result in conditions alien to man, for example, where there is no opportunity for privacy (the open plan house) or little physical contact with the ground (a high-rise apartment).[21] The judgments in this case are made not on the basis of human survival, which is not in doubt, but in terms of probable mental stress and discomfort to which such environments may contribute. Environments can thus be specifically designed to bring people together agreeably for some purpose, as in an amphitheater, or to engender a social relationship, as in the arrangement of seats in a park. Alternatively, design can prevent or discourage such possibilities.

Another way in which the influence of environment on behavior can be seen is in the way places assume meaning. A church, a cemetery, a library produce specific behavior conforming to the understood rules and meaning or symbolism of such buildings and places. Various types of landscape

may also result in specific behavioral response. This was in fact an important aspect of the eighteenth-century landscape gardens. Here the configuration of the landscape and the development of a sequence of changing views and experiences, including the introduction of allegorical and mythological allusions in the form of statuary, temples, grottoes, and other buildings, was intended to induce specific responses of sublimity, joy, amusement, sorrow, beauty, fear, awe—not all at once, but in sequence. The fullest response to these eighteenth-century situations demanded a high level of intellectual understanding and literary knowledge (Fig. 2.35).

The value of understanding the mechanics of visual sensation is, of course, obvious. Knowing how the eye works and transforms retinal images of constantly shifting light patterns into the visual world makes it possible for the designer to eliminate distracting situations which make life difficult. For example, our 180° peripheral vision exaggerates the sense of movement, and the closer the walls of a tunnel or passageway, the greater our sense of movement. Drivers tend to slow down on roadways lined with regularly spaced trees or when going under a bridge whose supports are close to the road. Perception of color and contrast can be manipulated to clarify territory and information about the environment. The painted crosswalk indicates a zone of relative safety. Finally, illusions can be created through the design of clues to space or depth perception to make areas seem larger, smaller, or wider, and also through the manipulation of perspective or with tricks, such as the trompe l'oeil.

Perception is a more complex process than just seeing. Through it, people select, organize, and interpret sensory stimulation into meaningful and coherent images of the world. Sensation shades into

perception as experience goes from the isolated and simple to the complex interactions characteristic of an ongoing awareness of the environment. The perceived environment normally contains so many objects and sensory stimuli that behavior is frequently less the result of a response to the total environmental influence than to specific elements selected through perception. Immediate experience then results from the interaction between sensory impulses from the environment and certain predispositions and states of mind in the individual which influence the selection and organization processes, and then give meaning to the result.[22]

The processes of selection and attribution of meaning or symbolism to the environment, or the development of an emotional response to aspects of the environment, clearly vary according to the individual. This fact is what makes the subjects of perception and behavior so complicated and so unlikely to produce universal rules. Although general patterns and principles are identifiable, what is seen by an individual is what he wants to see, or what he is looking for. Thus we can compare drawings and paintings of landscape or city views with photographs of the same scenes and realize the artist's selectivity and the particular emphasis which his vision or personality chose to pick out and stress. A good example is a mural on a building along the boardwalk of Venice, California. The artist has

20. Sommer, *op. cit.*
21. Humphry Osmond, "Function as the Basis of Psychiatric Ward Design" (sociopetal and sociofugal buildings), in *Environmental Psychology: Man and His Physical Setting*, edited by Harold M. Proshansky, William H. Ittelson, and Leanne G. Rivlin (New York: Holt, Rinehart & Winston, 1970).
22. Bernard Berelson, *Human Behavior* (New York: Harcourt, Brace and World, 1966).

Fig. 9.13 The artist selects and emphasizes whatever he is attracted to.

painted the view to be seen from that spot, but the scene is covered with snow, which has in fact never happened and is never likely to. It is an artist's fantasy (Figs. 9.14 and 9.15). Another case is the Thomas Hill painting of Yosemite Valley in the nineteenth century. The sides of the valley and the jaggedness of the peaks are exaggerated, reflecting Hill's sensation rather than what he really saw (Figs. 9.16 and 9.17). This is what differentiates painting or drawing from photography.

Previous experience and learning condition what we see and how we interpret it. The motive of the individual or the particular needs which seek fulfillment, or the interests, wishes, or desires of the individual, clearly influence perception at any particular time. In a *New Yorker* cartoon a couple in a furniture salesroom looking at a rather exotic lamp in the shape of a bird ask the salesman whether he has anything more ornate because, they explain, they are "nouveaux riches." That is to say, they see the lamp only in terms of what they believe to be fitting for a style of life they wish to adopt in the belief

Fig. 9.14 Mural, Venice, California.

Fig. 9.15 Venice, California.

Fig. .9.16 Yosemite. Painting by Thomas Hill (circa 1885). Courtesy Oakland Museum.

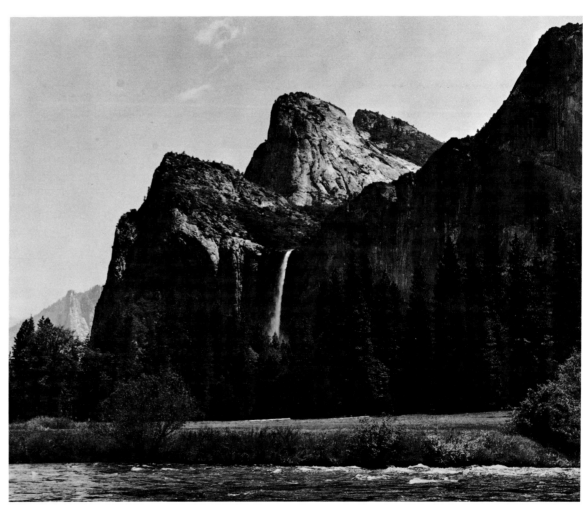

Fig. 9.17 Yosemite. Photograph by R. Burton Litton, Jr.

that it is in fact desirable, although the term *nouveau rich*, to those who coined it, was regarded as something to be avoided and distasteful. In another situation, mid-twentieth-century youth may describe the Taj Mahal as ticky-tacky. The significance of it, historically and architecturally, is merely incidental from the point of view from which they see it. For them it may be a materialistic manifestation of a form of society for which they have no sympathy, or it may merely be an incident on their journey in search of meditation and spiritual fulfillment with a guru in the foothills of the Himalayas. Alternatively, we may regard their attitude as simply a piece of antiestablishmentarianism. The two examples, however, show the extent to which perception, or at least the meaning given to objects and environments, is conditioned by variables in past experience, knowledge, age, socioeconomic class, and the personal motive of the individuals involved.

Another factor determining perception, or what is selected out of a great bombardment of stimulation, is the intensity or quality of a stimulus. An element or object in the environment can be so dominant because of its shape, color, contrast, and so on, that it cannot fail to be identified and selected by almost everyone, although its meaning and induced behavioral response will vary according to the individual.

The house is regarded in a variety of ways by different social and economic groups of society in certain Western cultures.[23] The perception of the home by the lower economic groups of society is frequently as a shell into which to withdraw for security. The middle-income professional member of society tends to regard the house as a piece of property to be looked after and improved. High-income groups tend to regard the home as a sort of hotel.

One other example of variable perceptions and be-

Fig. 9.18 To the youngster a tree is a playground and a challenge.
Photograph by R. Burton Litton, Jr.

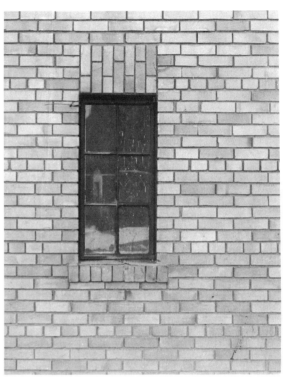

Fig. 9.19 The essence of beauty is a pattern which contains fluctuations.
Photograph by Peter Kostrikin.

havior can be seen in the case of a tree. In history, trees were regarded as symbols of fertility around which a form of religion and worship developed. Today the child will perceive the tree as a challenging object and his subsequent behavior will be to climb it and to use it as an element of play (Fig. 9.18). A teenager, on the other hand, depending upon the circumstances, may view the tree simply as a form that provides shade and gives uniqueness to

a spot, resulting in an attraction to it as a place to hang out with friends of the peer group. He may carve his initials on it. A passing adult will view the tree simply as a pleasing neighborhood feature and will associate it casually with environmental quality and possibly property values. The developer will

23. Clare Cooper, *The House as a Symbol of Self* (Berkeley: University of California Center for Planning and Development Research, Working Paper No. 120).

Fig. 9.20 Sacramento, California (1965).
Photograph by William A. Garnett.

view trees on his land in all probability as a good selling point, and he will therefore make efforts to protect them from damage and may even name the subdivision after the trees. Older people, on the other hand, will see the tree in terms of the possibility of falling limbs and the slipperiness of autumn leaves. Their impulse will be to have the tree severely pruned or cut down. A schizophrenic who has made a friend of this tree in an anthropomorphic way will respond appropriately to this event. And a street sweeper will have his own opinion.

For landscape architecture, another interesting theory about the interaction of people with the physical surroundings concerns aesthetic satisfaction. It has been suggested that the requirements for aesthetic enjoyment are simply the requirements for visual perception itself, raised to a higher degree. The essential thing in each case is to have a pattern which contains the unexpected. This seems to be the heart of what we call "beauty."[24] This is explained as follows. Our grasp and enjoyment of the world rest on two complementary neurophysical principles: the principle of response to novelty, change, and stimulation; and the principle of response to repetition or pattern. Our perceptual system thus paradoxically demands variety and new information while at the same time seeking regularity or pattern.

The brain, which is a pattern-selecting or pattern-perceiving system, can be thought of as consuming and requiring information as a stomach consumes food. It is argued that since this process of perception was vital in the evolution and survival of the human species, it will still have a strong influence in our lives today. It is further suggested that a major aspect in feeling pleasure in aesthetic satisfaction

24. S. R. Maddi and D. W. Fiske, *Functions of Varied Experience* (Homewood, Ill.: Dorsey Press, 1961).

may be related to the brain doing its job efficiently, that is, selecting patterns and novelties within it. Thus if fluctuations and patterns are basic to perception, these must also play a large part in aesthetic enjoyment. Aesthetic satisfaction, and therefore visual beauty, may be regarded either as a flux in which we can find a pattern or a pattern that contains unexpected fluctuations. A brick wall with its repetition of similar units provides a pattern. Changes and fluctuations occur, however, at different scales. At the scale of the bricks, the texture may vary or fluctuate. At the scale of the wall, a window becomes a fluctuation (Fig. 9.19). The same can apply to a fern frond which has a repetitive, identifiable structure with minor variations. Both are visually attractive because of these contrasts between a strong pattern and unexpected fluctuation within it.

In this chapter I have attempted to show the range of human characteristics, needs, and motives intrinsic to the people for whom we design. Second, I have attempted to indicate the way in which the environment may be regarded as a source of stimulus and a determinant of behavior. Third, I have tried to show

Suggested Readings

Recreation
American Academy of Political and Social Science, *Recreation in the Age of Automation.*
De Grazia, Sebastian, *Of Time, Work and Leisure.*
Friedberg, M. Paul, *Play and Interplay.*
U. S. Outdoor Recreation Resources Review Commission, *Reports,* 1962.
Williams, Wayne, *Recreation Places,* pp. 235–247, "Planning for Recreation."

The Physical Environment and Social Behavior
Alexander, Christopher, *The City as a Mechanism for Sustaining Human Contact.*

the mechanisms of perception and the variables that affect it and the relationship between perception and behavior. One of the major objectives of environmental design must be the development of a framework that facilitates rather than inhibits the fulfillment of individual needs without social conflict.

The evidence and concepts discussed here indicate the potential power of designers, whether they realize it or not, to influence human behavior. In the past there seems to have been a tendency to rely on personal experience for design concepts rather than on research into behavioral patterns, recognizing that all people—their perceptions, behavior, and satisfactions—are not alike and are quite unlikely to have taste similar to that of the designer. We seem to have slipped into a situation in which we preconceive environmental form in terms of a designation such as a house, a park, a town square, which is already a solution, rather than a statement of a problem.[25] This prevents the examination of alternative solutions more in keeping with the specific people for whom the environment is to be designed. This does not mean that everything has to be new.

Alexander, Christopher, Sara Ishikawa, and Murray Silverstein, *A Pattern Language.*
Ardrey, Robert, *African Genesis.*
Ardrey, Robert, *The Territorial Imperative.*
Chermayeff, Sergius, and Christopher Alexander, *Community and Privacy.*
Cooper, Clare C., *Some Social Implications of House and Site Plan Design at Easter Hill Village: A Case Study.*
Craik, Kenneth, "Environmental Psychology."
Department of the Environment, *The Estate Outside the Dwelling–Reactions of Residents to Aspects of Housing Layout.*
Dubos, René, *Man Adapting.*
Dubos, René, *So Human An Animal.*
Gans, Herbert J., *The Levittowners.*
Goffman, Erving, *Behavior in Public Places.*

Valid concepts need to be separated from stylistic panaceas.

Sommer has suggested that design should be seen as the development or enclosure of space in which certain activities can take place comfortably and efficiently, in which form must not only follow function but must assist it in every way, and in which the personal expression of the architect or landscape architect must yield to the function the building or landscape serves.[26] Design and the arrangement of space and environmental elements should then, when possible, fit the individual and his needs if these are clearly understood. If the individual's needs are not understood, the design should allow sufficient flexibility and choice for the individual to modify or use the environment according to his needs when they are recognized.

25. Raymond G. Studer and David Stea, "Architectural Programming, Environmental Design and Human Behavior," *Journal of Social Issues,* XXII(4) (October 1966).
26. Sommer, *op. cit.*

Hall, Edward T., *The Hidden Dimension.*
Hall, Edward T., *The Silent Language.*
Landmark 71, "User Feedback Studies."
Lynch, Kevin, *What Time is This Place?*
Maddi, S.R., and D. W. Fiske, *Functions of Varied Experience.*
Perin, Constance, *With Man in Mind.*
Peterson, Peggy Long, "The Id and the Image."
Proshansky, H. M. (ed.), *Environmental Psychology.*
Rapoport, Amos, *House Form and Culture.*
Shepard, Paul, *Man in the Landscape.*
Skinner, B. F., *Science and Human Behavior.*
Sommer, Robert, *Personal Space.*
Taylor, (Lord) Steven J.L., and Sidney Chave, *Mental Health and the Environment.*
Whyte, William H., *The Organization Man.*

10. CLIMATE AND MICROCLIMATE

This chapter deals with climate and microclimate as factors of design in landscape architecture. We will look at them in terms of the way in which they can become determinants of form, as at Sea Ranch. In addition, we will investigate ways in which microclimate can be specifically created by design and how the use of open space may be affected by it.

CLIMATE

Climate is the net result of several interacting variables, including temperature, water vapor, wind, solar radiation, and precipitation. Like topography, vegetation, and water, climate is a major component of the environment. The ideal climate for human comfort has been defined as follows: clean air, temperature in the 50 to 80 degree Fahrenheit range, humidity between 40 and 75 percent, air which is neither stagnant nor subject to severe prevailing winds, and protection from precipitation.[1] The goal in planning and design is to achieve this ideal.

In recent years technology has made it possible to counteract adverse climates by engineering devices. Adequate heating and cooling can be provided for any structure in the desert or the arctic, but at a considerable cost, which may be prohibitive for large sections of society. Moreover, the increasing demand for power is in itself a drain on resources and a potential threat to the environment. In many places the creation of a completely artificial climate would seem

to be a desirable goal, and some large shopping centers show that this is possible. But an entirely artificial environment can be maintained only in a limited area. The smog and air pollution of urban centers would still remain a problem. Besides all this, we cannot be certain that a completely controlled climate without the stimulus of change is in itself good for our health or psychological well being. The ecological repercussions of large scale climate modification by enormous domes or through the seeding of clouds to induce rainfall in the deserts are as yet undetermined. It seems more reasonable to design with climate rather than against it, to build and plant in such a way that the favorable aspects of a climate are taken advantage of and the unfavorable aspects are anticipated and ameliorated if possible. Temperature and air flow inside and outside a building can be modified significantly by orientation and siting, construction techniques, and tree planting.

In the past dwellings were designed to counteract at least some of the disadvantages of climates in which they were situated, in order to achieve an environment of health and comfort. In the hot, moist areas of the world, ventilation is vital. The veranda hut raised on piles in the humid tropics provides protection from the rain and at the same

1. Helmut Landsberg, "The Weather in the Streets," *Landscape*, 9 (1) (Autumn 1959).

Fig. 10.1 The veranda hut of the humid tropics combines ventilation with shelter.

Fig. 10.2 Aerial view of North African town: narrow streets create shade.

Fig. 10.3 Stone house with sod roof provides insulation in cold climates.

time allows air to circulate freely under and through the structure (Fig. 10.1). In Charleston, South Carolina, verandas or shaded porches were faced in the direction of the prevailing wind. The front porch in many instances became a side porch. In hot and sunny areas such as Italy, the Mediterranean, and Southern California insulation and the need for shade are the important factors. In North African towns we find narrow streets which prevent the sun from shining down into them (Fig. 10.2). The houses of ancient Rome were essentially windowless, thick-walled structures with inner courtyards and arcades providing shaded access to the rooms (Fig. 2.10). The marketplace of the Greek and Roman cities had colonnaded covered walks to provide public areas shaded from the heat of the sun. The thick adobe walls and covered arcades of the California missions did the same. All tourists in Italy know that temperatures inside the thick stone-walled churches are refreshingly cool in the heat of summer. In cold regions as in hot the key to comfort is insulation. The walls of traditional houses in central Europe become thicker in relation to their distance from the warm-

ing influence of the Atlantic Ocean, to compensate for the colder temperatures. In Norway and elsewhere thick stone or timber walls were frequently topped with sod roofs for further insulation from a cold and wet winter climate (Fig. 10.3).

The record of modern city building and house design has tended to ignore climates. The deep canyons of central city areas are frequently sunless and draughty. The free flow of natural air movements also has at times been disrupted in places where it would bring welcome relief. It is claimed that the average wind velocity in Detroit has been reduced by about half due to the placement of large buildings. Trees are cut down where shade would be welcome. Parking lots bring light-reflecting, temperature-raising desertlike characteristics to our cities (Fig. 10.4). Just as wind velocities tend to be decreased as cities are built up, so the temperatures tend to increase. This results from the high percentage of heat-absorbing surfaces and inadequate ventilation (Fig. 10.5).

Natural landscape, on the other hand, tends to stabilize temperatures and reduce the extremes. Plants act as an absorbent material in the landscape, "blotting up" heat and light, and also, as we will see, sound. The moisture dispelled into the atmosphere through transpiration contributes to the lowering or stabilizing of temperatures. Organic surfaces reradiate less heat than do inorganic materials such as concrete. In the summer the city may be as much as 10 degrees warmer than the countryside.

To what extent should green areas be considered the "lungs of the city"? Most statistics seem to indicate that the oxygen-replenishing characteristics of green vegetation is significant only in terms of vast areas of countryside or jungle, such as the Amazon Basin. According to Erich Kuhn, the effectiveness of

Fig. 10.4 Parking lots contribute to higher temperatures in urban areas.

Fig. 10.5 Light reflecting desert–like characteristics of cities raise temperatures.

urban parks to dispose of the carbon dioxide produced in cities by heating installations, exhausts, and so on, is scarcely worth calculating.[2] He cites the opinion of Camillo Sitte that a wooded area of 3 acres could absorb only as much carbon dioxide as four human beings would produce in the course of breathing, cooking, and heating. Martin Wagner has stated that to improve the air of Berlin to any marked degree, a green area of 3 million acres would be needed[3] (Golden Gate Park in San Francisco is 1,000 acres). If trees in cities are too few in number to photosynthetically improve the oxygen supply they do serve many other important microclimatological functions, such as dust and sound absorption, wind shelter, and temperature modification.

General climatic data describing the weather patterns in states and counties are usually easily obtainable. As planners and designers rather than meteorologists, our concern is with minimums and maximums of temperature, rainfall and the distribution of precipitation, the direction, force, and frequency of prevailing winds, days of sunshine, fog, snow, and frost, and so forth. In addition, extreme weather conditions resulting in flooding or other climate-caused disasters have been recorded in most places for a fairly long period of time. Thus by using recorded local occurrences and the overall general data, a fairly accurate image of the climate of a region can be compiled.

The maximum snowfall to be expected and the maximum wind speeds are important in the design of roofs and in building construction. In landscape, the greatest amount of rainfall that can be expected over any given number of years will be a critical factor in the design of drainage systems and culverts. The cooling power of the air and the degree of discomfort caused by heat and humidity will be in-

fluential in indoor and outdoor design, indicating the need for shade, covered walkways, wind shelter planting, and so on. The selection of plant material in landscape design must take into account the climatic conditions of temperature and wind, rain and sunshine.

MICROCLIMATE

Within the general climate patterns that make Detroit different from Los Angeles, London different from Rome, and so forth, there are detailed variations or microclimates. The term microclimate refers to the scope of the area studied and not necessarily to the size of the climatic differences, which may be great within close proximity. Unlike regional climate data, microclimatic information is not readily available. Local weather bureau statistics may be useful, but these are taken for the purpose of forecasting weather and tend to be taken in relatively undisturbed areas such as airports. Measurements of wind speed and direction, temperature variation, precipitation, fog, and sunshine may have to be specially taken (as at Sea Ranch) or, with luck, a local resident may already have such records for several previous years. Depending on the importance of the judgments to be made, intuitive conclusions can be drawn from an understanding of how microclimates arise, both in nature and in the man-made environment of buildings, paving, walls, and planting.

In the landscape, topography is the major determinant of microclimate. At night cold air falls down to the lowest points, and nighttime temperatures may be as much as 10 degrees lower and the humidity 20 percent higher in a valley than on the slopes. In addition, fog may form in the valleys by morning. When the free flow of cold air is prevented by tree plantations or buildings, "frost pockets" may be

Fig. 10.6 At night temperatures may be as much as 10°F lower at (A) than at the top of the slope. In daytime the effect will be reversed.

formed at higher levels. In the daytime the conditions are reversed: the valley bottom will tend to be warmer than at the ridges swept by winds, and the humidity will be lower. Thus the ridge and valley topography accentuates extremes of temperatures. And thus valley bottoms and frost pockets would be relatively unsuited for habitation. This may be interpreted in terms of indoor heating costs and outdoor comfort. The best place to site a house would be halfway up the south-facing slopes. This location would provide the best all-round living environment for many geographic regions in the northern hemisphere (Fig. 10.6).

Water also has a warming and cooling effect. Land on the lee side of a lake or ocean will be warmer in winter and cooler in summer. It may also contribute to the humidity, depending on the general temperature pattern. The larger the body of water, the larger its impact will be on the microclimate. In warm seasons the shores of lakes and oceans benefit from a

2. Eric Kuhn, "Planning the City's Climate," *Landscape*, 8 (3) (Spring 1959).

3. *Ibid.*

daytime breeze blowing from the water to the land as part of a larger pattern of cold/warm air exchange. This has a cooling effect (Fig. 10.7).

In Chicago the offshore breeze from Lake Michigan on the hottest days of summer will tend to lower the maximum temperature by about 10 degrees on the edge of the so-called Gold Coast, but the cooling effect of this is rarely felt more than ½ mile inland. Apart from the views of the lake, there is good reason therefore for the Gold Coast to be where it is (Fig. 10.7).[4]

In Toronto measurements taken on a clear winter night showed that the temperatures gradually decreased as one moved away from the lake to a point 200 feet higher in elevation and 7 miles away, with the addition of intervening high ground. The temperature difference was 30 degrees (+15 at the lake and –15 at the inland point). Thus, even within one city, very large variations can occur. If cities were planned in terms of climate alone, they would no doubt be different from those laid out according to transportation networks or real estate operations, which, in the case of Toronto, seem to have been completely at odds with the climatic environment.[5]

Temperature can also be affected to a small degree by variations in soil. A dry soil (sand, gravel, and the like) tends to result in higher temperatures and lower humidity; wet soils, loams, and predominantly clay soils in poorly drained marshy areas tend to cause lower temperatures and higher humidities. Although they are small in magnitude, in certain situations, such as siting a house, the differences might be significant.

Plants and natural vegetation are good indicators of microclimate. For example, the day on which similar flowering trees come into bloom in a city frequently varies according to their location. This is due to differences in shelter and sunshine. The wind-clipped characteristics of trees in certain locations indicate the relative exposure of these areas to strong winds and their prevailing direction. The temperatures inside forests are usually higher at night and cooler during the day than in adjoining open land. Plants that thrive best in moist, cool situations will be found in areas of higher precipitation or north-facing slopes. It may be deduced that such areas are more moist and cooler (Fig. 11.4).

The sun is perhaps the most constant climatic factor. It is always there and, except for clouding over, its effect and seasonal change are predictable. The effect of the sun varies according to the latitude and the season, which cause changes in its intensity and the angle at which its rays strike the earth. The surface of the land or its vegetative cover and shade patterns also affect surface temperatures.

Data from Arizona indicate the temperature variations that can occur. With an air temperature of 108 degrees (160 degrees on the roof of a house), the ground temperatures varied depending on the surfaces and whether they were in the shade of a tree or not. Thus it was found that the temperature in full sun on concrete was 110, on asphalt 124, and on grass 95 degrees. In the shade the surface temperature of the concrete was 100 and that of the grass 90 degrees. At 4 feet above the ground in full sun the temperature over concrete was 96 and that over asphalt 102 degrees. The extremes were grass in shade, 90 degrees, and asphalt on its surface, 124 degrees. Even in the shade the difference between concrete and grass was 10 degrees (Fig. 10.8).[6]

As the sun appears to move during the day, so the area of shadow changes in position and extent. These dimensions can be calculated and shade patterns projected for different times of day and year

NORTH

Fig. 10.7 Land at water's edge benefits from a cooling breeze in summer and warmth in winter.

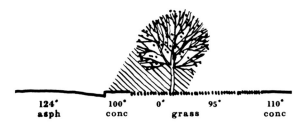

| 124° asph | 100° conc | 0° grass | 95° conc | 110° conc |

Fig. 10.8 Surface temperatures vary according to the surface and exposure.

(Fig. 10.9). The use of outdoor spaces is related to these shade patterns. Siting a tall building on the south side of an urban square in a cool summer climate puts the whole area into shade at the lunch hour, which will ensure that it is not used for eating or any other social purpose. In a hot climate a park without shade will be unusable. Natural daylighting can be modified by shade patterns cast by trees and buildings. Glare can also be reduced in this way.

4. *Architectural Forum*, 86 (March 1947).
5. *Ibid.*
6. *Ibid.*

Fig. 10.9a Azimuth angles of the sun for December and June at 38° latitude, and the degrees of altitude of the sun for the same months. (Source: Graphic Standards.)

Fig. 10.9b Extent of shadow cast by building A (50' high) and building B (30' high) in December.

Fig. 10.9c Extent of shadow cast by building A (50' high) and building B (30' high) in June.

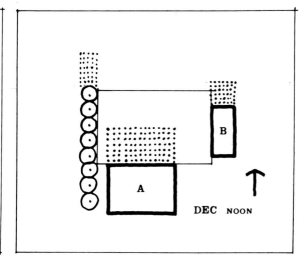

Fig. 10.9d Plan of shadows cast December, 8 a.m.

Fig. 10.9e Plan of shadows cast December, 10 a.m.

Fig. 10.9f Plan of shadows cast December, noon.

Fig. 10.9g Plan of shadows cast December, 2 p.m.

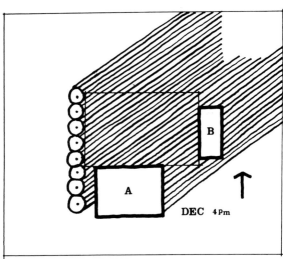

Fig. 10.9h Plan of shadows cast December, 4 p.m.

Fig. 10.9i Composite of December shadows for the day shows no part of the open space is in full sun all day.

Fig. 10.9j Composite of June shadows shows much of the open space is in full sun all day.

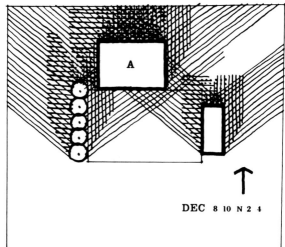

Fig. 10.9k With building (A) moved to the north side of the open space, even in December a considerable portion of it is in full sun all day.

After temperature and precipitation, perhaps the next most important aspect of weather is wind. There is a difference between the shelter offered by windbreaks composed of plants and that offered by solid screens, fences, or buildings. Solid screens tend to create a turbulence on the lee side, which reduces the extent of the shelter. By contrast, the permeability of plant material, which permits certain amounts of air to move through the screen, results in less turbulence and a greater total area of shelter. The extent of shelter from a natural windbreak depends on the degree of permeability and its height. In general, the totally sheltered zone to the leeward will probably be about thirty times the height of the shelter belt. Small reductions in wind speed may be important in erosion control and agriculture, but for human purposes it may be desirable to be more specific about the reduction in wind velocity, which is significant. If a 20 percent reduction of wind speed is taken as the criterion, then the protected zone will be between fifteen and twenty times the height of the planting. A 50 to 60 percent reduction in the original wind speed might be even more realistic in areas where strong winds prevail. In this case the area of protection would extend to only between six and nine times the height of the shelter belt. If the trees were 50 feet high, then the zone of shelter would lie between 200 and 500 feet (Fig. 10.10). The greatest shelter begins in fact a distance of four or five times the height from the belt, and the wind speed tends to be increased at the ends. There is also an area of reduced velocity on the windward side. The movement of air through and around natural windbreaks is a science. It is of extreme importance in the development of microclimates and in understanding the microclimates that may already exist on a site. The width of a shelter belt is not necessarily a variable in the amount of shelter it will provide from wind.

Air movement or winds are equally affected by buildings. Wind tunnels are important devices by which to predict the flow of air around and over buildings. Models can be tested in this way. Predicting the effects of large new buildings in the landscape and especially in cities is important if a livable street-level environment is to be maintained. Draughty corridors and wind-swept corners can be inadvertently created or, as in Detroit, the free flow of cool air as a ventilation system may be prevented by the placement of buildings and the relationships of one building to another. In cities air flow between buildings is more important than air movement around any building considered in isolation.

A series of wind tunnel experiments at the Agricultural and Mechanical College of Texas offers some generalities about the flow of wind in relation to single buildings and the degree of shelter they provide (Fig. 10.11).[7] They show that as the building gets wider, the area of shelter in fact decreases. However, as the length of the building is varied, keeping the width and height constant, the area of protection does increase. Thus the longer the building, the greater will be the eddy space or shelter zone. But the degree to which the wind is reduced is not calculated in these studies. The height is also a significant variable. The higher the building, the greater the zone of protection. The pitch of the roof can also have an effect on the shelter caused by a building. Thus the shape and form of buildings can be seen to have a distinct impact on the surrounding microclimate factor of wind, and therefore on temperature and comfort, and this in turn affects the way in which adjacent spaces may be used and should be designed and planted.

Noise pollution has become a significant environmental problem. Noise may be considered a factor of microclimate. It has been believed for some time that tree planting could reduce sound levels, but without any evidence to prove it or on which to base guidelines. Recently research has been done in Germany, where the sound-absorbent quality of specific plants has been found to vary according to leaf size and density of foliage. Other experiments have been conducted in Nebraska. Shelter belts planted as a soil conservation measure in the 1930s have been

7. Benjamin Evans, *Natural Air Flow Around Buildings* (College Station: Texas A & M College System, 1957).

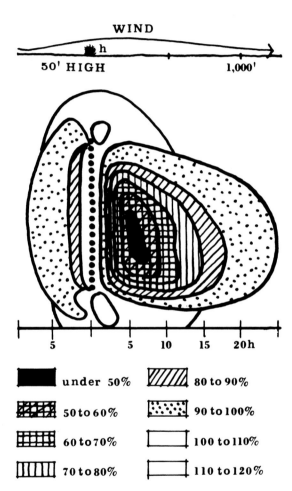

Fig. 10.10 Degree of shelter from wind expressed as a percentage of the original velocity. Dimensions are measured in multiples of the height of the windbreak. See also Fig. 6.35.

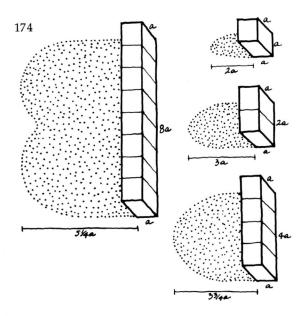

Fig. 10.11a Extent of shelter from wind provided by a building increases in proportion to its length. Based on *Natural Air Flow Around Buildings*, by Benjamin Evans (1957).

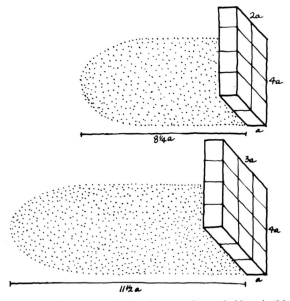

Fig. 10.11b Extent of shelter from wind provided by a building increases in proportion to its height.

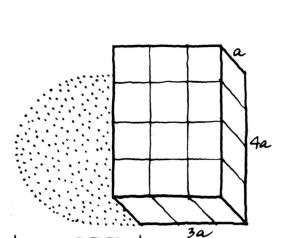

Fig. 10.11c Extent of shelter from wind provided by a building is hardly effected by its width.

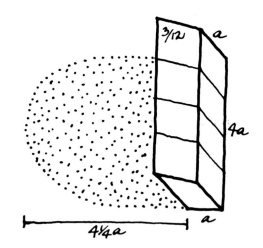

Fig. 10.11d The roof pitch of a building effects the extent of shelter from wind.

used in tests to evaluate their effectiveness in reducing sound. Many were very wide, frequently consisting of five or six rows of different tree types, often several miles in length. Studies made on the shelter belts placed noise sources on one side, and scientific measurements were taken on the other.[8]

The results showed that trees and shrubs have a high potential for absorbing sound. Reductions of sound levels (attenuations) on the order of 5 to 8 decibels were common and attenuations of 10 decibels (approximately half as loud) were not unusual for wide belts of tall, dense trees. The relative placement of noise screens between sound source and protected area is of great importance: a screen placed relatively close to a noise source is more effective than one placed close to an area to be protected. Thus plantings to screen noise from a freeway should be alongside the road. The study states that urban residential property was effectively screened from passenger car noise with a single row of dense shrubs backed by a row of taller trees totalling a depth of 20 feet. However, screening of rural areas from freeways where large trucks account for much of the noise requires wider belts consisting of several rows of tall trees in dense plantings. The sound-reducing planting belts would have to be a minimum of 100 feet in width.

Some other work has been done on the reduction of noise emanating from high-speed motorways or freeways in England. It is not concerned with the use of planting but rather with solid vertical barriers and grading. The results, summarized in Fig. 10.12, show that considerable reductions can be achieved.

Although the general climate is essentially unalter-

8. David Cook and David Haerbeke, *Trees and Shrubs for Noise Abatement* (U.S. Forest Service and University of Nebraska, 1971).

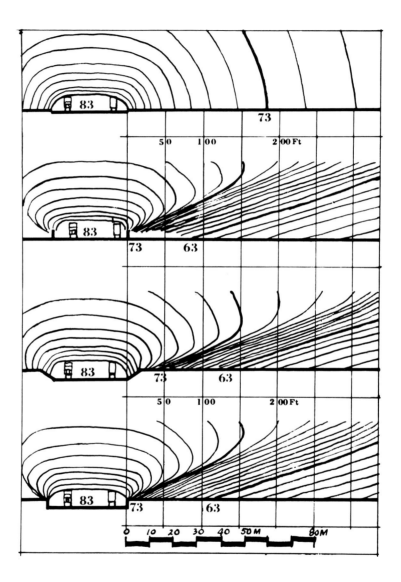

Fig. 10.12   Sound modification with physical form. Based on "Designing Against Noise from Road Traffic," Building Research Station Current Paper 20/71.

able, the climate of a specific portion of the land can be influenced easily and altered by design. Put another way, advantage can be taken of existing microclimatic variations if they are recognized. The siting of buildings to take advantage of warm conditions in winter and cool in summer is clearly an advantage, providing a more pleasant environment, permitting extended use of the outdoors, and cutting heating and cooling costs indoors. Landscape design and planting, careful siting, and architectural design combine in the development of a livable microclimate. The use of outdoor areas is affected by wind and shade, noise and temperature. These are critical indices of environmental quality.

Suggested Readings

Architectural Forum, "Microclimatology," March 1947, pp. 116–119.

Building Research Station, Current Paper 20/71, "Designing Against Noise from Road Traffic."

Caborn, James M., *Shelterbelts and Windbreaks*.

Cook, David, and David F. Haerbeke, *Trees and Shrubs for Noise Abatement*.

Dickinson, Jim, *New Housing and Traffic Noise*.

Eckbo, Garrett, *Art of Home Landscaping*, pp. 18–23.

Geiger, Rudolf, *The Climate Near the Ground*.

Olgay, Victor, *Design with Climate*, pp. 1–23, "General Introduction", pp. 44–53, "Site Selection," pp. 74–77, "Shading Effects of Trees and Vegetation."

Fig. 10.13   50' hedges of pine shelter farmsteads against winter winds and snowstorms in Shimani prefecture, western Japan.

11. PLANTS AND PLANTING DESIGN

Why should plants have such symbolic and aesthetic importance in our lives, in parks and gardens, window boxes and pots? It is not surprising that primitive man and early civilizations held plants in esteem. Indeed plant forms have been used in architectural decoration since ancient times (Fig. 11.1). Beyond their obvious value as food, fiber, and building materials, plants were the very essence of life, exhibiting growth and reproduction. The major religious faiths described paradise gardens at the beginning of time or at the end of life. Specific plants assumed symbolic significance in various cultures. Certain trees were sacred, and tree worship was perhaps the first form of religion. Trees were thus symbols of fertility, long life, knowledge, and temptation. The lotus was the symbol of upper Egypt, and the fig tree was honored and worshipped by the peasants for its wood, fruit, and shade. The olive, vine, date palm, acacia, and avocado similarly were imbued with symbolic significance. A more recent example is the rowan or mountain ash, which is found in almost every old Scottish garden and gardens of Scots overseas. It was believed to be capable of warding off evil spirits. Similarly, the lilac seems to have a traditional and symbolic place in American gardens.

The evolution of more sophisticated religions, the urbanization of society, and the development of an agriculture industry has changed the intimate relationship between plants and people which existed up to the nineteenth century. We are now unlikely to eat the food we see growing in the local fields, and we are even less likely to be treated for illness with potions made from medicinal herbs grown in our gardens. Today we are left with a somewhat inexplicable and apparently irrational love for plants and trees, which seems to have grown out of our heritage and belongs perhaps to our animal origins and instincts. Thus we legislate the preservation of trees, protest the removal of ancient oaks and chestnuts, and allocate public funds to preserve the last virgin stands of redwoods. In Britain the second most popular adult leisure occupation, according to a recent study, is gardening. In recent years the popularity of indoor plants indicates even more the intensity of our need to nurture and cultivate plants and to watch growth. We are also fascinated with plants in composition with topography and have designated landscapes as areas of outstanding natural beauty, and we go and admire these as though they were paintings. In recent times some scientists, although notably not biologists, have imbued plants

Fig. 11.1 Ancient Egyptian columns. Capital detailing derived from (a) palm leaf, (b) lotus bud, and (c) papyrus bud.

with feelings similar to but of a lower order than an- imals'. Other people feel anthropomorphically about plants and would take to criminal court those responsible for the deaths of large trees due to care- less construction.

As landscape architects, we come heir to this tra- ditional and changing involvement with plants. We are preceded by a long line of distinguished planters for profit and pleasure; and these have not always been mutually exclusive objectives. In the seven- teenth century John Evelyn recommended that En- glish gentlemen should replant their estates to re- plenish the diminishing supply of oak for shipbuilding.[1] In the eighteenth century the English landscape garden included the entire agricultural scene as an important aspect of the concept (Fig. 2.36). In both cases the adornment of the landscape with copses and hedgerows of oak and beech provided a source of valuable timber at a later date. More recently there have been conflicts between profit and pleasure. In England some consider the use of faster growing coniferous species suitable for shorter term forestry alien to the character of the English landscape. Another potential conflict in agriculture lies in the trend toward larger fields suited for modern machin- ery and more efficient production, which will alter the characteristic and loved pattern of small irregular en- closures, hedgerows, and woods in Europe and on the East Coast of the United States. Lumbering practices in the forests of the United States have also begun to conflict with Federal agencies' interest in their use for recreation.

The nineteenth-century planters J. C. Loudon, William Robinson, and Gertrude Jekyll developed

1. John Evelyn, *Sylva* (London: J. Martyn, 1664).

the art of planting design using the wide variety of trees, shrubs, and herbaceous plants which became available as a result of world-wide botanical expedi- tions and plant breeding. Planting for aesthetic ef- fect and pleasure thus reached its zenith in the late nineteenth and early twentieth century, being sup- ported and maintained by numerous trained and skilled gardeners. Horticultural societies, flower shows, and the horticultural industry grew and thrived on the intense interest and zeal of plant en- thusiasts from all walks of life.

Before discussing specific uses of plants in design, we must deal with the problem of organizing the enormous amount of material available for use. To do this plants are considered in terms of six classifi- cations: (1) ecology; (2) botany; (3) horticulture; (4) aesthetic values; (5) growth and survival of plants; and (6) use of plants in design.

ECOLOGICAL COMMUNITIES

The distribution of species—that is, where plants are found naturally—is a function of their genetically established tolerance range. This corresponds with the range of environmental conditions which allows the growth and reproduction of a given species if the seeds or spores are present. Temperature, water, and soil are the major limiting factors to plant distri- bution. The mosaic of vegetation which results is a response to overall world-wide general limiting fac- tors and, at a smaller scale, to local variations in growing conditions: river banks, hot dry slopes, moist woodlands, and so on. Each plant has a natu- ral range (Figs. 11.2 to 11.7; see also Fig. 6.10).

In nature we find minute alpine plants and enor- mous trees, creeping plants, herbaceous perennials and annuals, those with long life spans and short,

those which can withstand drought and desert con- ditions and those which thrive best in marshland or rain forest, those which can tolerate frost and those which cannot. The greatest variety exists in the trop- ics; the least in the arctic.

Native or indigenous plants are those associated with specific regions. In general, they are likely to have the closest fit in their own regions and should be selected for use whenever possible and desirable. Plants can be classified by natural communities, which usually include the whole range of plant types from trees to herbaceous. Thus we talk of the oak/ maple community, the redwood forest community (Fig. 11.8), and so on. Each consists of a characteris- tic series of plants in tree, shrub, and groundcover layers.

The plants we use are not new, but their use in design requires them to be located, propagated, and made available in commercial quantities. Plant selec- tion and breeding have produced some genetic var- iations not found in nature. These cultivars and var- ieties have been developed in greatest profusion in flowering plants such as roses, chrysanthemums, and dahlias. It is possible also to "design" street trees according to an ideal specification of size, dur- ability, leaves, and so forth. The Modesto ash and the thornless honey locust are examples of specially bred improved varieties for street tree planting.

BOTANICAL NOMENCLATURE

The botanical classification orders the mass of plant material into families, genera, species, and varieties according to similarities in flower, fruit, leaf, and so on. Thus the Fagacea family includes the genera oak (*Quercus*), beech (*Fagus*), and alder (*Al- nus*). This taxonomy is useful in tracking down un-

Fig. 11.2 The geographical range of Red Spruce (picea Rubens). (Based on Silvics of Forest Trees of the United States Agricultural Handbook No. 271, U.S. Department of Agriculture, Forest Service, 1965.) Distribution is related to temperature range, soil type, rainfall and elevation above sea level. Red spruce attains maximum development in the higher parts of the Southern Appalachian Mountains, where the atmosphere is more humid and the rainfall heavier during the growing season than in other parts of its range.

The largest existing forested area lies in the Great Smokey Mountains National Park where all sites above 4,500' (1600 M) which are not occupied by beech or heath are occupied by forests of red spruce and fraser fir. (Shelford, Victor E., "The Ecology of North America", 1965)

Fig. 11.3 Local variations in soil, temperature and moisture result in a mosaic of vegetation within the generalized range of a particular species. Thus, we find in the headwaters of the Little Pigeon River in the Great Smokey Mountains National Park that there is a tendency for tulip/oak to be in the deep valleys and on north-facing slopes, whereas red spruce is found on south-facing slopes and a higher altitude. Oak/chestnut occurs on south-facing slopes of broad valleys (Shelford). (Map based on F. H. Miller, 1941, U.S. National Park Service.)

Fig. 11.5 Vaca Mountains, California. A low rainfall area (15″). Soil and moisture must be exactly right for tree growth. Warm south slopes are bare. Heavier vegetation of blue oak and digger pine clothe the cooler northern slopes.
Photograph by R. Burton Litton, Jr.

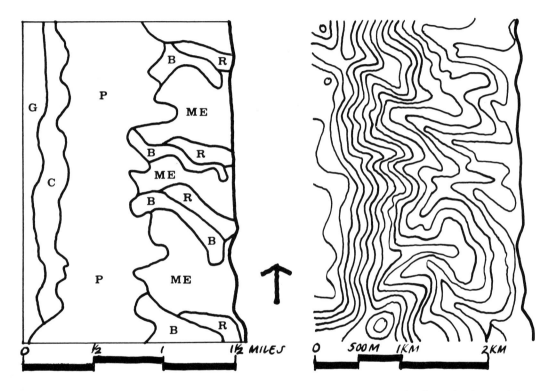

Fig. 11.4 Distribution of vegetation at Inverness, California. The wind–swept ridge is covered with grassland (G) and chapparral (C). The higher slopes with shallow sandy soil are covered with Pine (P). The north–facing, moisture–retaining slopes favor California Bay (B) and riparian vegetation including alder and willow occupy the valleys. Introduced planting dominates the built–up residential areas (M.E.)

Fig. 11.6 Grand Teton Range, Jackson Lake, Wyoming. Vegetation mosaic related to soil type. Lodgepole pine prefers the coarse, highly drained soils of glacial morraines. Sagebrush grows on the finer soil of the alluvial flats.
Photograph by R. Burton Litton, Jr.

Fig. 11.7 Desert conditions of climate and soil are extremely restrictive and support a specialized flora.
Photograph by R. Burton Litton, Jr.

Fig. 11.8 Despite deep shade cast by a redwood forest, it contains other species in a "community": California laurels, Pacific madrone and alders may be found mixed with the redwoods. The forest understory might include vine maple, rhododendron and vaccineum. A low growing broad-leafed shrub layer might include seedlings of understory trees, big leaf maple, hazel, and California blackberry and bracken. A herb layer frequently includes redwood sorrel.
Photograph by R. Burton Litton, Jr.

known species within flora. It also gives plants universal Latin names which are the same the world over and therefore useful in specifications. They are more reliable than common names, which vary from place to place. For example, the genus *Liriodendron tulipifera*, of the Magnoliaceae family, is known in some places as the tulip tree and in others as the yellow poplar.

HORTICULTURAL TYPES

The horticulturist uses botanical nomenclature but classifies plants essentially by form into trees, shrubs, herbaceous and annual plants, groundcovers, and vines. This is a useful breakdown of the plant kingdom for landscape architecture and design. In briefly reviewing each type, mention of certain design implications will be inevitable.

Groundcovers are defined as low-growing, prostrate, surface-covering plants which can be used for erosion control on slopes or to make a pattern to be seen from above, as in a parterre. As a surface, such plants—provided they have low maintenance needs—are cheaper than concrete or paving. They absorb heat, moisture, and dust, and control erosion. Groundcovers vary in form, leaf size, color, and texture (Figs. 11.9 and 11.10). Low, creeping plants like fragaria or ajuga spread close to the ground. Prostrate plants like juniper grow taller and spread farther to shade out and cover the ground with dense foliage. Low-growing dense shrubs like hypericum do the same job, but with a different visual effect.

Fig. 11.9 Juniper used as a ground cover.

Fig. 11.10 Hypericium used as a ground cover.

Fig. 11.12   Privet hedges at Radburn.

Fig. 11.13   Strong planting of elms in Chicago. Being deciduous, their form changes seasonally.

Fig. 11.11   Shrubs forming a visual and physical separation.

Shrubs range from approximately 3 to 10 feet in height, are defined as woody plants, and are often multistemmed and low branching (Figs. 11.11 and 11.12, also 12.2, 12.3). Low-growing shrubs can be arranged to divide space at ground level, a physical separation rather than a visual one. Larger shrubs growing above eye level will define space. Plants with thorns can increase the physical effect of shrubs planted as barriers to separate areas. Shrubs may be grown in their natural form for flowers and fruit or, on the other hand, may be clipped or pruned into shape. Hedges are the result of clipping shrubs, achieving strict divisions of various heights and textures within a limited space (like a fence). Some plants are more adaptable to making hedges than others. Dense branching and foliage such as those of cypressus and privet are excellent. The possible height of the hedge depends on the plant selected.

Trees are defined as having a single stem and growing to a height greater than 10 feet (Figs. 11.13 to 11.15). They are subdivided into deciduous (for example, liquidambar, London plane), broad-leaved evergreen (southern magnolia, camphor), and coniferous (Scots pine, cedar). Broad-leaved evergreens tend to cast year-round and denser shade than deciduous trees. They are therefore most suitable for hotter climates. Trees allowed to grow to maturity will occupy a considerable amount of space, the actual height and spread depending on the species. The rate of growth varies according to the tree and the environmental conditions. It is especially true of conifers that as they grow, so their form may change. Since even the fastest growing tree will take some time to reach full size, tree planting may be done in two stages. Close planting to encourage upward growth may be specified first with the intention of thinning to one or two specimens at a later date. This concept is expressive of the dynamic nature of landscape architecture.

In recent years moving large, established trees to achieve a more mature effect quickly has become popular (Fig. 11.16). This is not a new idea: there

Fig. 11.14 Camphor trees, a medium–sized broad leafed evergreen.

were tree-moving machines in the nineteenth century. The technique is widely used today with a high rate of success. Small to medium sized trees can be dug up on a site, boxed for a few years, and returned after a project has been completed. Soil preparation is extremely important, as are various techniques for preventing transpiration during the moving procedure. It should be recognized, however, that the growth of such moved trees will probably be retarded because of root damage. The tree will take a few years to adapt. In areas where growth is fast, it may be just as effective to plant vigorous young trees in the first place. This will also allow us to watch the early rapid growth of the tree, which in itself is peculiarly satisfying and educational.

Some vines need support, others twine or cling. Combined with an overhead structure, vines can provide delightful shaded areas (Fig. 11.17). The walls of buildings can be covered for insulation and to reduce glare. Wire fences can be transformed into green fences. Many vines, like clematis, have con-

Fig. 11.15 Canary pines makes a strong vertical statement.

Fig. 11.16 Mature tree being replanted.

Fig. 11.17 Vines provide a shaded roof terrace in Italy.

Fig. 11.18 Classic English mixed flowers border at Sissinghurst.

spicuous flowers, others are leafy evergreen or deciduous types. Grapes may be grown in suitable climates.

Herbaceous plants and bulbs, herbs, and annuals are usually grown for their flowers, although many also have attractive foliage. Almost everybody likes flowers, and they are planted for pleasure. The work and labor involved in planting and properly maintaining the herbaceous border of the nineteenth and early twentieth centuries have made this form of gardening and use of herbaceous plants almost impossible from an economic point of view (Fig. 11.18). In addition, the modern designer's obsession with sculpture and form in the 1940s and 1950s relegated herbaceous flowers to the enthusiast's private yard. "Bedding out" brings welcome relief to shopping areas and places of civic importance (Fig. 11.19).

Flowers should be seen close up and with simple backgrounds. Seats should be placed close to raised flower beds or boxes (Figs. 11.20 and 11.21). Containers are popular in Northern Europe where the winters are long and flowers are an especially welcome relief in the summer. In Stockholm planting in the public places is replaced overnight from municipal greenhouses, so that there is no time when the containers are empty. Window boxes are standard elements of every apartment (Fig. 5.15).

AESTHETICS AND DESIGN

Thus far we have seen that plants come in a variety of shapes, sizes, and types and that their natural distribution is related to environmental factors. Now let us turn to more precise criteria for the selection of plants in design. Our fourth consideration in landscape design is the aesthetic attributes of plants. There are many variables, including leaf and flower, their color and size, shape and texture, the form of

Fig. 11.19 Flowers in containers can be restocked or removed when out of bloom.

the whole plant, and seasonal variation (Fig. 11.22). These are some of the visual qualities that can combine in design.

FITNESS

The fifth consideration used in the selection of plants concerns conditions and requirements for their growth and survival. In addition to the selection of plants suitable on the basis of these criteria, clearly planting conditions and subsequent maintenance are also critical for survival and healthy development.

To ensure their survival, plants must be chosen with an understanding of their growth requirements, tolerances, or preferences of soil and climate and, of course, an understanding of the principles of vegetative growth in general. The real world compared with the nursery environment from which new plants come is a hard place with varied conditions of light, water supply, soils, and bugs. Once

Fig. 11.20 Seating placed in relation to flowers and both set off the beaten track in the foreground. Copenhagen.

Fig. 11.21 Seats and flowers. Copenhagen.

Fig. 11.23 Plastic plants.

Fig. 11.22 Gunera Manicata.

Fig. 11.24 A large single tree defines space.

planted in a project, the plant must adapt to the new conditions. The soil provides support for the plant and a reservoir of water and nutrients. Excessive compaction of the soil makes root growth difficult, and lack of certain minerals in impoverished soils of urban areas restricts growth. Waterlogged conditions and badly drained soils will kill most plants or impair normal growth. Water is extremely important and must be available naturally or by regular and deep irrigation.

Wind is an environmental factor most plants are sensitive to although some are more tolerant than others. For example, liquidambar is vulnerable to wind, whereas Monterey cypress can tolerate not only wind but also the salt spray of the sea. Evergreens are typically susceptible to soot and dust, which clog the pores through which the plant transpires. Deciduous trees, which produce new leaves each season, can survive better. Light is also obviously a critical factor, since photosynthesis takes place only in the presence of sunlight. Some plants, however, are better adapted to shade conditions than others, due to their evolution in the understory of a natural forest. Temperature is also critical and freezing is a clear cut-off point. From freezing up to 80 degrees is the most favorable temperature range, but some plants require lower and higher temperatures. Altitude, latitude, and geomorphology delineate natural growth zones. Reflected heat or glare from walls and pavement can also cause leaf burn.

Maintenance after planting is extremely important and has a strong bearing on plant selection. There are four main considerations. The first is water:

plants must have it to grow and in dry regions there must be periodic irrigation of nonnative plants. Drainage is also important and soil must not be allowed to become waterlogged. The second need is a program of fertilization that will provide nutrients in poor soils to stimulate growth and the establishment of plants. Third, weed control is essential to avoid competition for the moisture and nutrients intended for the selected plants. Control is effected by hoeing or by preemergent weed killers. Finally, pruning is important in terms of the ultimate form of trees and shrubs, the quality and development of hedges, grass and lawns, and so on. Pruning is a skill which helps to maintain the form of the tree or shrub but reduces the amount of foliage and shade. In fruit trees, of course, it is essential to productivity, and in flowering plants it is critical in the production of blossom (e.g., roses).

Some plants need less maintenance than others. Watering can be reduced for native plants once established. Pruning is not needed for some plants. Grass needs regular cutting, whereas most groundcovers do not. Quick-growing, spreading plants will reduce the amount of weeding necessary. Thus the maintenance factor and associated costs should be carefully evaluated in the selection of plants for functional or aesthetic reasons. Plastic plants may seem to be the ideal answer to the maintenance problem; no water, no fertilizer, no pruning, only an occasional light dusting (Fig. 11.23). Yet the public outrage in Los Angeles over the installation of plastic trees and shrubs on a highway median strip demonstrates that people are not yet as insensitive as some bureaucrats seem to think.

Our sixth and last concern is selecting plants to perform some design purpose or function. The process is complex, combining all the objective preferences of soil, water, temperature, and other factors, with a clear understanding of the problem to be solved with the planting (Fig. 11.28). First, then, the purpose of the planting must be clearly defined. Plants should never be used to fill leftover spaces; their positioning and selection should result from and be part of the solution to a design problem. Plants are material just as paving is and can be used according to much the same principles. Just as with paving, maintenance and replacement costs are additional considerations.

Plants can be used to give form and quality to a design. Used formally and volumetrically they can structure space as effectively as architectural forms. Shrub plantings and hedges can define areas like the walls of a room, enclosing space and screening out unwanted views. Spreading trees or vines on trellises can give a canopy or ceiling effect (Fig. 11.24). Both provide a delightful tracery of cast shadows. Plants can articulate space into outdoor rooms, and the use of plant texture and color can be manipulated to produce a variety of environmental qualities. At Villandry, plants are clipped into "architectural" forms and arranged to enclose large open spaces (Fig. 11.25). Hedges of yew at Sissinghurst are as precise as walls and create background textured surfaces for flowering plants (Fig. 11.26). Hawthorns in Chicago's Lakeside Park, planted close together, form an "architectural" tunnel from within and strong linear form seen from outside (Fig. 11.27). The elms in the same park enclose or define

Fig. 11.25 Villandry. Clipped limes provide strong architectural definition.

Fig. 11.26 Yew hedges at Sissinghurst define space as precisely as the walls of a room.

Fig. 11.27 Gothic tunnel of Hawthorn, Chicago.

PLANT MATERIALS SELECTION SYSTEM

Plant Data Coding Form

Department of Landscape Architecture
University of California, Berkeley
Russell A. Beatty, Assistant Professor
Thomas G. Dickert, Assistant Professor   November 1971

INSTRUCTIONS CARDS 1–3:

1. Leave cols. 1–4 and 72–80 blank.
2. For those columns noted "see CODING LIST", use the coding descriptors as applicable (enter 1 to 7). For those descriptors not applicable enter 0.
3. For all other columns enter 1 if descriptor is applicable to plant; if not applicable, enter 0.
4. Sources: For each descriptor used (other than 0) a reference letter and page number should be provided in adjacent box. Letters should be recorded as listed in the Plant Bibliography. Example: A-23 refers to reference A, page number 23.

CARD 1—Functional Characteristics

see Coding List

PLANT TYPE — **POTENTIAL USES** — **DISTINGUISHING CHARACTERISTICS** — **GENERAL GROWTH DATA** — **FOLIAGE**

Col	Descriptor
1–4	Plant Number
5	Tree
6	Shrub
7	Vine
8	Herbaceous
9	Annual
10	Bulb, etc.
11	Fern
12	Palm
13	Cactus-succulent
14	Grass
15	Erosion/bank control
16	Groundcover
17	Windbreak
18	Physical barrier
19	Hedge
20	Screen
21	Street tree
22	Container
23	Fire resistant
24	Deer resistant
25	Espalier
26	Grove
27	Canopy
28	Bark
29	Emphatic
30	Fall color
31	Flowers
32	Fruit
33	Foliage
34	Fragrance
35	General plant form
36	Seeds
37	Thorns
38	Winter effect
39	Seasonal character
40	Form
41	Form (cont)
42	Habit
43	Habit (cont)
44	Texture
45	Min. height range
46	Min. height (cont)
47	Max. height range
48	Max. height (cont)
49	Min. spread range
50	Min. spread (cont)
51	Max. spread range
52	Max. spread (cont)
53	Growth rate
54	Longevity
55	Longevity (cont)
56	Bark
57	Foliage density
58	Foliage color
59	Foliage color (cont)
60	Leaf surface
76	Card number
72–80	blank

CARD 2

see Coding List

FLOWER — **FRUIT** — **PROBLEMS** — **PESTS** — **DISEASE** — **PROPAGATION**

Col	Descriptor
1	Flower significance
2	Flower color
3	Flower color (cont)
4	Begin bloom
5	Begin bloom (cont)
6	End bloom
7	End bloom (cont)
8	Fruit significance
9	Fruit color
10	Fruit begin
11	Fruit begin (cont)
12	Fruit end
13	Fruit end (cont)
14	Short-lived
15	Short-rooted
16	Voracious roots
17	Brittle
18	Dirty
19	Thorns
20	Poisonous
21	Unpleasant odors
22	Aphids
23	Scale Insects
24	Mites
25	Borers
26	Leaf miners
27	Caterpillars
28	Leaf chewing beetles
29	Deer
30	Rabbits
31	Oak root fungus
32	Powdery mildew
33	Verticilium wilt
34	Fireblight
35	Anthracnose
36	Rusts
37	Chlorosis
38	Cuttings
39	Division
40	Layering
41	Seeds
42	Spores
43	Grafting
44	Rhizomes
45	Runners
73	Blank
76	Card number

the larger spaces of the design, separating roadways from the green lawns (Fig. 11.13). The classic avenue is another example of the use of planting to structure space and direct attention and movement through the landscape. Depending on the scale, the sense of division or enclosure of space with trees is inferred rather than actual, whereas hedges and shrubberies tend to produce physical and visual barriers (Fig. 8.19). In the regional landscape, forest clearings are spatially defined by the trees (Fig. 8.18).

Plants can be used in design to emphasize circulation and give information about a place. Planting can be situated and designed to indicate edges, to accent junctions, to emphasize directional lines, or to act as a physical barrier. At the city scale, street tree planting can give identity to areas or to major streets or routes. The boulevards of Paris or any of the Beaux Arts civic developments demonstrate the use of trees to emphasize city form. The changes in natural variations in vegetation around a pond provide an excellent ecological indicator of edge from which principles for more designed situations may be derived.

Fig. 11.28 Card 1 and 2 of a 4-card computer plant material selection system. All the characteristics of plants are listed, including their tolerances and growth requirements, maintenance problems and needs, size, rate of growth and design potential. The retrieval system provides the designer with a selection of plants which correspond to his specification. System developed by Professor Russell A. Beatty, assisted by Professor Thomas G. Dickert, Department of Landscape Architecture, University of California, Berkeley (1972).

Fig. 11.29 Ivy planted to control erosion on a highway embankment.

Erosion control is an extremely important function of plants. They hold together soil with their root structure, thus preventing it from being washed away down banks or causing landslides. Another function of the plant is to prevent the rainfall from falling with its full force on bare ground. By reducing the rate of runoff, planting contributes to the conservation of moisture and the replenishment of groundwater resources. Turf, ivy, and native vegetation are excellent for this purpose (Fig. 11.29).

Another important functional use of plants is in microclimate control. At Sea Ranch and Cumbernauld we have seen the importance of tree belts to break the wind and provide areas of shelter, originally for crops and livestock, later for houses and schools when the use of the land changes. Fine-leaved trees help to diffuse the wind. Conifers are especially suitable (but they must also be wind tolerant) and mixtures of small and large trees in multiple rows are especially effective (Fig. 10.10).[2] Tem-

peratures can be affected also by the shade cast by trees in warm climates (Fig. 10.8). In addition, the transpiration of water vapor from plants may in the quantity of a forest have an additional cooling effect. The seasonal shading characteristic of deciduous trees is particularly important in places with hot summers and cold winters. Plants are also beneficial to some degree in keeping the air fresh and the level of pollution down. Certain types of plant are well suited to catch dust by virtue of their texture and form. As we have seen, noise can be controlled by planting if the scale is large enough. To all these "air conditioning" effects may be added the possibility of providing agreeable scents, albeit this is a temporary effect. Nicotiana and other plants such as *Viburnum fragrans* can be selected especially for this attribute. The smell of orange blossom on a hot night in the Imperial Valley of California is memorable.

Gardening and landscape design need not simply involve the solving of "problem areas"; they should be rich and joyous, intricate, and interesting. Thus one final point to be made concerns the process of simplification which has occurred in the agricultural landscape and which now afflicts the domestic landscape. To some extent this is the result of a misinterpretation of modern landscape architecture. The designers and the nurserymen and the magazines have influenced new gardens and parks, housing developments, and industrial estates to such an extent that they all tend to look alike. The variety of plant material that exists is essentially unused and is becoming restricted in design to a limited number of well-tried favorites.

2. J. M. Caborn, *Shelter Belts and Windbreaks* (London: Faber and Faber, 1965).

In summary, the selection of plants is concerned with the following questions: Will the plant grow and survive? Will it do the job intended? Will it require low maintenance? Will it add delight and quality? And are the plants commercially available on the market?

Suggested Readings

Buckman, Harry O., and Nyle C. Brady, *The Nature and Properties of Soils*, pp. 1–15, "The Soil in Perspective."

Colvin, Brenda, and Jacqueline Tyrwhitt, *Trees for Town and Country*.

Gardner, Victor R., *Basic Horticulture*, pp. 13–23, 81–150.

Robbins, Wilfred W., T. Eliot Weier, and C. Ralph Stocking, *Botany, An Introduction to Plant Science*, pp. 9–12, "Sub-divisions of Botany," pp. 61–71, "Physiology of the Cells," pp. 172–183, "Soil and Mineral Nutrition," pp. 202–214, "Photosynthesis and Respiration," pp. 303–322, "The Plant as a Living Mechanism."

Robinette, Gary O., *Plants, People and Environmental Quality*.

Robinson, Florence Bell, *Palette of Plants*.

Robinson, Florence Bell, *Planting Design*.

Weddle, A. E., ed., *Techniques of Landscape Architecture*, pp. 176–193, "Tree Planting," by Brenda Colvin.

Fig. 11.30   Photograph by William A. Garnett.

12. LANDSCAPE ENGINEERING

Grading or landscape engineering is a fundamental technical aspect of landscape architecture concerned with the development of the site plan into three-dimensional reality. It involves the remodeling of existing land form to facilitate the functions and circulation of the site plan. Thus a knowledge of grading technology is useful in the site planning process. Grading is the adjustment and connection of given or required levels. Detailed leveling is needed to make connections between architecture and landscape, between indoors and out (Figs. 12.1 to 12.3).

The site-to-structure relationship is a visual as well as a functional matter. The floor levels of build-ings should be higher than the surrounding ground. Surfaces adjacent to and outside buildings should also slope away from the building so that rain water will not easily enter the structures or undermine foundations.

The aesthetic aspects of grading can be seen at Foothill College (Chapter Seven). The original landscape was extensively reshaped to fit the buildings and open space into buildable and usable land. The sensitivity with which this was done resulted in a landscape that did not look as though it had been remodeled. Buildings were set well back from the edge of the hill, permitting them to sit comfortably on level ground (Figs. 7.8, 7.9, and 7.10).

There are two principal relationships between buildings and land. The land may be graded or adjusted to suit the architectural or engineering requirements, or the architecture may be adapted to meet variations in ground level so that the original surface is disturbed less (Fig. 12.4). Buildings that stand on pilotti and do not touch the ground at all require little grading except to provide access. The land will be disturbed to some extent during construction and will have changed light and moisture factors under the structure. On the other hand, construction that assumes conventional foundations results in a building-to-ground relationship all around the structure. Single-level houses on steep hillsides

Fig. 12.1 Grading is the connection of given or required levels. A house with two floor levels with indoor/outdoor relationships from each.

Fig. 12.2 The change in level is hidden by planting.

Fig. 12.3 Steps connect the two levels.

191

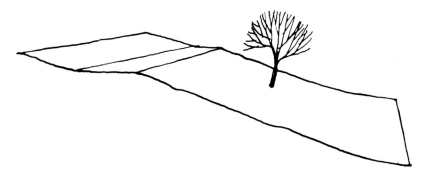

Fig. 12.4a A sloping site.

Fig. 12.4c A single storey house set on conventional foundations requires considerable cut and fill resulting in steeper slopes at each side of the lot.

Fig. 12.4b A single storey house set on stilts leaves the ground relatively undisturbed. The tree can be saved.

Fig. 12.4d A split–level house with retaining walls maintains shallow slopes at each side of the lot and the tree can be saved. The house is closely related to the form of the landscape.

require extensive cut and fill grading, eliminating the original soil relationship. Psychologically, there is perhaps more satisfaction in a house or a building being directly on and related to solid land; but ecologically it may seem better to disturb the land as little as possible. A bulldozer may be thought of as an extension of the primitive digging stick of earlier times. Being on the earth, dug into it, is probably a positive urge and need. Yet the crudeness with which the land is frequently terraced in hillside sub-

divisions may lead to unstable conditions resulting in erosion, landslides, floods, and a complete destruction of the ecosystem (Fig. 6.6 and 12.5). The appropriate way to site buildings depends on a careful analysis of the land, its slope, soil, geology, and so on. In addition, the initial decision to build in any area should result from land suitability studies (Chapter Six), so that truly destructive processes can be prevented or special construction techniques instituted to match the conditions.

THE PRINCIPLES AND TECHNOLOGY OF GRADING

Let us now proceed to the more conventional problems in which buildings and use areas are sited on suitable land and in which the site plan essentially creates a new and working landscape to replace the existing "natural" condition. The technology of grading represents a unique skill of landscape architecture and is connected with the process of placing

Fig. 12.5 Graded and leveled building sites on hilly terrain, Los Angeles (1955). Photograph by William A. Garnett.

the diagram of the site plan onto a given topographical landscape. Our concern is not only with fitting or connecting buildings to the land but also with siting use areas such as playing fields, parking lots, and circulation routes. All of these have specific criteria for slope, foundation depth, and drainage.

Landscape engineering is concerned with economical development and with sensitivity to the existing conditions. The basic principles and goals of grading may be summarized as follows.

1. The ground surface must be suitable for the intended purpose or use.

2. The visual result should be pleasing; indeed the purpose of the grading may be purely aesthetic, to screen views or create symbolic land form.

3. The resulting ground surface must have positive drainage.

4. The grading plan should attempt to keep the new levels as close as possible to the original state of the land. In nonurban areas especially, existing landscape represents an ecological balance, a natural drainage system, and a developed soil profile.

5. When ground is reshaped it should be done positively and at the scale of the machinery. Grading machinery is by definition gross in nature and subtle details are difficult to achieve except by hand labor.

6. Topsoil should be conserved wherever possible. It may be stripped, stockpiled, and reused after heavy grading.

7. In the grading operation, the quantity of cut should approximately equal the amount of fill. This eliminates the need to import soil or to find a place to dump unwanted material.

Grading plans are technical documents and are instruments by which we show and calculate changes to the three-dimensional surface of the land (Fig.

12.13). Contour lines are used to indicate the extent of that change. Depending on the scale, contours show relative elevation at intervals of 1 foot, 5 feet, or more. Existing contours are shown as dashed lines. The proposed new land form is shown by solid lines drawn where this varies from the existing form. The difference between these lines shows where land is to be cut and where filled and, in general, the extent and nature of the change. Such drawings, showing two sets of contour lines, express the difference between the existing condition and the design intent. From these drawings quantities of cut and fill can be calculated. The plans must be accurate if calculations and therefore cost estimates are to be reliable.

Grading and site planning take care of the adjustment necessary between fixed levels and structures within the boundaries of the site. Such fixed or control elevations include the levels of existing trees or vegetation to be retained, existing and proposed buildings and roads, the levels at the boundary of the site, existing land forms to be included in the design, lakes and natural swales, existing and proposed underground utilities. Such levels constrain the reshaping possibilities.

The terminology of the grading plan is simple. *Contour lines* are abstractions which join all points of the same elevation above a fixed datum. *Spot elevations* provide additional information beyond that given by the contour lines. They indicate micrograding; that is, specific levels that lie between the intervals of the contour lines. They show level differences needed to ensure drainage on "flat" surfaces and to indicate specific levels at important points in the plan. Typical locations at which spot elevations are shown are at tops and bottoms of steps, tops of retaining walls, outside entrances to buildings and their inside floor elevations.

Another term frequently used is *grade* or *gradient*. This refers to the rate of slope between two points, expressed as a percentage, or as a ratio of horizontal distance to vertical change in elevation, or as an angle. Thus a 1% slope is the same as 100–1. A 10% slope is the same as 10–1 or a 6° angle. A 50% slope is the same as 2–1 or a 26°30' angle, and a 100% slope is 1–1 or a 45° angle. Key variables in figuring gradients are the horizontal distance between two points and the vertical change in elevation.

Frequently the surface has to be changed to provide some specific gradient or to fit into some maximum or minimum slope criteria. The process of developing a grading plan involves the manipulation of the three factors: *gradient (G)*, *horizontal distance (L)*, and *difference in elevation* between two points *(D)*. If, for example, the existing G between two points 100 feet apart is too great for an entrance road (say 15%), then either the vertical difference must be made less (10 feet) or the horizontal distance must be increased (to 150 feet). The variables interact as follows.

$$G = \frac{D}{L} \qquad L = \frac{D}{G} ; \qquad D = L \times G$$

Altering these variables produces solutions with different economic and aesthetic implications (Fig. 12.6).

In landscape design there are generally accepted maximum grades. These figures have been developed by engineers, architects, and landscape architects from experience and practice. They become determinants of form in site planning, and they are also economic factors. For example, walks and paths usually have a crowned cross section and if possible should not have a longitudinal gradient of more than 6% in areas of cold winters, or 8% in milder climates where frost is not persistent. These are pre-

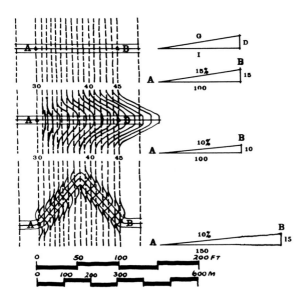

Fig. 12.6 A road from A to B in plan 1 would have a gradient of 15%. By cutting into the hillside and extending the road length beyond the plan area, the gradient between A and B can be reduced to 10% (plan 2). Alternatively, a gradient of 10% can be achieved within the plan area and without extreme changes to the land as shown in plan 3. The length of road is increased, however.

ferred slopes for long distances of path. For shorter distance, ramps with a gradient of up to 12% can be used; over 12%, steps become the most reasonable way to overcome changes in level, but they should be avoided wherever possible. For wheelchairs and bicycles, steps are an obstacle and a hazard. Flights of three or fewer steps become an irritation for movement, although they can serve as informal seat-

Fig. 12.7 (a) and (b) Two grading solutions fitting playing fields into uneven terrain. In both cases the cut balances the fill. Solution (a) is perhaps the most sensitive of the two, but might have some disadvantages.

ing, especially on school grounds and college campuses (Fig. 8.4).

Steps are purely functional in changing elevation in the shortest possible space and are subject to preferred dimensions derived from the physical act of walking developed over centuries of building in both vernacular and Renaissance modes (Figs. 8.20 and 8.32). For example, one "rule" states that the riser multiplied by the tread should equal approximately 74 inches. This allows alternative dimensions, for example, 6-inch riser and 12-inch tread, 5-inch riser and 15-inch tread, 4-inch riser and 18-inch tread. As the riser is reduced, so the tread becomes longer. However, when the tread becomes excessively long, incorporating more than one step, then the rhythm of walking and the dimensions of a stride must enter into the calculations. Designers should measure and record steps they find comfortable.

Roads and driveways also have preferred maximum gradients. Although 6% is considered desirable, 8 to 10% is permissible for short distances. In exceptional cases (in San Francisco, for example, where fortunately the weather is mild) streets are found at 15% and more. These standards and rules of thumb must be viewed in terms of the specific problem to be solved and its context of geography, custom, and use.

In the cut and fill process necessary to fit use elements with criteria of flatness onto land of variable slope, the procedure is as elementary as it sounds. However, depending on the type of material and the compaction process, the quantity of cut should be calculated to be about 5 percent more than would appear to be theoretically necessary for the fill. This is due to the fact that when loose material from a cut is filled, the compaction makes it take up less volume. This is important in large scale grading where 5 percent may be a considerable quantity. Cross sections, which are an essential technique in developing a grading plan, are used in the calculations of cut and fill quantities. Computing is done most accurately with a planimeter, which measures the cross sections of a cut and fill area. The average of the cross section is multiplied by its length to give the volume (Fig. 12.7).

Existing trees in a landscape which is to be altered require special care if they are to survive (Fig. 12.8). The vulnerable area around a tree trunk varies according to its rooting characteristics. In general, however, it is possible to develop some principles which, with the foregoing proviso, apply to most situations. The vulnerable area on the ground equals the spread of the tree plus an additional one-third of that on each side. Trees tend to extend their feeder roots, which take up nutrients in solution, beyond the drip line. This zone is therefore particularly important for the health of the tree, and the inner zone is important for its physical support. To be absolutely certain of the tree's survival, no grading, cut, or fill should take place in the total vulnerable area. The levels or elevations of this surface then become control elevations as discussed earlier.

Sometimes, however, total conservation is impossible. If it is necessary to cut to a depth more than 6 inches in the vicinity of the tree, no more than one-third of the vulnerable area should be cut. In this case, since some structural and feeder roots may be lost, the tree should be pruned to reduce the weight to be supported and the demand for nutrients and water. If, on the other hand, the levels around the tree have to be raised in excess of 4 inches, it may be saved by taking measures to keep air and water in the same relationship to the roots as in the existing condition. Twelve inches of coarse gravel should be laid over the entire vulnerable area under the fill as shown in Figure 12.8. Drainpipes laid vertically to the top of the fill will allow air to circulate freely. With this technique, the relationship of the roots to air will remain essentially the same and the adjustment the tree will have to make will be relatively gentle. Further horizontal drains may be needed to maintain the water table at the original level. None of these techniques can be considered particularly satisfactory. Even if the trees do survive, their growth may be affected. In addition, the way in which trees grow naturally out of the ground is an important aspect of their aesthetic quality.

The machinery that will do the grading can be an economic constraint and a determinant of form. Several factors influence the cost of the grading operation, and under tight budget situations these factors should indicate the most suitable methods. For example, in the cut and fill process it is best and most economic that the cut area be as close to the fill area as possible. If the cut is 2 miles away from the fill area, the length of haul will increase the cost of the operation. Sometimes the nature of the material being excavated can affect the time involved. Clay and silt and loam are easy to load, spread, and compact, whereas sand is harder to handle, as are shale and

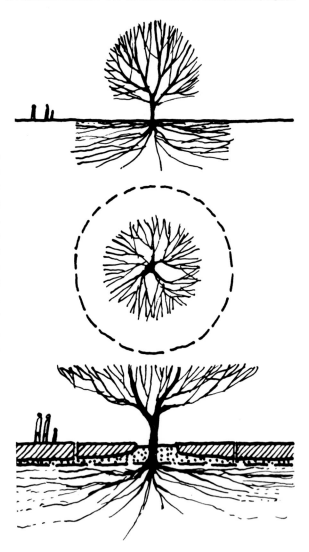

Fig. 12.8 (a) The vulnerable area around a tree is equal to its spread plus one-third.
(b) A system of filling land over the vulnerable area which attempts to maintain the original relationship of air and water to the trees' roots.

Fig. 12.9 Brick retaining wall with "weep holes."

hard pan. Thus the nature of the material may extend the time or incur excessive wear and tear on machinery, both increasing costs.[1] Soil analysis can thus be seen to relate to grading. Machinery of different types and sizes has specific minimum turning circles. Therefore in terms of the ease and speed with which the work can be done, the type of machinery available is an important factor that may influence certain aspects of the grading plan. Curved grades with gentle shapes are easier to create than are specific angular grades. Finally, there are certain maximum slopes beyond which some machinery cannot operate.

In grading we should be sure that the surfaces which result are stable. As the banks or graded slopes increase in steepness, so the amount of surface water that runs off will increase and with it the greater possibility of soil erosion (depending on the vegetative cover). The less steep the banks are, the better. Basically the type of material forming the banks dictates the maximum slopes that are possible by virtue of its natural angle of repose. Thus solid

rock may be cut almost vertical at, say, ¼–1; this will be safe for banks not greater than 20 feet high. On the other hand, fill with broken rock will have an angle of repose of approximately 1–1 (a 100% slope, or 45°). Average soil has an angle of repose of about 55° for cut and 17° for fill. What is safe, in equilibrium or in balance, depends on the nature of the soil or material being excavated and compacted for fill. In certain situations of geology and soil, slopes of greater than 25% are considered unsafe.

Another reason to keep slopes as gentle as possible is maintenance. Grass cutting machinery is not practical at slopes greater than 30%. Thus the permissible slope will depend on a number of factors, including the nature of the original material, whether the surface of the slopes is planted, paved, or grassed, and what kind of drainage provisions are made at the top and bottom of banks. It is generally best to stay away from the maximums represented by the angles of repose. Retaining walls should be considered in situations where changes in elevation cannot be accommodated with acceptable slopes. Retaining walls are devices that can take up differences in elevation abruptly; they are expensive, requiring reinforcing if they are over 3 feet in height. Gravel backfill and "weep holes" at the base of the wall are needed to relieve the pressure and weight of rain water behind the wall (Fig. 12.9). Being architectural elements, retaining walls of any material can be used as an effective design technique to link buildings or structures to the landscape. Where land is excessively steep, flat areas can be achieved only with retaining walls or decks.

Since grading by definition involves disturbance of the land surface, the maintenance of soil conditions which will permit plant growth is an important concern. Good soil is a valuable resource, the product of thousands of years' evolution; it should not

be disposed of lightly. The less disturbance to the surface topsoil, the better. If big changes are needed, the topsoil should be stripped, stored, and reused. Even so, the structure and its relation to the soil profile will be altered. In urban situations where the soil has already been disturbed or built on, the problem may be the development of fertile soil suitable as a growing medium. This is a matter of fertilization and cultivation and possibly importation of topsoil.

SURFACE DRAINAGE

Rainfall is the usual source of surface water. When it falls, a proportion of it percolates into the soil, the amount depending on the soil type and vegetative cover. Another proportion of it drains or runs over the surface of the land to some low point on the site. Another proportion may flow off the site, and some will evaporate. That portion of the rain which does not enter the soil or evaporate is called runoff. In grading and construction provision must be made for this runoff, so that flooding will be avoided and valuable topsoil will not be lost by erosion. One of the functions of the grading plan is to shape the ground in such a way that rain water will flow through the site to collecting points without causing washouts (Figs. 12.7 and 12.13). It is therefore economical and usual to grade the land in such a way that water is collected in channels, grass swales, or gutters (depending on the nature of the project) and directed around buildings and away from major use areas into either natural channels or, in urban areas, into drain inlets connected to a storm sewer system.

Predictions of water runoff quantities are necessary in order that the size of the pipes or swale dimensions can be calculated and provided adequately

1. Brian Hackett, "Land Form and Cost Factors," *Landscape Architecture* 56 (6) (July 1964).

so that they can cope with the worst possible conditions. Historical climate data are used to provide 100-, 50-, 25-, or 10-year storm expectancies. The frequency selected depends on whether occasional flooding would be acceptable, as on playing fields and recreation areas. An agricultural engineering formula is frequently used in which the quantity of water (Q) arriving at any point in a watershed is derived from a combination of several variables.

$$Q = ACi$$

The variables are the area of the watershed in acres (A), a coefficient of runoff (C), and a quantity derived from the amount of rain that can be expected for a selected storm frequency combined with the farthest distance that a drop of water will have to run before reaching the collecting point (i).

The coefficient of runoff is the most interesting variable. It varies according to two site factors: the condition of the surface and the topography or slope. The coefficient represents the percentage of rain which is not absorbed or delayed before reaching a specified point or drain inlet. Tables have been prepared to give values for a variety of conditions. For example, in urban areas where 30 percent of the surface is estimated to be impervious (roofs, roads, and so on) in a generally flat landscape, 40 percent of falling rain will become runoff for drainage purposes. With a similar percentage of impervious surface in a situation of rolling terrain, the runoff may rise to 50 percent. As the amount of impervious surface increases, the quantity of runoff increases. With building roofs and roads that have runoff coefficients between 85 and 100 percent, it can be seen that urban conditions in areas of heavy rainfall either throughout the year or at selected times within the year pose very serious drainage

Fig. 12.10 Crematorium, Stockholm. Gunar Asplund (1937–40).

problems in the design of open space and paved plazas. By contrast, in more natural situations the runoff is considerably less.

To the variables of surface cover and topography is added soil, which can have a considerable impact on the quantity of water that becomes runoff. Thus in a wooded landscape on flat ground with open sandy loam soil the runoff will be about 10 percent. In the same situation but with a heavy clay soil the runoff may be as much as 40 percent. As the topography becomes steeper, the rate of runoff increases. The coefficient of runoff on hilly land with slopes of between 10 and 30% with sandy soil will be about 30 percent, which will double if the soil has a high clay content.

These figures are significant not only for drainage purposes but also for water conservation. Paul Sears argues that the longer water can be kept on or in the land, the better for mankind.[2] Delay of the water cycle in its land phase is desirable, and in certain circumstances spreading water over the land and allowing it to percolate into the soil, replenishing groundwater, is preferable to immediate removal by storm sewers.

For drainage purposes there are some minimum gradients for surfaces. Drainage, especially around buildings or use areas such as playing fields, must

be positive. Water must flow if ponds and puddles are to be avoided. It is therefore undesirable to have dead level surfaces. The minimum gradients vary according to the nature of the surface and/or its permeability. For example; the minimum gradient for asphalt is between 1.5 and 2%. For smooth finished concrete the minimum is 1%, whereas on coarser, exposed aggregate the minimum would be 2% since water will not flow as easily over the rougher surface. Bricks laid in sand need a minimum of 1%, whereas brick paving laid with grouted joints needs 2%. Lawns and grass areas should have a minimum of 1% in the open and 2% adjacent to buildings and in grass swales.

The design of a storm sewer system is properly the work of an engineer. However, drain inlets are surface manifestations of the hidden underground system. Their position and elevation are related to economics and the constraints of water flow technology. They are the places where landscape design meets engineering, requiring collaboration between the two. They must be designed as part of the surface treatment or pattern rather than incorporated as afterthoughts, as so often seems to happen.

2. Paul B. Sears, *The Living Landscape* (New York: Basic Books, 1962).

Just as there are minimum gradients to facilitate positive drainage, so there are maximums. These are important in erosion control. Groundcover or grass planting on banks of 25% or more is absolutely necessary to prevent erosion and excessive runoff. In solving drainage problems without a storm sewer system, that is, in natural swales or streams, it is important to know what the effect of the runoff will be downstream. Silting up of streams and channels may occur, thus reducing their capacity to remove water from the area at a subsequent time (Figs. 6.5 and 6.6).

Roof gardens require very rapid drainage since the weight of water added to soil, paving, and plants places stresses on the structure. The slopes on paved surfaces in such situations should be greater than slopes normally required. Special lightweight and porous soil at least 12 inches in depth should be used in planting beds with subsurface drains to remove excess water.

VISUAL CONSIDERATIONS

In addition to all the functional considerations, grading also has visual implications. The created land form can have an aesthetic appearance in its own right, as at the Stockholm Cemetery (Fig. 12.10) or at Foothill College (Fig. 7.9). In addition, land form can help to screen out undesirable views such as parking lots and freeways (Fig. 12.11). With the addition of planting, earth mounds can provide a quick and effective visual barrier and also wind shelter (Fig. 6.39). The sunken fence, product of the eighteenth-century landscape garden, is also a grading technique devised to conceal the boundary fence, the division between pastureland and garden (Fig. 2.34). Topographic changes may also be devised to separate circulation and social uses in site

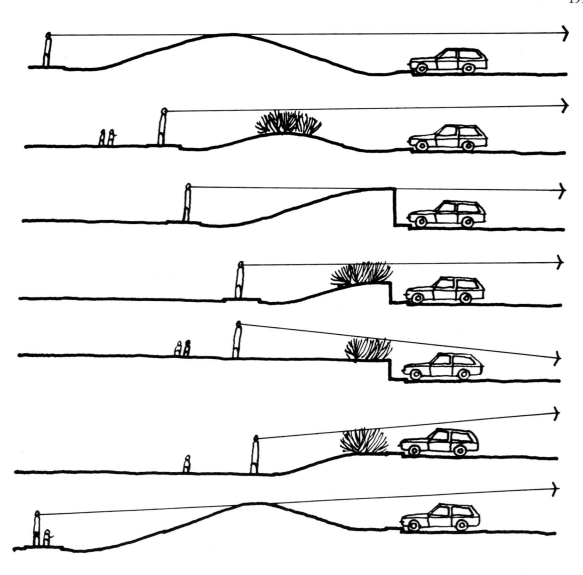

Fig. 12.11 Land formland form combined with retaining walls and/or planting, and differences in relative levels can be used in design to conceal and separate.

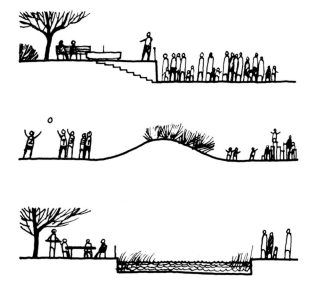

Fig. 12.12 Articulation of levels to separate circulation and use areas.

planning and detailed design (Fig. 12.12). Geometric land shaping as opposed to natural form can produce interesting and exciting results, as the wind protection earthworks at Sea Ranch show with bold angular forms (Fig. 6.39). Land forms that are not imitations of nature are especially appropriate where new landscapes are being made in the restoration of derelict land or in the disposal of excess fill. Open-air theaters provide other opportunities for creative land shaping.

CASE STUDY

Discussion of a small and simple case study may help to show the interrelationship of the grading principles and goals outlined here. The success of the Church project seen in Fig. 12.13 depended on

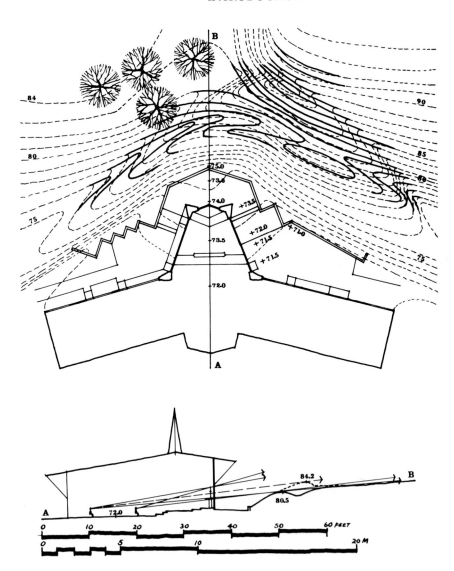

Fig. 12.13 a) Grading plan deals with drainage on the hillside and on the paved surfaces. Useable space is provided around the church and the steepness of the original slope is reduced. b) Section.

a careful assessment of regrading possibilities. There were three requirements. First, the provision of level paved open areas for outdoor meetings and for after church social hours. Second, the grading had to produce a stable slope out of one that was too steep and subject to slides and provide a drainage swale halfway up. Third, the view from the window behind the altar was involved in the regrading. From the church the visual line caused by the top of the existing bank seen from the window cut across a very beautiful but delicate cross on the altar. Visually, whatever line resulted from the regrading should therefore be either above or below its present location to eliminate this aesthetic conflict.

Cross sections through the site resulted in the dimensions for the paved areas, the acceptable slopes, and the location, depth, and gradient of the drainage channel. Levels obtained from the cross sections were transferred to the contour plan, and proposed contours were drawn, which when implemented would result in the desired cross section. The quantities of cut and fill could be calculated from these lines, and since more cut was needed than fill a suitable area nearby was located to dispose of the excess. The paved courtyards also had to be graded so that the paved surface would drain away from the building and into a French drain (removing the water from the immediate area but not off the site).

This simple example illustrates how various problems were solved. The existing unstable bank was graded to a more acceptable slope and a drainage swale was provided at the top, both contributing to its greater stability. Retaining walls were also used to reduce the slope, and level areas were provided outside the doors of the church. The visual background to the altar was also made more simple, eliminating the visual conflict.

The translation of the grading plan and its elevational details into reality is in itself a creative process. Surveys are never totally accurate and the bulldozer can be only roughly specific. Supervision demands creativity in connecting up disparate levels in the spirit of the original design and with regard to the basic concepts of drainage, erosion control, visual effect, and maintenance. Thus minor adjustments are always needed on site, and the design process continues into the execution or implementation of the work.

In summary, grading is the means by which we modify the surface of the land to meet the requirements of a design and program. The extent to which surface changes can normally be made depends on the control elevations of the site and fixed elements on its surface. Further determinants of form are maximum gradient criteria for roads, paths, and slopes, the balance of cut and fill, bank stability, erosion control, and surface drainage. Economics, soil conservation, and the characteristics of earth-moving machinery are further variables in the specific transformation of site plans into three-dimensional reality. In addition to these functional matters, the shaping of the land in relation to use for visual impact is also fundamental to the process of surface articulation in landscape architecture.

Suggested Readings

American Association of State Highway Officials, *A Policy of Geometric Design of Rural Highways.*

Ayres, Quincy Claude, *Soil Erosion and Its Control*, pp. 83–99, "Rainfall and Runoff," pp. 20–38, "Factors Affecting Rate of Erosion."

Beazley, Elizabeth, *Design and Detail of the Space Between Buildings.*

Crowe, Sylvia, *Garden Design*, pp. 101–105, "Land Form."

Cullen, Gordon, *Townscape*, pp. 175–181, "Change in Level."

Eckbo, Garrett, *Landscape for Living*, pp. 79–85, "Earth, Earthwork."

Hackett, Brian, "Land Form Design and Cost Factors," *Landscape Architecture*, July 1964, p. 273.

Halprin, Lawrence, *Cities*, pp. 116–127, "The Third Dimension."

Lynch, Kevin, *Site Planning*, pp. 125–128, "The Grading Plan."

Nichols, Herbert Lownds, *Moving the Earth.*

Parker, Harry, and John W. McGuire, *Simplified Site Engineering for Engineers and Architects*, pp. 124–129, "Contours," pp. 133–153, "Use of Contours," pp. 155–165, "Cut and Fill."

Simonds, John O., *Landscape Architecture*, pp. 25–35, "Nature Forms, Forces and Features."

Weddle, A. E., ed., *Techniques of Landscape Architecture*, pp. 55–72, "Earthworks and Ground Modelling," by Brian Hackett, pp. 73–89, "Hard Surfaces," by T. Cochrane.

In Chapters One and Six I reviewed some of the factors and changes that indicate the need for a reorganization of our environment. The needs of an expanding population have to be fulfilled without destroying natural resources. I have tried to develop an environmental theory responsive to this concept which can contribute to the location and building of new communities and the revitalization of established but decaying cities. In it, natural and ecological factors interact with social needs and behavioral analysis in a creative process called landscape architecture, which includes as indispensable ingredients aesthetic sensitivity and a concern for visual quality. The theory assumes a technology for construction and implementation and implies methodologies for evaluating resource data and environmental quality.

I have tried to stress the interrelationship of the scales of operation from regional planning to detailed design, and I emphasize further by means of the matrix (Fig. P. 1) how the subject areas of the various chapters interact. Thus history and climate (5) can be discussed in terms of early solutions to the problems of counteracting the adverse effects of weather. The social implications of regional landscape planning (10) is a subject dealing with perception and evaluation of landscape, its "imageability," and the socioeconomic pressures of the recreation industry. The relationships between site planning and regional policy (8) are represented by the concept of the environmental impact statement in which the effect of a project is measured in terms of regional impact. The use of social analysis in the development of a site plan (15) deals with development of a program that will provide those facilities most desired by the users in a form which can be used. The influence of climate and microclimate on the use of open space (23) is a subject concerned with behavioral analysis and the technology of microclimate. There are innumerable ways in which each specialized area of knowledge relates to others.

By now it must be clear that landscape architecture is a very complex profession involving a wide range of possible tasks with many scientific and technical inputs. It is a profession involving interdisciplinary relationships on the basis of which decisions about the planning and design of the environment are made. At the same time, it is a profession of judgment—value judgments requiring an attitude of stewardship and responsibility to alternative futures and a commitment to environmental health and fitness for human use. The landscape architect may be seen as a bridge between the natural scientist and the land developer and economist, and as an advocate for society attempting to secure the wise use of resources and the prevention of catastrophic consequences resulting from ill-considered social intervention in the ecosystem.

We must remember that theory without implementation has little use. It is necessary therefore to develop a political ability at various levels so that good design will be understood and built by the client and planning policies will be approved by the community, then legislated, and enforced. Finally, we must be equipped to study the effects and results of our work so that improvements can be effected from experience and, as a consequence, the theory improved through practice.

Fig. P.1

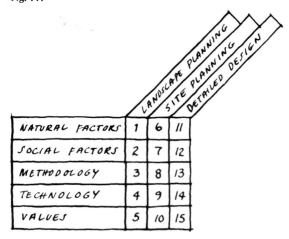

Fig. P.2 The five basic components of landscape architecture apply at all scales. Each number represents a possible synthetic phase in the process of landscape design and planning.

BIBLIOGRAPHY

Alexander, Christopher. *The City as a Mechanism for Sustaining Human Contact*. Berkeley, Calif.: State University Center for Planning and Development Research, Working Paper No. 50.

———, Sara Ishikawa, and Murray Silverstein. *A Pattern Language Which Generates Multi-Service Centers*. Berkeley, Calif.: Center for Environmental Structure, 1968.

———. *Notes on the Synthesis of Form*. Cambridge, Mass.: Harvard University Press, 1964.

American Academy of Political and Social Science. *Recreation in the Age of Automation*, Paul F. Douglas, et al., eds. Philadelphia, 1957.

American Association of State Highway Officials. *A Policy of Geometric Design of Rural Highways*, rev. ed. Washington, D.C., 1966.

American Society of Landscape Architects. *Colonial Gardens: The Landscape Architecture of George Washington's Time*. George Washington Bicentennial Commission, 1932.

Ardrey, Robert. *African Genesis*. New York: Atheneum, 1963.

———. *The Territorial Imperative*. New York: Atheneum, 1966.

Ayres, Quincy Claude. *Soil Erosion and Its Control*. New York, London: McGraw-Hill Book Co., 1936.

Baker, Geoffrey H., and Bruno Funaro. *Parking*. New York: Reinhold, 1958.

Bates, Marston. *The Forest and the Sea: A Look at the Economy of Nature and the Ecology of Man*. New York: Random House, 1960.

———. *Man in Nature*. Englewood Cliffs, N. J.: Prentice-Hall, 1961.

Beazley, Elizabeth. *Design and Detail of the Space Between Buildings*. London: Architectural Press, 1960.

———. *Designed for Recreation: A Practical Handbook for All Concerned with Providing Leisure Facilities in the Countryside*. London: Faber and Faber, 1969.

Belknap, Raymond, and John Furtado. *Three Approaches to Environmental Resource Analysis*. Washington, D. C.: Conservation Foundation, 1967.

Berral, Julia S. *The Garden: An Illustrated History*. New York: Viking Press, 1966.

Blake, Peter. *God's Own Junkyard: The Planned Deterioration of America's Landscape*. New York: Holt, Rinehart & Winston, 1964.

Breckenfeld, Gurney. *Columbia and the New Cities*. New York: Washburn, 1971.

Brookes, John. *Room Outside, A Plan for the Garden*. London: Thames and Hudson, 1969.

Buckman, Harry O., and Nyle C. Brady. *The Nature and Properties of Soils: A College Text of Edaphology*, 6th rev. ed. New York: Macmillan, 1960.

Building Research Station. *Current Papers*, no. 20. "Designing Against Noise From Road Traffic." London: H.M.S.O., 1971.

Butler, George D. *Introduction to Community Recreation*, 3rd ed. Prepared for the National Recreation Association. New York: McGraw-Hill Book Co., 1959.

Caborn, James M. *Shelterbelts and Micro-Climate*. Great Britain Forestry Commission Bulletin No. 29. Edinburgh, 1960.

———. *Shelterbelts and Windbreaks*. London: Faber and Faber, 1965.

Chadwick, George F. *The Park and the Town: Public Landscape in the 19th and 20th Centuries*. London: Architectural Press, 1966.

———. *The Works of Sir Joseph Paxton, 1803–1865*. London: Architectural Press, 1961.

Chermayeff, Serge, and Christopher Alexander. *Community and Privacy*. Garden City, N. Y.: Doubleday, 1963.

Church, Thomas D. *Gardens Are for People: How to Plan for Outdoor Living*. New York: Reinhold, 1955.

Clark, H. F. *The English Landscape Garden*. London: Pleiasdes Books, 1948.

Cleveland, Horace W. S. *Landscape Architecture: As Applied to the Wants of the West*. Pittsburgh: University of Pittsburgh Press, 1965.

Clifford, Derek. *A History of Garden Design*. London: Faber and Faber, 1962.

Colvin, Brenda. *Land and Landscape: Evolution, Design, and Control*, 2nd ed. London: J. Murray, 1970.

———, and Jacqueline Tyrwhitt. *Trees for Town and Country: A Selection of Sixty Trees Suitable for General Cultivation in England*, 3rd rev. ed. London: Lund, Humphried, 1961.

Cook, David, and David F. Haerbeke. *Trees and Shrubs for Noise Abatement*. Research Bulletin 246, The Forest Service in cooperation with the University of Nebraska College of Agriculture, 1971.

Cooper, Clare C. *Some Social Implications of House and Site Plan Design at Easter Hill Village: A Case Study*. Berkeley, Calif.: Center for Planning and Development Research, University of California, 1965.

Coyle, Davis C. *Conservation, An American Story of Conflict and Accomplishment*. New Brunswick, N. J.: Rutgers University Press, 1957.

Craik, Kenneth H. "Environmental Psychology," in *New Directions in Psychology*, Vol. IV. New York: Holt, Rinehart & Winston, 1971.

Creese, Walter. *The Search for Environment: The Garden City Before and After*. New Haven, Conn.: Yale University Press, 1966.

Crisp, (Sir) Frank. *Medieval Gardens*, limited ed. London: John Lane the Bodley Head Ltd., 1924.

Crowe, Sylvia. *Garden Design*. London: Country Life, 1958.

———. *The Landscape of Power*. London: Architectural Press, 1958.

———. *The Landscape of Roads*. London: Architectural Press, 1960.

———. *Tomorrow's Landscape*. London: Architectural Press, 1956.

Cullen, Gordon. *Townscape*. New York: Reinhold, 1961.

———. *The Concise Townscape*, new ed. London: Architectural Press, 1971.

Darling, F. Fraser. *Wilderness and Plenty*. New York: Ballantine Books, 1971.

———, and John P. Milton, eds. *Future Environments for North America*. (Record of the 1965 Conservation Foundation Conference, Warrenton, Va.) Garden City, N. Y.: Natural History Press, 1966.

Dasmann, Raymond F. *Environmental Conservation*, 2nd ed. New York: John Wiley & Sons, 1968.

———. *The Destruction of California*. New York: Macmillan, 1965.

De Grazia, Sebastian. *Of Time, Work and Leisure*. New York: Twentieth Century Fund, 1962.

Department of the Environment. *The Estate of Outside the D.WELLING (Reactions of Residents to Aspects of Housing Layout)*. London: H.M.S.O., 1972.

Dickenson, Jim. *New Housing and Traffic Noise: A Design Guide for Architects*. London: H.M.S.O., 1972

Dickert, Thomas, ed. *Environmental Impact Assessment: Improving the Process*. Berkeley, Calif.: University of California Extension, 1973.

Dober, Richard P. *Campus Planning*. New York, Rheinhold, 1963.

Downing, Andrew Jackson. *Landscape Gardening and Rural Architecture*, 10th ed., rev. by Frank A. Waugh. New York: John Wiley & Sons, 1921.

Dubos, René. *Man Adapting*. New Haven, Conn.: Yale University Press, 1965.

———. *So Human an Animal*. New York: Charles Scribner's Sons, 1968.

Dutton, Ralph. *The English Garden*. London: B.T. Batsford, 1937.

Eaton, Leonard K. *Landscape Artist in America: The Life and Work of Jens Jensen*. Chicago: University of Chicago Press, 1964.

Eckbo, Garrett. *Art of Home Landscaping*. New York: F. W. Dodge Corp., 1956.

———. *Landscape for Living*. New York: Architectural Record, with Duell, Sloan & Pearce, 1950.

———. *Urban Landscape Design*. New York: McGraw-Hill Book Co., 1964.

Fabos, Julius G., Gordon T. Milde, and V. Michael Weinmayr. *Frederick Law Olmsted, S.R., Founder of Landscape Architecture in America*. Amherst: University of Massachusetts Press, 1968.

——— (with Richard Careaga, Christopher Greene, and Stephanie Williston). *Model for Landscape Resource Assessment*. Amherst, Mass.: Department of Landscape Architecture and Regional Planning, 1973.

Fairbrother, Nan. *Men and Gardens*. London: Hogarth Press, 1956.

———. *New Lives, New Landscape: Planning for the 21st Century*. New York: Alfred A. Knopf, 1970.

Fein, Albert, *Frederick Law Olmsted and the American Environmental Tradition*. New York: G. Braziller, 1972.

———. *Landscape into Cityscape: Frederick Law Olmsted's Plans for a Greater New York City*. Ithaca, N. Y.: Cornell University Press, 1968.

Fox, Helen. *André le Nôtre, Garden Architect to Kings*. New York: Crown, 1962.

Freidberg, M. Paul. *Play and Interplay*. New York: Macmillan, 1970.

Gans, Herbert J. *The Levittowners: Ways of Life and Politics in a New Suburban Community*. New York: Pantheon Books, 1967.

Gardner, Victor R. *Basic Horticulture*, rev. ed. New York: Macmillan, 1951.

Geiger, Rudolf. *The Climate Near the Ground*. Coupta Technica, Inc., trans. Cambridge, Mass.: Harvard University Press, 1963.

Giedion, Sigfried. *Space, Time and Architecture: The Growth of a New Tradition*, 5th ed. Cambridge, Mass.: Harvard University Press, 1967.

Goffman, Erving. *Behavior in Public Places: Notes on the Social Organization of Gatherings*. New York: Free Press of Glencoe, 1963.

Gothein, M. Louis. *The History of Garden Art*. Walter P. Wright, ed.; Laura Archer-Hind, trans. London and Toronto: J. M. Dent & Sons; New York: E. P. Dutton & Co., 1928.

Graham, Dorothy. *Chinese Gardens: Gardens of the Contemporary Scene*. New York: Dodd, Mead & Co., 1938.

Green, David. *Gardener to Queen Anne, Henry Wise and the Formal Garden*. London, New York: Oxford University Press, 1956.

Gutkind, Erwin A. *Our World From the Air: An International Survey of Man and His Environment*. Garden City, N.Y.: Doubleday, 1952.

———. "Our World from the Air: Conflict and Adaptation," in *Man's Role in Changing the Face of the Earth*, William L. Thomas, ed. Chicago: University of Chicago Press, 1956.

Hackett, Brian. *Landscape Planning: An Introduction to Theory and Practice*. Newcastle Upon Tyne: Oriel Press, 1971.

Hadfield, Miles. *Gardens*. New York: Putnam, 1962.

Hall, Edward T. *The Hidden Dimension*. Garden City, N. Y.: Doubleday, 1966.

———. *The Silent Language*. Greenwich, Conn.: Fawcett Press, 1967.

Halprin, Lawrence. *Cities*. New York: Reinhold, 1963.

———. *Notebooks, 1959–71*. Cambridge, Mass.: MIT Press, 1972.

Hazlehurst, Franklin H. *Jacques Boyceau and the French Formal Garden*. Athens: University of Georgia Press, 1966.

Horiguchi, Sutami. *Tradition of Japanese Gardens*. Tokyo: Kokusai Bunka Shinkokai, 1962.

Howard, (Sir) Ebenezer. *Garden Cities of Tomorrow*. F. S. Osborn, ed. London: Faber and Faber, 1951.

Hussey, Christopher. *The Picturesque: Studies in a Point of View*. London and New York: Putnam, 1962.

Huth, Hans. *Nature and the American: Three Centuries of Changing Attitudes*. Berkeley: University of California Press, 1957.

Hyams, Edward S. *The English Garden*. London: Thames and Hudson, 1964.

———. *A History of Gardens and Gardening*. New York: Praeger, 1971.

International Federation of Landscape Architects, 9th Congress. *Landscape Architecture in Japan*. 1964.

International Union for Conservation of Nature and Natural Resources. *Towards a New Relationship between Man and Nature in Temperate Lands*. Morges, Switzerland: IUCN, 1967.

Jellicoe, Geoffrey A. *Studies in Landscape Design*. London and New York: Oxford University Press, 1960.

Jellicoe, Susan, and Geoffrey Jellicoe. *Water*. London: A & C Black, 1971.

Jourdain, Margaret. *The Work of William Kent: Artist, Painter, Designer and Landscape Gardener*. London: Country Life; New York: Charles Scribner's Sons, 1948.

Kahn, Herman. *The Year 2000*. New York: Macmillan, 1967.

Kassler, Elizabeth B. *Modern Gardens and the Landscape*. New York: Museum of Modern Art, Doubleday, 1964.

Landmark '71. Berkeley: Department of Landscape Architecture, University of California, 1971.

Leopold, Aldo S. *A Sand County Almanac, and Sketches Here and There*. New York: Oxford University Press, 1950.

Lewis, Philip H. *Regional Design for Human Impact*. Kaukauna, Wisc.: Thomas, 1969.

Litton, R. Burton. *Forest Landscape Description and Inventories—A Basis for Land Planning and Design*. U.S. Department of Agriculture, Forest Research Paper PSW49, Berkeley: U.S. Department of Agriculture, 1968.

———. "Landscape and Aesthetic Quality," in *America's Changing Environment*, R. Revelle and H. H. Landsberg, eds. Boston: Beacon Press, 1970.

Lockwood, Alice G. B. *Gardens of Colony and State: Gardens and Gardeners of the American Colonies and of the Republic before 1840*. New York: Charles Scribner's Sons, 1931–1934.

Lovejoy, Derek, ed. *Land Use and Landscape Planning*. Aylesbury: Intertext Publishing, 1973.

Lynch, Kevin. *Site Planning*. Cambridge, Mass.: MIT Press, 1962.

———. *What Time is This Place*. Cambridge, Mass.: MIT Press, 1972.

McHarg, Ian L. *Design with Nature*. Garden City, N. Y.: Natural History Press, 1969.

———. "Ecological Determinism," in *Future Environments for North America*, Frank Darling, ed. Garden City, N. Y.: Natural History Press, 1966.

Maddi, S. R., and D. W. Fiske. *Functions of Varied Experience*. Homewood, Ill.: Dorsey Press, 1961.

Marsh, George Perkins. *Man and Nature*, David Lowenthal, ed. Cambridge, Mass.: Harvard University Press, 1965.

Massingham, Betty. *Miss Jekyll: Portrait of a Great Gardener*. London: Country Life, 1966.

Masson, Georgina. *Italian Gardens*. London: Thames and Hudson, 1961.

Meyerson, Martin. *Face of the Metropolis*. Prepared for the National Council of Good Cities. New York: Random House, 1963.

Morse, Edward S. *Japanese Homes and Their Surroundings*. New York: Dover, 1961.

Muir, John. *Yosemite and the Sierra Nevada*, Charlotte C. Mauk, ed. Boston: Houghton Mifflin, 1948.

Mumford, Lewis. *The Brown Decades: A Study of the Arts in America*, 2nd rev. ed. New York: Dover, 1955.

Newsom, Samuel. *A Thousand Years of Japanese Gardens*, 3rd ed. Tokyo: Tokyo News Service, 1957.

Newton, Norman T. *Design on the Land; The Development of Landscape Architecture*. Cambridge, Mass.: Belknap Press of the Harvard University Press, 1971.

Nichols, Herbert Lownds. *Moving the Earth: The Workbook of Excavation*. Greenwich, Conn.: North Castle Books, 1955.

Odum, Eugene P. *Fundamentals of Ecology*, 2nd ed. Philadelphia: Saunders, 1959.

Olgay, Victor. *Design with Climate*. Princeton, N. J.: Princeton University Press, 1963.

Parker, Harry, and John W. McGuire. *Simplified Site Engineering for Architects and Builders*. New York: John Wiley & Sons, 1954.

Patri, Tito, David C. Streatfield, and Thomas J. Ingmire. *Early Warning System*. Berkeley: University of California, Department of Landscape Architecture, 1970.

Perin, Constance. *With Man in Mind: An Interdisciplinary Prospectus for Environmental Design*. Cambridge, Mass.: MIT Press, 1970.

Peterson, Peggy Long. "The ID and the Image," *Landmark '66*. Berkeley: Department of Landscape Architecture, University of California, 1966.

Pevsner, Nikolaus. "The Genesis of the Picturesque," *Architectural Review*, Vol. 96, November, 1944, pp. 139–166.

Proshansky, H. M., ed. *Environmental Psychology*. New York: Holt, Rinehart & Winston, 1970.

Rapoport, Amos. *House Form and Culture*. Englewood Cliffs, N. J.: Prentice-Hall, 1969.

Reps, John W. *The Making of Urban America: A History of City Planning in the United States*. Princeton, N. J.: Princeton University Press, 1965.

Ritter, Paul. *Planning for Man and Motor*, Elmsford, New York: Pergamon, 1964.

Robbins, Wilfred W., T. Elliot Weier, and . Ralph Stocking. *Botany: An Introduction to Plant Science*, 2nd ed. New York: John Wiley & Sons, 1957.

Robinette, Gary O. *Plants, People and Environmental Quality*.

U. S. Department of Interior. Washington, D. C.: G.P.O., 1973.

Robinson, Florence Bell. *Palette of Plants*. Champaign, Ill.: Garrard Press, 1950.

———. *Planting Design*. New York: McGraw-Hill Book Co.: London, Wittlesey House, 1940.

Rubensteinn Harvey. *A Guide to Site and Environmental Planning*. New York and London: John Wiley & Sons, 1969.

Scientific American. *Cities*. New York, 1965.

Sears, Paul B. *Life and Environment*. New York: Teachers' College, Columbia University, 1939.

———. *Where There is Life*. New York: Dell, 1962.

Shepard, Paul. *Man in the Landscape: A Historical View of the Esthetics of Nature*. New York: Alfred A. Knopf, 1968.

Shepheard, Peter. *Gardens*. London: MacDonald and Company, in association with Council of Industrial Design, 1969.

———. *Modern Gardens*. London: Architectural Press, 1953.

Shepherd, John C., and Geoffrey A. jellicoe. *Italian Gardens of the Renaissance*. New York: Charles Scribner's Sons, 1925.

Simonds, John O. *Landscape Architecture*. New York: F. W. Dodge, 1961.

Siren, Osvald. *Gardens of China*. New York: Ronald Press, 1949.

Skinner, B. F. *Science and Human Behavior*. London/New York: Macmillan, 1953.

Sommer, Robert. *Personal Space: The Behavioral Basis of Design*. Englewood Cliffs, N. J.: Prentice-Hall, 1969.

Sorenson, Carl Theodore. *The Origin of Garden Art*. Kobenhavn: Danish Architectural Press, Arkitektens Forlag, 1963.

Stein, Clarence S. *Toward New Towns for America*, new American ed. New York: Reinhold, 1957.

Stroud, Dorothy. *Humphry Repton*. London: Country Life, 1962.

———. *Capability Brown*. London: Country Life, 1950.

Tamura, Tsuyoshi. *Art of Landscape Gardens in Japan*. Tokyo: Kokusai Bunka Shinkokai (The Society for International Cultural Relations), 1935.

Tandy, Clifford, consultant ed. *Handbook of Urban Landscape*. London: Architectural Press, 1972.

Taylor, Geoffrey. *The Victorian Flower Garden*. London, New York: Skeffington, 1952.

Taylor, (Lord) Stephen J. L., and Sidney Chave. *Mental*

Health and the Environment. Sidney: Longma Green, 1964.

Thomas, William L., ed. *Man's Role in Changing the Face of the Earth*. (From the 1955 International Symposium on Man's Role in Changing the Face of the Earth.) Chicago: University of Chicago Press, 1956.

Tobey, George B. *A History of Landscape Architecture*. New York: American Elsevier, 1973.

Tunnard, Christopher. *American Skyline: The Growth and Forms of Our Cities and Towns*. Boston: Houghton Mifflfififi 1955fi

———. *Gardens in the Modern Landscape*, 2nd rev. ed. London: Architectural Press; New York: Charles Scribner's Sons, 1948.

———, and Boris Pushkarev *Man-Made America—Chaos or Control?* New Haven, Conn.: Yale University Press, 1963.

Twiss, Robert, David Streatfield, and Marin County Planning Department. *Nicassio: Hidden Valley in Transition*. San Rafael, Calif., 1969.

Udall, Stewart. *The Quiet Crisis*. New York: Holt, Rinehart and Winston, 1963.

U.S. Outdoor Recretion Resources Review Commission. *Outdoor Recreation for America: A Report to the President and to the Congress*. Washington, D.C., 1962.

Villiers-Stuart, Constance M. *Gardens of the Great Mughals*. London: A. and C. Black, 1913.

———, *Spanish Gardens, Their History, Types and Features*. London: B. T. Batsford, 1929.

Way, Douglas S. *Terrain Analysis: A Guide to Site Selection Using Aerial Photographic Interpretation*. Stroudsburg, Pa.: Dowden, Hutchinson and Ross, 1973.

Weddle, A. E., ed. *Techniques of Landscape Architecture*. New York: American Elsevier, 1967.

Whyte, William H. *The Last Landscape*. Garden City, N. Y.: Doubleday, 1968.

———. *The Organization Man*. New York: Simon and Schuster, 1956.

Williams, Wayne. *Recreation Places*. New York: Rheinhold, 1958.

Wright, Richardson Little. *The Story of Gardening: From the Hanging Gardens of Babylon to the Hanging Gardens of New York*. New York: Dodd, Mead, 1934.

Zube, Ervin H., ed. *An Inventory and Interpretation of Selected Resources of the Island of Nantucket*. Cambridge: University of Massachusetts, Cooperative Extension Service, 1966.

———. *The Islands: Selected Resources of the United States Virgin Islands and Their Relationship to Recreation, Tourism, and Open Space*. Prepared for U.S. Department of Agriculture by the Department of Landscape Architecture, University of Massachusetts, 1968.

INDEX